My Story

A Memoir of Love and Transformation

Elizabeth Marie Rolfe

NEW PATHWAY BOOKS

Calgary, AB, Canada

Prologue

I've heard it said that a book's prologue is the part most people skip over and do not read at all. But, would you eat dry toast and expect it will be more delicious without the butter? Butter makes eating, or in this case reading, so much more delightful and certainly improves the taste and whole experience. When you grasp how a story came about in the first place, the meaning is enhanced and expanded. And this is the purpose of these few lines before my story begins.

It was several years ago while I was in mid-sentence conveying to my grandson, Brad, just how the times have changed since I was his age, when he voiced an epiphany question. "Why don't you write your memoirs, Granny?"

Strange as it seems, that very thought had been percolating in my mind for a long time. You see, I've been writing ever since I was 'knee high to a grasshopper,' that is, most of my life, and I had occasionally imagined myself doing just that, writing my autobiography.

So I answered his question with my own, "Who would read my memoirs?"

He promptly replied, "I would."

And now I'm hoping YOU will read my memoirs, too!

The book you hold in your hands is a fulfilment of my desire to write an accurate account of my life for my family. And, as often is the case, I just required a mere nudge in the right direction to follow through and accomplish it. It is my wish that you will read my book, remembering as you do, I've thought about each of you with a great deal of love as I've written My Story. I've also prayed your life will be blessed with good times and joyful adventures, so you may one day write your own historic journey of trekking through life, just as I have.

1. In the Beginning

All of us are writing a story by simply living out our lives year after year, or as we might say, page after page. John Eldredge, the author of the book *Epic* says, 'A year goes by like a chapter from a novel.'[1] I totally agree. We are indeed telling the story of our lives as we live it day by day. The following pages tell *My Story* just as I lived it and it is not a work of fiction. When you've read what I've written, you'll have learned more about me than you've ever known before and my hope is that you will have enjoyed taking the journey.

Telling *My Story* comes easy for me as I've known for a long time that I'm definitely a storyteller. Not everyone you meet is a storyteller, but without a doubt you know if you are one. The way I've acknowledged this discovery about myself is to have written regularly in a journal. I first began doing this more seriously over forty years ago, floundering at first, but soon getting the hang of it and enjoying it. Why would I want to record my thoughts on paper? Well, journaling helps me exercise my gift of being a storyteller. It allows me to reveal and express my deep inner self that is so often hidden away, far below the surface. I get to know myself through journaling, the person I really am at the very core of my being.

My story begins at my birth on the 15th day of December in the year 1930, amid an era of suffering and hard times known as The Great Depression or 'dirty-thirties'. Of all the places in the world I could have been born, I believe the little town of Cardston in the province of Alberta is where I was destined to arrive. That small, sleepy town lies nestled in the low foothills of southern Alberta with a sweeping, panoramic view of the Rocky Mountain range to the west. I always loved those towering mountains and when I moved away from them in my teen years, I very much lost my sense of direction. For you see, as a child, those Rocky

---

1 John Eldredge, *Epic: The story God is telling and the role that is yours to play.* Thomas Nelson, Inc. Nashville, Tennessee, 2004.

Mountains always pointed me to the west and I didn't realize I was born with a serious direction deficit!

Cardston was, and always has been, very much a Mormon town because it was settled by pioneers of that religion in 1887. The Church of Latter Day Saints, or Mormons as they are called, built their first Mormon Temple outside of the United States in my hometown of Cardston, thus making it somewhat famous, if only to the Mormons. That same Temple, as I'll explain later in my story, was my playground as a teenager. My friend and I labeled it 'our private stomping ground,' which may sound odd, but will make sense when we get there. Every nook and cranny of that huge marble Temple was as familiar to me as the back of my hand.

My birth took place at home, not in a hospital. You see, I had a Grandmother who was not only the mother of ten children, but was also a highly experienced midwife. My mother's mother had delivered a great many infants in her life and was, to her credit, a doctor-of-sorts as well. Qualified doctors were as scarce as 'hen's teeth,' as the old-timers used to say back then, so it was only natural my Grandmother would be there to help me take my first breath of life.

My Grandmother's name was Elizabeth Ann Sanders and I was named Elizabeth Marie in her honour, which has always meant a great deal to me. That is even though I've been called by my second name, Marie, all my life. Only my birth certificate and driver's license disclose that I'm really Elizabeth.

I was the fourth child born to Tony and Ella Posing. My parents were both born in the United States, but migrated to the vicinity of Cardston, where they met and were married in 1919. It was eleven years later that I was born and welcomed into the family by my two older brothers and a sister, Harold, Floyd, and Hazel.

I'm not sure another mouth to feed was actually welcomed in those grim Depression years. However, my sister Hazel, who was six at the time of my birth, was thrilled. She had shyly requested a doll with a 'skin head' for Christmas and along I came ten days early on December 15th. To her, I was a wish-come-true and she nurtured me like I was her very own baby. She was in the first grade at school and would hurry home to hold and cuddle me every day. Such joy for me! Like a lot of other youngsters in those days, Hazel's mode of travelling to school was on a horse with her two older brothers, which spoke of their togetherness.

2. My First Few Years

Despite Hazel's good care of me most of the time, there were two minor accidents which happened while I was still in diapers. The only reason I know about these two events is because Hazel related them to me many times over the years. I felt each time she told me was an act of contrition on her part, as those two episodes seemed to weigh heavy on her conscience. The first incident came about when Hazel was rocking me in her little red rocker and I was bundled up in her arms. Being an enthusiastic six year old, she rocked so hard the rocker went over backwards and I went flying. She received a harsh scolding even though I was wrapped up so tight I was unhurt. The episode was so etched in her memory she never forgot it.

The second incident came about when I was almost a year old, but not yet walking, and it was of a more serious nature. Hazel carried me into the kitchen and sat me down on the open oven door, as she had a habit of doing. Unfortunately, on this particular day, Mother had just removed freshly baked bread from the oven and the oven door was exceptionally hot. My skin was burned and blistered! But Mother was quick to act with a home remedy. She quickly shredded up mounds of the raw potatoes she had peeled and set aside for supper and applied them to my scorched bottom as a cooling poultice. I cried and cried with pain, or so I've been told. Of course, I was too young to recall the experience. However, I was always aware of the dimpled skin I could feel on the back of my upper legs, making me feel damaged somehow. But I didn't share this with anyone, especially Hazel. Perhaps it was the remembrances of these misadventures that bound Hazel and I together in some mysterious way. She always had the heart of a mother toward me and did become a real surrogate mother to me later on when I was in my teens.

Meanwhile, the deeply-rooted Depression of the 1930's continued on and on, making life very difficult for families everywhere. History books say few countries were as severely affected at that time as Canada. Able-bodied men were desperate to find a paying job and the entire population was suffering hardships of every kind imaginable. My Dad was a citizen of the United States, having been born in Illinois, only coming into Canada as a young man before he married. In desperation now, and needing some sort of work to support his family, he crossed over the nearby U.S. border between Alberta and Montana, thinking surely 'the grass must be greener' over there. But he found, to his disappointment, jobs were just as scarce in the United States and was forced to return to Canada.

By the time I was two and a half years old and there was still no relief in sight from the economic downturn, another baby was added to our family, my brother Buddy. He was given the name of Herman John, but nicknamed Buddy right from birth. He was to be the last of my siblings. It was also about this time that my Dad came up with what some people said was a 'crazy idea.' To provide a living for his family, he decided to round up some of the untamed, wild horses that roamed free on the open prairies and sell them across the United States border. With wheat being at an all-time low price per bushel, farmers could not afford to buy machinery and had to use horses to work their land. So Dad knew his horses would be in high demand. But as he found out soon enough, supplying these wild horses was not only very difficult work, it was dangerous work, though it did earn him some much needed money. He persevered at the job until it ultimately led him to other forms of work on the American side of the border. As a result, he was away from home a lot.

My grandmother, Elizabeth Ann Sanders.

Whenever Dad did return, he would often spend time playing games with all of us. As I reminiscence back to that time, I'm reminded of a very special game Dad would play with me. He'd cross his knees one over the other and have me straddle his upper foot. He now became the horse and I was the rider. He'd bounce me up and down vigorously on his foot, in what was my galloping 'pony ride.' Often I'd start out a little shy, but soon my giggles would turn into peals of laughter and then I'd end up with hiccups, all the while enjoying every minute.

My Dad's favourite song back then was a rather popular tune of the day sung on the radio by Gene Autry. It was entitled

Floyd, Mother, Hazel, Dad & Harold.

Sharing their ride to school.

Springtime in the Rockies. One fetching memory of Christmas time that I've stored away is when Dad wanted us children to sing his special song for him. Hazel and my two older brothers tried their best, but they weren't singers and could not carry the tune. I was too young and shy to sing out loud, even though I knew all the words from hearing it so many times. Just the same, we each got a treat out of Dad's special sack of hardtack Christmas candy. It was such a luxury for us to have candy. Even now, I can summon up the feel of that smooth, ribbon-shaped bon-bon slowly melting in my mouth, tasting ever so yummy, as well as a little bit extravagant.

All the words of my Dad's much-loved song have lingered with me to this very day. Perhaps because I remember, too, that the next year my Dad went away again and didn't come back for a long, long time. To me, it seemed like forever and ever. Those special lyrics are unforgettable to me. They call me back to the heart of that little girl I was, humming that tune and 'mouthing' the words, all the time wishing my eyes were blue and not brown.

> When it's springtime in the Rockies,
> I'll be coming back to you
> Little sweetheart of the mountains
> with your bonnie eyes of blue.
> Once again I'll say I love you,
> while the birds sing all the day.
> When it's springtime in the Rockies,
> in the Rockies far away.

3. My Early Childhood

Before I even started going to school, our family moved to a house I remember so very well. It had a porch around it and we always referred to it as the house with the wrap-around-porch. I'm so glad there was a photograph taken of Buddy and me standing in front of the house as I have no other snapshots of that time.

The picture of us was taken with an old Brownie Box Camera, the only camera most people ever owned back then. And it was about the time of this picture-taking that a major catastrophe almost happened to me. At least, that was what my older brother Harold told me. He was ten years my senior and remembered all the details of the near-tragedy and related it to me when I was old enough to understand.

The incident came about when I was making my way across an empty field that lay between our house with the wrap-around-porch and my Grandmother Elizabeth's house. I was not alone that day, as our little white dog Nicky followed close at my heels like always. Wherever I went, Nicky went with me! I had watched my three older siblings taking this short-cut through the field to Grandmother's house many times. Nevertheless, what I failed to understand at four years of age was that the vacant field was also a pasture for a herd of cows, and amongst those cows was a ferocious black bull. Unfortunately, the bull spied me as soon as I climbed through the barbed-wire fence that day, though I was unaware of it. With his massive head lowered to the ground, he brandished his twisted horns and headed towards me without any hesitation. I was definitely his target!

My brave little dog Nicky was immediately alert to my dangerous situation, whereas I was looking straight ahead and unaware of being in any jeopardy. Nicky wasted no time in rushing towards the bull, barking like mad for all he was worth. Harold told me how he couldn't help laughing as he watched the little 'fluff-ball' of a dog fearlessly charge at the enormous bull on my behalf. Then what took place in the following moments astounded even Harold! The yapping 'pint-size' dog seemed to puff-up to double his size and, just as if he had wings, flew aggressively against the attacking bull, causing the beast to stop dead in his tracks.

My brother, who was a good distance away, was amazed and offered up a cheer. As for me, I wasn't even aware I had an audience and continued my trek nonchalantly across the field, parting the barbed-wire fence and scrambled through out of harm's way, even if I didn't know it! Then, as always, Harold revealed the happy ending to my story, saying, "I watched you amble up Grandmother's back stairs and disappear through her screen door."

I am four and Buddy is 15 months.

As I reflect now on what happened that day, I can only say my guardian-angel must have been on duty for me at that precise moment. Otherwise I would not have lived out *My Story* as I have. Or perhaps, just perhaps, Nicky was my guardian-angel. What do you think?

4. Family

With all of my Dad's connections in the United States, he eventually found steady work across the border and remained there waiting for times to improve in Canada. And after a while, he was offered a chance to lease a good-sized ranch in Greenough, Montana and seized the opportunity, as he was a rancher at heart. My Dad then returned to Cardston with a plan to relocate the whole family to the Montana ranch. But by now, Mother had grown used to living on her own and was not enthusiastic about joining him. Nonetheless, she did let Harold leave school to go with his Dad, saying the rest of us would follow later. We never did.

When Floyd reached his sixteenth birthday in 1938, he asked to go and join his Dad and brother on the Montana ranch. Floyd loved horses and wanted the chance to ride them and Mother sent him on his way. Dad tried unsuccessfully to convince Mother there was a life for her and the rest of us there with him, but she never answered any of his letters. Even a tear-stained note from Harold was unable to persuade her, or so my Dad told me in later years.

Thereafter, my Dad and two brothers lived on their own in Montana and our family was permanently broken apart. And afterwards, Mother referred to herself as a widow or even a divorcee. But the truth was she was neither. My Mother and Dad were still married and would remain so all their lives, despite the divorce papers Mother had drawn up by a lawyer stating Dad was missing and declared dead.

And so, Hazel, Buddy and I continued living our lives without any further connection with our Dad or our two older brothers. It seemed to be what our Mother wanted. This final break in the family took place about the time we moved from the house with the wrap-around-porch and took up residence in an old abandoned hotel on Main Street in

Cardston. It was definitely not a nice place to live, although I was too young to make that judgement at the time. The old hotel had not only been abandoned, but condemned, and was destined to be torn down. However, it became home for us. The enormous structure with its many rooms was very time-worn and worse for wear, but I suppose it was the best Mother could afford. If Mother had to pay rent, it must have been very little, as all the people who lived there were poor like us.

My mother was free from her marriage, but it seemed she was still not happy and carried a load of bitterness around in her heart. She was bitter about how 'life' had treated her or that was the way she phrased it anyway. She was stubbornly independent and would not ask for a 'handout,' as Mother described the Government Relief Plan, set up to help those in need during those bleak years leading up to the World War in 1939. To support us all, she worked at a variety of odd jobs around the town of Cardston. I remember her as a chambermaid, a waitress and as a short-order cook in a café. Like most women of her generation, she had only an elementary school education which didn't give her many options when it came to employment. The meager wage Mother earned was barely enough to get by on. So our family of four was 'as poor as church mice,' as was said about the desperately poor in those days.

5. The Old Hotel

The outdated, age-old hotel was a dark and dingy place that needed many repairs which, of course, were not going to be done now that it was condemned. I didn't like the place! In fact, it seemed to affect my health and I became sick a lot and had frequent nightmares. Once I even became seriously ill with a feverish earache that caused me to become delirious and to have hallucinations. I recall Mother putting cold cloths on my burning forehead as there was no such thing as antibiotics available to cure us in those days. Not that we could have afforded penicillin anyway. Yet to know Mother was keeping a close eye on me was very comforting, even though she didn't say much. I still felt she cared.

Mother was an extremely private person, always keeping her emotions to herself. And looking back, I believe this was the very trait that affected her marriage to my Dad. Many years later, he told me how Mother had never been one to communicate her thoughts or for that matter any of her feelings either. I don't know why she was like that because she grew up in a big family surrounded by nine siblings. Or perhaps that was the reason!

I do not have good memories of the people who lived in the old hotel. In particular, there was a Mr. Flannigan whose room was at the opposite end of the hall from us. Mother called him her 'boarder.' Sometimes she would send me down the hall with a plate of food she had cooked for him, but I never wanted to go because I was afraid of him. He seemed so old and scary to me, with his grey-bearded face and bad-smelling breath.

I was plagued for years with a persistent dream, or rather a night-mare, in which Mr. Flannigan would be in bed with the covers turned back waiting for me to open the door. And although I was petrified with fear in my nightmare, I would continue moving down the hall towards his room. The hallway was very strange in my dream too, with many portions of the floor-boards missing. Somehow I had to get over or around these dangerous gaps in the floor since underneath, there was a pit of terrible darkness and I was afraid of falling into that abyss. This persistent nightmare pursued me for years and I'd wake up frightened and upset. Even when I grew older and moved away from Cardston, it continued to haunt me. Do persistent nightmares plague others too, I wonder?

Among the other people living in the old hotel at the time we did was Curtis, a man in his mid-twenties who lived there with his older brother, Dave. Both Buddy and I didn't like either one of them because they were mean and obnoxious to us. They told off-coloured jokes and laughed at us when we naively 'didn't get it.' Curtis especially enjoyed planting ter-rible doubts in my mind about my Dad. My childhood memories of Dad were hazy at best and Curtis insisted he knew my real father and said he was a no-good drunken Indian from the local Reserve. We all knew the Blood Reserve bordered our town of Cardston. To make his point fur-ther, Curtis said my brown eyes and hair proved what he said was true, I really was a native Indian! This mixed me up terribly and confused my young mind.

Buddy was also teased with horror stories about his juvenile chubbi-ness. He was told he was going to be so repulsively fat when he grew up he wouldn't be able to buy clothes big enough to fit him. People would laugh at him! And he would have to join the circus as the fattest man alive. There were also some horrible stories and jokes about our Mother as well. This was all so very troubling to me and being the oldest, I wanted to protect us from hearing such vicious lies, but I didn't know how.

6. The Car Lot Miracle

Usually Buddy and I avoided Curtis and his brother as much as possible. Yet one day, there was a big accident and we desperately needed the help of any adult we could find, and it was Curtis who came to our rescue. He accomplished such an act of heroism that day, Buddy and I were impressed and so were our new friends, Lois and Grant. They were with us when the major catastrophe occurred.

Lois was my age and her brother Grant was younger than Buddy and they had recently moved into the same old hotel where we lived. The four of us played together every day and our favorite game to play was a made-up one, which we nicknamed 'Cars.' This game was a whole lot of fun for us. Behind our old hotel there was a dump yard of old abandoned cars and this was our playing field. The game was really just a game of tag, the difference being the old deserted cars were where we hid ourselves until someone spied and tagged us. Climbing over the top of those abandoned cars and hiding inside them made it a very dangerous game to play, as a lot of the old relics were 'topsy-turvy' and resting precariously on their sides or even upside down. Being kids though, we were not mindful of the danger and continued to play our game day after day. That is, until the big accident! It still stands out with great clarity in my memory.

The youngest of our group was Grant, who weighed next to nothing, but could move with the speed of sound. And that day, he ran like a streak of lightening to find a hiding place and jumped onto a shell of a car that leaned unsteadily on its side. His weight was just enough to make it topple over with a loud crashing sound that reverberated in our ears. Grant was pinned by his neck to the ground with the collapsed car on top of him. We all ran to look at him under the car and his face was whiter than a ghost, which sent us all screaming for help.

As I mentioned before, the first adult we came upon was that terrible guy Curtis, who Buddy and I disliked so much! But today, we were thankful for anyone to help and begged him to come to the over-turned car and free our friend Grant before he died. With one mighty heave that old vehicle was lifted off Grant's body. It was an incredible sight to see! And Grant, even though he was dazed and didn't yet have any colour in his face, was not seriously hurt after the weight was raised off and he could breathe again. Later on, Curtis tried to lift up that same monstrous car again, just to prove how strong his muscles were. And he was not able to do it! The car wouldn't budge an inch off the ground.

All of us who had witnessed Grant's release from underneath the car felt like we'd seen a miracle. And I have to admit, the whole ordeal did put a lot of fear in our hearts about future accidents taking place. As a result, we quit playing our game of 'Cars' that very day and I think it was a wise decision, don't you? We still hung out with our friends, but after that experience we looked for more subdued and less dangerous games to play. And I remember that later that summer, we even vied for a spot in the Mayday parade in Cardston and marched proudly down Main Street.

In the parade, I was dressed in a costume as Little Bo Peep, sewn by Mother on her trusty little portable Singer sewing machine, and I carried a tall shepherd's crook. We had made the crook from a long willow branch that we laboriously wrapped in roll after roll of crepe paper. This took ages! Lois marched as Hiawatha in a borrowed buckskin costume while Grant rode a decorated tricycle, waving a Union Jack which was our Canadian flag at that time. Why Buddy wasn't in the photo I don't know, but the picture brings back one of my good childhood memory captured on film.

Another nice thing I remember about my years as a youngster is that we didn't have any 'street people' living on our streets as we see today. Street people simply didn't exist then. Not one! But, we did have a 'bag-lady' who I recall was taunted by the kids of the town. It gives me pangs of remorse even thinking of it. She was an elderly woman, bent over in stature and appeared very scary to us. Why? She wore long black dresses and a wide-brimmed black hat that surely did give her a 'witchy' appearance. She wandered up and down the streets collecting little things such as lost buttons, coins and bits of this and that, stuffing them in the huge black bag she carried. A rumour circulated that she secretly had scads of money hidden under her mattress, but of course, no one was brave enough to check it out. And why was that? For fear she'd put a hex on them, whatever that was? The poor unfortunate woman! Whatever became of her? I don't know whether the tale of her hidden wealth was true or not as it all remains a mystery in my past. Does every small town have their own brand of odd characters?

Me, Grant & Lois

7. Elementary School

I was very bashful and self-conscious when I started grade school and was prone to blushing when I was embarrassed, which was often. I felt this was a real handicap. Also, I was older than most of my other class-mates as Mother had kept me home from school an extra year, so I was almost seven when I started. I felt awkward about being older than the others in my grade, as if I had failed somehow and it plagued me all through my early elementary school days. Yet, I loved school and had a desire to learn as far back as I can remember. The public school was always a long walk for me and I dreaded being late for class. Rules about being late were very strict in those days. If you were late three times in a term you got the strap and I knew kids who had! I was never late! Not even once. But I was often scared I might be and would sometimes run part of the way to school just to be sure. Do you think I may have been a 'worrywart'?

It always seemed natural to me to want to please my teachers, but my shyness definitely got in the way. I was so thankful when I didn't have to stand up and read out loud like we were asked to do from time to time. I would blush in embarrassment and go 'red as a beet', as we used to say. I didn't like every eye on me! I suppose I felt insecure, perhaps due to my unstable home life, I don't know. I recall that I did not do well at sports at school either, as I wasn't very coordinated. When we were chosen for sports teams, I usually got picked near the end as the popular kids were chosen first. Was it a popularity contest? It seemed like it was to me. As a kid I wanted to play as much as anyone else in order to improve at the game. I felt hurt waiting so long to be picked, even though I pretended it didn't matter.

There were several popular girls in my class and I secretly wished I was one of them and not me! One was a girl with golden hair and I noticed she wore the same dress for a week at a time. At first I thought she was poor like me, but then I discovered her parents were born in Holland and tended to be on the thrifty side. I envied her in more ways than one, especially in our Social Studies class, when we had to identify our racial origin. Why did it matter anyway? Were we not all born here? For us children, it was very rare back then not to have been born in Canada.

I would have loved to be Dutch, but I had to say I was German, as Mother told me Dad's people came from there and we could only claim the ethnic origin on our father's side of the family. Our country was in the early war years now and there were terrible battles overseas raging against Germany. Everyone frowned upon being of German descent because of Hitler and the war. So both Buddy and I felt mortified when we had to admit our father was German. And it wasn't until many years later that I discovered my Dad wasn't German at all. His ancestors came from Luxembourg, a separate country between Germany and France with its own King. So I was equally French and German and I would have happily claimed to be of French ancestry. Funny the things you remember.

As a pupil in the elementary grades, I enjoyed learning about all the interesting countries and discovering new places I'd never even heard of. Getting to draw them on a world map was fun, too. Art was one of my

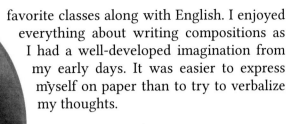

favorite classes along with English. I enjoyed everything about writing compositions as I had a well-developed imagination from my early days. It was easier to express myself on paper than to try to verbalize my thoughts.

I'm 10 years old.

8. The Car Wreck

By the time I was ten and in grade four, Mother had moved us again and we were now living in the worst possible house yet. It was an awful, old two-story house I hated with a passion. What made me hate it? It was infested with BED BUGS! And I'll never forget the awful bites I'd wake up and find on my body in the morning, for those ugly red creatures did their biting in the dark of night. Buddy and I couldn't scratch those itchy spots either or they'd flare up into big red welts and the kids at school might ask questions. We lived in that horrible house for more years than I want to remember and kept the bed bugs a secret. But that is not to say we didn't constantly complain about them to Mother. Why wouldn't we, it made us hate going to bed!

It was only a short time after we moved into that dreadful house that Hazel quit school and got married. She was just seventeen years of age. I was undeniably sad! Her choice of a husband, so it turned out, was none other than Curtis! Yes, that awful person Buddy and I disliked so much from the old hotel days. His nasty remarks and distasteful jokes were well remembered. But of course, I kept those feelings hidden from Hazel, as she was dear to me and I couldn't tell her I disliked the man she was marrying. No, not for the world! I was silent and explained to Buddy that our dislike for Curtis was our private little secret and he must not tell anyone.

After their wedding, which was done quietly and without much fan-

Hazel at 17 years of age.

fare, I'd go to visit Hazel where she lived across town. I would walk there after school when Hazel was alone and it gave us time together. She liked to style my hair and she'd roll it into pin-curls all over my head, fastening each curl with a bobby-pin as was the fashion then. I couldn't help noticing how my wonderful sister seemed to have lost some of her delightful sparkle. I wasn't sure why, but I could guess. Curtis hadn't changed one iota over the past years and was still as rude and obnoxious as ever. That was my opinion of him anyway.

To explain my ongoing judgmental attitude towards Curtis, I'll have to describe one of our Saturday night chicken suppers. You see, it wasn't unusual for Mother to take Buddy and me over to Hazel's place late on a Saturday afternoon. Then, as it grew darker outside, Curtis would pile as many of us as possible into his old worn-out, rattle-trap of a car and we'd head out for 'some excitement', as Curtis always called it!

Buddy and I rarely ever had a chance to ride in a car, so we were keen to go and would jump right in. It wasn't always a joy ride for me though! Dave, the older brother of Curtis, would often come along and share the back seat of the car with us, to my dismay. You see, Dave would put his hand on the seat when we were climbing in, so I might 'accidently' sit on his hand. At least that was his plan. Even the thought of him trying to slip his hand up under my skirts made me terribly mad and I'd protest in a loud voice. Naturally, everyone in the car heard my complaining and usually that took care of the problem. Then, once we were all settled in the car again, Curtis would yell out, "Look out chickens, here we come!" Away we'd go in a cloud of dust to steal several chickens for our supper.

Buddy and I knew from experience that we had to stay inside the car on these trips, as the job had to be done quickly and quietly in the pitch-dark. A lot of people in our town back then kept chickens in their backyards, so it was easy to locate a chicken-coop. However, it was not so easy to find one without a barking dog.

Once Curtis and his brother retrieved the chickens, their necks would be rung and they'd be flung into a gunny-sack and then hidden in the trunk of the car. After that, we'd return home and Hazel would fry up a chicken supper and it would always be finger-licking good! I didn't ever hear her express an opinion on all this, but I don't think it was something she was enthusiastic about either. The idea of venturing out to perform this thievery was always instigated by Curtis or Dave, so in my child's mind, they were the thieves and the rest of us just went along for the ride. I was a real naïve youngster, wasn't I?

One particular Saturday night, everything went terribly wrong. Before a chicken-coop could even be located, our car was involved in an accident on the far side of town. Just which of the two cars involved didn't obey the stop-sign, I can't say. But I do recall our vehicle was broadsided in the middle of the intersection by the town taxi cab. The force of the collision sent our fully-loaded car right off the road and turned it over completely. I will always remember the ferocious sound of that impact! It was ear-splitting, as metal collided with metal. Then, inside our car, there was a strange sensation of dirt from the car's floor showering us from above as our car rolled over upside-down and finally righted itself again on its wheels in the roadside ditch. We were all flung around in the car, as it was long before the use of seatbelts. Mother was sitting beside me in the backseat and in trying to be helpful, I guess, shoved my head down hard to avoid flying glass. I saw 'stars,' inasmuch as my head hit hard against the seat in front of me and I received a nasty gash on my forehead. And then, just at that very moment, I heard someone in the car yell, "Get out and run," and all of us in the car promptly moved into action!

Our car was left where it had come to a stop in the ditch and we made a quick retreat back across town as fast as our legs would carry us. I was holding somebody's handkerchief against my bleeding head as I raced along and we were half-way home before I realized I wasn't the only one who was hurt. Mother was having difficulty breathing and it really scared me! Once we arrived at Hazel's doorstep, she quickly attended to our needs with bandages from her medicine chest. Then Mother, standing silently by, took a seat and passed-out from her injuries. Someone voiced the fear she might have fractured some ribs, but when Mother came around, she claimed she was fine and would just rest a spell on the bed. Denial was always Mother's way of handling things. Even so, I felt sorry for her in her pain.

Of course, every one of us was pretty shaken up by what happened and there was no chicken supper on the table that night! Once our stomachs settled down, we ate bologna sandwiches which Hazel fixed for us from her larder. The following Monday morning, I went to school with a sizable scab on my forehead and a fictitious story of how it happened. Telling the truth would certainly have gotten us all in trouble, wouldn't it? Later on when my scab fell off, I was left with a life-time dent in the bone of my forehead, a souvenir of that sorry adventure.

9. The Gold Mine

Did I say we were a dysfunctional family? Well, in case there is any doubt left, I have to divulge Mother's tale of the lost gold mine up in the Alberta hills! Buddy and I had heard Mother repeat her story more times than we could count and it was always exactly the same. She alleged her two brothers knew the whereabouts of a mysterious lost gold mine where a pot full of gold nuggets was hidden. Thinking back now, perhaps Mother thought inventing such a story would help us put up with the poverty we lived in better. So, perhaps she may have meant well? Anyway, this is how the story unfolded:

When Uncle Bud and Uncle Juke were on a hunting trip on horse-back up in the Rocky Mountain range in the distant past, they supposedly came upon an old caved-in mine entrance. And being curious, the two of them poked around until they broke into the old deserted mine and found a big rusted cast-iron cooking pot, buried in the dirt floor. When they pried off the lid they found it was full of gold nuggets left behind by some gold miner, who had likely been forced to leave in a hurry. There were lots of solitary miners living like hermits up in those hills and they were vulnerable to attacks, or at least that was Mother's version of the story.

Always at this point in the account, which was as familiar to us as a nursery rhyme, I would ask the same question. "Then why aren't both of our uncles rich men now?"

Mother had her answer ready. "They kept only a sample of the gold nuggets and reburied the rest because they had to apply for a deed in order to claim the mine as their own." Then, like always, she would add in a near whisper. "That's why it has to all be kept a secret."

Those two uncles of ours lived in Cardston and when either one of them dropped by, Buddy and I would listen carefully, in case the gold mine was ever discussed. It never was! After many years of Mother saying, "Just wait until our gold mine comes in," I decided it must be a figment of my mother's imagination. Naturally, she flatly denied that she'd made the tale up, even when I pressed her for the truth. Finally, one day she surprised me and said she'd prove to me that her story was true. I was ready to listen. She then produced a small cloth bag with a number of tiny gold nuggets in it. They were convincing alright, but I still had my doubts that the lost gold mine story was an authentic one.

Time moved on and the big secret of the 'lost gold mine' was often the topic of our private conversations at home. That is, until the day I accidently happened to find a letter stored away in an old shoe-box upstairs. It was from Mother's sister in California, an aunt I'd never met. She had moved to southern California with her husband years before when I was still a baby. Curiosity being part of my nature, I read the open letter and was astounded to read that my aunt was sending some gold nuggets in the letter to my mother. The nuggets were mementos from a mountain holiday in California, my aunt said, where she'd been instructed in the art of panning for gold. The little nuggets were her reward and she wanted Mother to have them. What a discovery! The mystery of the gold nuggets and the 'so-called' gold mine was solved, as far as I was concerned anyway.

Mother, of course, stuck stubbornly to her original story of her brothers and the gold mine and it was some decades later, when we were all adults that my brother Floyd divulged the fact that he knew about the secret gold mine. We were visiting him in Idaho, when he confessed he'd always wanted to go looking for that lost gold mine up in the Rocky Mountains. What did he say! I couldn't believe my ears! It was revealed then, that my three older siblings had also been raised on the same myth Buddy and I had listened to for years. And because it was a secret we hadn't discussed it openly, even with each other. To this day, I'm really not sure Floyd believed my version of the story. I suppose for him, it was a lot like giving up a wishful dream that might still come true someday.

10. The Sheep Farm

The summer when I was eleven and Buddy was nine, we enjoyed the best summer vacation away from school we'd ever had. Normally we did nothing all summer, but play and lay around, but this year Hazel invited us to come and spend a few weeks with her on a farm near Fort MacLeod, Alberta. Hazel and Curtis had been hired to manage and tend a huge flock of sheep on a sheep-farm over the summer that year. Buddy and I were excited to go because we missed Hazel and we'd never seen a sheep-farm before. It was a great holiday for us being around the sheep and romping with the Collie sheepdog. We roamed the open spaces and climbed up on giant boulders that lay in the fields of the farm.

We even tamed a couple of the docile sheep so we could ride them like they were small ponies. We'd hang on to them around their necks, clutching handfuls of their thick woolly coats to keep from falling off. We had a ball! The sheep were like pets to us and we gave names to our favorite ones. What calm and peaceful temperaments they possessed. Their gentle bleating at night soothed us to sleep in our beds, as we lay there listening to their soft-pitched, quivering cries.

We also made friends with two raccoons that summer, a male and female we nicknamed Queenie and King. Whether they were really a girl and a boy, who knows? We really enjoyed pampering them like pets. However, this escapade called for us to be very brave, as raccoons can

Right: Me riding a sheep.
Below: Buddy and I perched high up.

sometimes be vicious creatures. But Queenie and King must have been an especially good-natured pair of raccoons, because we were able to train them to come to our doorstep for a treat of cow's milk. At first, we were very timid to touch them while they were busy slurping the milk up, but after a while they let Buddy and I stroke their wiry heads and their long stripped backs. It was a very scary business, but for some reason Hazel allowed us to do it. Their teeth were sharp and they had extra-long claws and were certainly wild. Regardless of what might have happened, we never did receive a scratch or a bite and enjoyed our relationship with them. I guess our guardian angels were once again sitting right there beside us.

That summer on the farm was a mixture of happiness one moment and of fear the next, for me. I was afraid a 'tallying up' of accounts might have to come about between Hazel's husband and me. I still had an intense dislike for Curtis and he was well aware of it! I did my best to avoid being around him, but it was impossible to do on the farm. He was still drinking a lot, and it took many bottles of beer to quench his thirst each day. Frequently, he would offer me a bottle which I would not accept and always politely said, "No thank you." His glaring scowl told me a day was coming when his accumulating anger would erupt.

And then it did! On an exceptionally hot day, which always made Curtis bad-tempered anyway, he cornered me when I was alone in the yard. Before I knew what was happening, he had completed his mean stunt. He grabbed me by the arms and lifted me up, turning me over in the air, so I was upside-down. I struggled, but my weight was nothing compared to his strength. Then he freed one hand and slowly poured a whole bottle of beer into my upturned face hoping to force some of it down my throat. I clenched my teeth and held my mouth firmly shut. The rank-smelling beer ran up my nose and completely drenched my whole head. I was saturated with the stinky stuff, and dreadfully mad and upset. I broke away from his clutches and ran down the path to the river and washed the foul smell off myself as best as I could. A great many tears ran down my face at the unfairness of it all. I felt violated and I resolved never to lay eyes on my awful brother-in-law again. Of course, that meant not returning to the house. Even so, my mind was made up!

It wasn't long before Hazel's voice began calling my name, but I hid until the sun went down and the shadows of darkness covered everything. I was too mad to be afraid. When my stomach began to growl with hunger, I crept into the garden and ate some raw carrots. I estimated I could last a long time with all the rows of vegetables growing there. All the while, the wind carried Hazel's voice to me as she called my name over and over again. And as her loving voice resonated in my ears, I began to let go of my anger. After all, I wasn't mad at Hazel! Finally, she won my heart over and I returned to the house and was restored safely into her loving arms once more. I decided that night, having someone who really loves you makes the world a much better place, even though existing in this world with all its heartbreaking burdens is difficult to endure at times.

I remember it was later that same summer when Hazel patiently taught me how to dance just like the grown ups do. She good-naturedly showed me the slow waltz steps and the faster fox-trot paces. It was so much fun being taught to dance by my precious sister. We'd turn the radio up loud and she'd take the lead, twirling me round and round the kitchen floor as we sang the lyrics to the Hit Parade tunes. We knew every word of the top ten popular songs, despite the fact that neither of us could carry the tunes very well. All the same, a certain kind of joy swept over us and all our cares took flight in those special moments of dancing with our arms around one another, surrounded by the strains of the music we loved.

When I turned eleven, I found out what it was like to work for a wage, albeit for only one day. Mother was cleaning houses for a living now and on this particular Saturday was not feeling well. She asked me to take her place and do the housecleaning of a regular customer. I couldn't say no, could I? So, I started out early and walked to the far side of town where the house was situated in one of our wealthy neighbourhoods. I worked hard all day long for the lady and at the end was asked to wash an assortment of her husband's socks, before I left. Ugh! That was the final straw for me and to top it off, I was handed a one dollar bill for my day's pay.

I returned home more than a little upset. "Did the lady pay me this dollar because I'm only a kid?" I asked Mother.

"No," she answered, "that's the same as she pays me."

Right then and there, I decided I was never going to make my living cleaning other people's houses. No way! And can you imagine having to hand-wash a pile of stinky socks as part of your measly dollar pay? That definitely was pushing things too far in my estimation.

11. Dance Lessons & Baptism

It was later in that same year of 1942, when I was almost twelve that I dreamed of becoming a famous dancer on the stage or in the movies. I begged Mother to let me start taking dance lessons. She had once again changed jobs and was now the laundress at the Cardston hospital, definitely the best job she'd ever had and with greatly improved wages, to boot! It made me ecstatically happy when Mother gave-in to my pleading for lessons as I just knew I'd been born to dance!

Me in my ballet costume.

The dance lessons were once a week and cost only fifty cents for instruction in ballet, as well as toe dancing and tap dancing. Such a bargain! Our dance instructor was Kay, a beautiful, blonde eighteen year old girl who had recently graduated from the Cardston High School and was opening up her new dance studio. Her father was a local businessman who owned the only two movie theatres in town and the dance lessons were given in one of them. Kay's personality turned out to be every bit as charming as her looks and it wasn't long before her class of seven students all adored her, including me. There were huge photographs of Hollywood's top stars hanging on the walls of her dance studio, and I recall thinking Kay's family must be 'filthy rich' since each picture was autographed personally to them. Imagine! It certainly made the place look extraordinarily classy.

And it was at dance lessons where I first met Laurene, who immediately became my very best friend. We both loved learning to dance and getting dressed up in our costumes when the annual dance finale came around. Laurene was ever so pretty with black hair and green eyes and was older than me by two years, but that never mattered to us. I loved Laurene from the start and it seemed to be a very mutual friendship for us both. Laurene and her family had a great in-

Laurene and I.

fluence on my young life. Why was that? They were very strict Mormons in every sense of the word and talked a lot about their religion quite naturally in front of me. However this did not bother me at all. For you see, it was through their influence that I was introduced to a desire to know God for myself.

Up to that point in my life, I knew nothing about God, as Mother had never mentioned religion of any kind or taken us to church. So when I asked Mother if she had any objections to me having a Mormon friend, her answer was as I expected.

"Do as you please," she said. Getting advice from Mother was like 'getting blood from a turnip,' or at least that was my way of describing it. I knew Mother had been raised Presbyterian by her parents, but for some reason she had quit attending for as far back as I could remember.

And so, that very day I accepted the challenge of becoming a Mormon and my friend Laurene encouraged me to attend Sunday school classes with her, which I did. The classes were held in the Mormon Tabernacle, which was their church. I don't recall any of the other people I met there, but my friendship with Laurene grew immensely. Those instruction classes were where I began to learn about Mormonism and how they were the only people going to heaven when they died. And naturally, this made me feel anxious about my own eternal destination. Where was I going? I didn't know!

So I asked Mother if I could get baptized and become a Mormon and she gave me her usual reply, saying, "Do as you please." So, I made plans to become a member of the Church of the Latter Day Saints by being baptized in the Mormon Temple, which was where all their baptisms were performed. I was twelve-and-a-half years of age.

When the scheduled day of baptism arrived, I was nervous about going by myself and so I talked Buddy into coming with me. He had just turned ten years old and said he definitely wanted to go to heaven, too! What a sight we must have been, a pair of scared, straggly young waifs determined to seal their eternal fate once and for all. But beyond any fear, I was filled with excitement! Entering the mysterious marble Temple was going to satisfy my curiosity about what the interior of that massive place looked like. And believe me, it turned out to be much more overwhelming than I even expected.

The beauty on the inside of the Temple struck me with awesome delight! The room where we entered had a spectacular storybook appearance about it, hardly appearing real at all. The two of us were ushered into change rooms and handed white robes to put on. Following that, we were led down a corridor into a huge central room which was entirely filled with brilliant light, so dazzling to our eyes it almost blinded us. And there in the center of the room stood a gorgeous circular pool, with water in it as blue as the sky on a hot summer's day. Two humongous lions carved out of marble were guarding either side of the entrance to the sparkling pool where our baptism would take place. Were we going to be baptized into heaven? It seemed like it to me.

A tall man in a white robe, like the ones we wore, summoned us into the center of the pool. And there we were baptized one by one, me first and then Buddy. The man tipped us over backwards and completely dunked us under the water. Not once, but three times!

I was greatly relieved when the water part of the baptism was over. But my brother and I were not finished yet! We were instructed to memorize the Mormon's Thirteen Articles of Faith and to return in one week's time in order to repeat them from memory before a Church Elder. We were entirely too young to grasp it all, but we obeyed and followed through. Getting baptized surely did made us feel better and even months later, in the cold of wintertime with our feet propped-up on the oven door for warmth, Buddy and I were still reliving our experience of baptism. But now, we were fully convinced that heaven would resemble the inside of the vast Temple and it comforted us to know where we were going.

The Mormon Temple in Cardston.

12. Friendship

Getting to know Laurene and becoming bosom-friends with her brought such a whole lot of happiness into my life. Her family was respectable and lived in a nice home only two blocks from where I lived in the condemned, bed bug filled house. But of course, that was my secret! We went to dance lessons and the movies together and generally spent every weekend in each other's company, but always at Laurene's house. Her family didn't seem to mind me coming around as often as I did and besides, my house had those 'skeletons-in-the-closet,' didn't it?

During the sunny days of summer, Laurene and I would often wander over to the Mormon Temple grounds and hang out there. It soon became our very favorite place to go. It was so restful among the cool marble alcoves set in the outside walls of the Temple, especially in the heat of the day. We learned how to make ourselves invisible to the many gardeners working there as we knew every nook and cranny of that giant edifice, including the best places to hide.

If we did sometimes snitch the occasional flower, it was usually one of the enormous chrysanthemums which we would tuck into our hair and imagine we were on some exotic island faraway, just like we saw depicted in the Dorothy Lamour movies. We claimed all the beautiful flowers that flourished on the Temple grounds as our very own.

Posing at the Temple.

The Temple grounds were our private hideaway and a place to escape to, not that Laurene had anything to escape from, other than an annoying younger sister. Whereas, I had all my dysfunctional family stuff, didn't I? The two of us basked for hours in the peaceful silence of the parkland surroundings. It was indeed a newfound refuge for me.

Laurene and I grew inseparable. In Sunday school class, we would whisper and write notes to each other and generally act like the teenagers we were. For this reason, I didn't learn much more about the serious side of the Mormon teachings, let alone become indoctrinated by them. Still, it did affect the way I lived and held my standard of behavior to a high-level. You might say, it kept me on the 'straight-and-narrow' and caused me have a desire for an honest life before God, which worked out to my benefit in the long run.

As friends, Laurene and I encouraged each other by reading books and poetry to each other. And because we both possessed such romantic hearts, we loved and memorized the long poem called *The Highwayman*. The Scotsman, Alfred Noyes, wrote that wonderful poem back in 1906, long before our time. We spoke those lilting lines of poetry to each other, over and over again, so much so that I've been able to recall them all these years later. Yes, I can still recite all eighty-five verses of that poem today! It takes over six minutes to do it, too! How incredible our brains are, to have that huge storage capacity. Do try it for yourself. Memorizing is loads of fun!

As well as poems, Laurene and I read a whole pile of books together, but *Anne of Green Gables*, by Lucy Maud Montgomery, was our number one favourite. We even made a blood pact, Anne-style, by pricking our index fingers and mixing our blood together. Why would we do such a crazy kid thing? So we could make pledges to each other. Yes, indeed! One of them I'll never forget was to remain kindred spirits always and to never get married in our lifetime on earth. It seems like a preposterous idea to me now, but that's because I was a child then and I left such childish things behind me when I grew up.

Laurene.

Whenever we walked anywhere, Laurene and I always linked our arms, one through the other, and thought of it as a sign of our togetherness. We surely didn't think of it as embarrassing, as some might today. And, believe it or not, in the movies we'd hold hands. Yes! I recall us doing it all the time! If the movie had a scary part, Laurene would grip my fingers so tight it would be painful. And she had long fingernails which intensified my suffering. Yes, it was kid stuff alright, but definitely part of our culture back then.

In those years, I often had 'sleep-overs' at Laurene's house on Friday nights in the summertime. When all the household members were asleep, we would 'raid' the refrigerator and were delighted if we found leftovers there. And I remember it seemed like their family often had liver for Friday's supper. So we'd divide any thick, chewy slab of leftover liver between us before climbing out the window of her second-floor bedroom onto the roof. Then, we'd lie on our backs on the warm shingles, nibbling our chunk of cold liver and contemplating the moon and the stars. It was a special game we played and we designated it our 'moon-gazing' time.

On those evenings out there in the darkness, we'd share our innermost secrets, gazing with wonder at the spacious night sky so magnificent and gloriously spread out high over our heads. And we'd try to count every star. An impossible task! There are zillions of twinkling stars up there, like jewels hung in space. But even before counting the stars, we would have a race to see who could spot the first star of the night. Once we found it, we'd recite the familiar old English nursery rhyme that went like this. Remember?

> Star light, Star bright,
> First star I see tonight,
> I wish I may, I wish I might,
> Have this wish I wish tonight

You've probably said that little verse over and over again many times yourself, haven't you? Everyone has! And how impossible it is to view that indescribable sky at night, in its awesome splendor, and not believe that behind its beauty and majesty there is a God who designed it all. In *Psalm 8,* we are told to consider, "...how the moon and the stars were set into place by the work of God's hands." But of course, I'm jumping ahead aren't I? That disclosure came much later in my span of my life.

And getting back to that scene on the rooftop ... as well as wishing on the first star of the evening, which Laurene and I always did, we would also count each and every falling star with their tails of fire and light trailing out behind them. It kept us so amused and entertained that the hours would literally fly by like they had wings. This nearly always resulted in us getting to sleep at a very late hour, so we were real 'sleepy-heads' on Saturday mornings!

13. The Movies, a Bike Ride and a Peacock

Our junior high school, at that time, combined our three different grades into one Drama Class, so my closest and dearest friend and I shared the same acting class every week. We volunteered for any part in a play no matter how small. We were anxious to expand our acting abilities! Our love of drama was likely influenced by all the movies we watched in those years during the 1940's. We went to them all and it was no wonder, as theatre tickets were a mere fifteen cents each, or ten cents for a Saturday matinee. A real entertainment bargain!

My favourite movie actress at the time was the gorgeous Lana Turner and one day I mailed a request to her studio for a picture. Stamps were so cheap back then, a paltry three cents each! To my delight, I received an authentic photograph of Lana, autographed in her own handwriting, in ink no less. I was thrilled and straightaway made additional appeals for photos of Dennis Morgan and other leading stars I idolized at the time. I've held on to that collection to this very day. Yes, I was a really big fan of the movies and *Gone with the Wind* was my favourite. I saw it countless times after it won ten Oscars at the Academy Awards Ceremonies in 1940.

Before we had movies to watch, we only had radios and our imaginations. And in those days of radio listening, the spooky programs were always my favorites, like the *Inner Sanctum* with its squeaky door and another mystery called *Only the Shadow Knows*. The opening sequences of those programs would make shivers go up my spine as a kid. It's something I haven't forgotten.

In our town, as I said before, we had two theatres, one showing movies and the smaller one was where Kay gave us our dance lessons every week. Remember her father owned both theatres. Once a year in May, a big dance revue was held in order to show off what we had learned all year. It was always a big extravaganza. And so, in 1944 the revue was once again anticipated as a major gala event, this year headlined as *The Spring Parade*. As the rehearsals got under way, Kay spoke to our senior class of seven, confiding that she was expecting a picture perfect performance from us as we were her most experienced students. It put a load of pressure on us, but we loved Kay and promised to practice very hard so she wouldn't be disappointed.

In the big dance revue, our senior group was to dance four numbers together and then Kay would pick five of us to do solo numbers. The idea of dancing on the stage alone was my wildest dream come true. My big chance! But I also knew it would be extremely scary. So when the parts were given out, I was surprised and a little scared, but on 'cloud nine' with delight. Kay had chosen me to do a solo dance number as a peacock! I just knew Mother would create a beautiful peacock costume for me to wear.

Laurene, however, was not happy. She was mad! Her solo number came at the very end, as a wicked witch! She knew it was because of her jet-black hair and for once I wasn't envious of her lovely head of hair and was glad mine was just ordinary brown.

Yet, neither of us realized at the time it might be a close call as to whether either of us would participate in the dance revue at all. The reason being that one week before the big revue that year, Laurene decided to teach me how to ride a bicycle. The story unfolds as follows:

It was early on a sunshiny Saturday morning when the two of us set out for me to realize what would be my remarkable victory! I wanted to feel confident, but riding a bike lined up with my inability to swim, both of which seemed to be entirely beyond my capabilities. However, Laurene had no doubt at all about teaching me and had brought her older brother's bike along with her to carry out the task.

We walked out of town on the main highway, which was gravel back in those days and not paved as they are today. The gravel made a terrible surface to ride a bike on, but I wasn't worried so much about that, I just wanted to get it over with! Before long, Laurene announced it was time to begin the lesson and I was ready. As it was a boy's bike, I was told to climb up and straddle the bicycle bar and balance there while she got the bike moving forward. Then, with full confidence as my instructor, she scrambled up onto the seat behind me and we were under way.

Unfortunately, in my nervousness my hands clutched the handle bars so tight it was a battle as to which one of us had control of the bike's navigation. The bike started to wobble back and forth across the highway with both of us pulling on the handle bars. Then suddenly in the distance, a car loomed out of nowhere and came rushing toward us. Laurene headed for the ditch, or was it me steering? All I know is we flew off the road and were thrown head over heels into the rocks and grimy mud of the ditch. Thankfully, neither of us was killed, but we didn't come out of it unscathed either. The oncoming car went whizzing by, leaving us standing forlornly in the horrible ditch with our legs cut and bleeding. What a mess we were!

Then, simultaneously, the reality of it all dawned on us and we groaned, "What have we done?" Our dance revue was taking place the following Saturday! Oh the pangs of conscience that escaped our lips as we looked down and beheld our wounded legs. Incredible as it seems, we did manage to both be in *The Spring Parade* revue the following week after all. But we were aided by many flesh coloured Band-Aids to conceal our numerous nicks and cuts.

Mother came through with a beautiful peacock costume for me, too. It consisted of a gorgeous midriff top and tights made from a rich purple 'sparkle' material which had been supplied by my teacher Kay. And the peacock part of the costume was delightful as well. It was an exquisite tie-around-skirt that parted in the front and flowed out behind me to the floor. On it were rows of ruffles in all the colours of the rainbow, sewn on by Mother, using her trusty little Singer sewing machine once again. She had outdone herself in creating a truly fabulous costume and it cost next to nothing to make either. Mother had fashioned the ruffles out of coloured crepe paper! How very smart! I couldn't wait to perform my solo as a peacock and when my cue arrived, Kay whispered in my ear, "Strut like a peacock" and so I did!

As I recall, there was only one glitch leading up to my much awaited peacock dance and it turned out to be one of my all-time most embarrassing moments. It happened after our final dress rehearsal when Kay asked me to stay afterward so she could speak with me. Privately, she explained very nicely that I needed to take care of the stubbly new-growth of dark hair in my armpits. I was mortified, but not so naïve I didn't understand what she was referring to. I know my face turned every shade of scarlet, but I managed to nod in agreement. Looking back now to that awkward moment, I realize it mustn't have been an easy task for a young teacher to inform her pupil about such a thing. Then again, she wanted my performance to be flawless and from that perspective, I'm grateful that she cared enough to do it.

Dancing my solo that night to an overflowing theatre audience made me ecstatically happy! Afterwards, Kay told me I'd accomplished my dance with excellence and she was very proud of me. I thought my heart would burst with the intense pleasure I felt.

And another thing to rejoice over was that the wicked witch decided to be a happy witch after all. What a relief! She danced her solo number in marvelous form, which pleased me as well as her. What a perfectly amazing evening we experienced!

In retrospect, although I was scared to be alone on the stage that night, I was in high spirits because I was honouring Kay's trust in me. And through it all, I was able to give great joy to Mother too, who proudly applauded me from her seat in the audience.

Mother and I.

14. Sink or Swim

Have you ever wondered why some enjoyable things in life are so hard to achieve? For me it was the knack of being able to swim. I've often pondered why I didn't learn to swim as a child or even as a young adult, as it's not like I haven't tried. Perhaps it's due to the fact that swimming in deep water can trigger a sense of fear in me, even if I don't like to admit it. And perhaps my hope of becoming a swimmer was dashed with my very first attempt!

It happened way back, in the second summer that Laurene and I were friends. We were wishfully looking through the Sears catalogue one day when we saw these astounding one- piece bathing suits. We had earned extra babysitting money and saved it up, so we could easily afford them. We filled out the catalogue forms requesting two in matching turquoise satin and posted them away.

The weekend the bathing suits arrived by mail was the same weekend our two month summertime vacation from school began, much to our delight. We donned the turquoise beauties and hastily made our way to the banks of the Old Man River, which wound its way through the center of our town. Why the river? We had no such thing as an Aquatic Centre to swim in back then. We had only one choice and that was the river.

Slowly we ventured into the surging depths, still chilly from the spring run-off despite the summer sun. When the water had reached almost to our midriffs, our eyes spied them. A shoal of SNAKES coming rapidly towards us from upstream! I'll never forget that display of swimming snakes. Yikes! Only their heads appeared above the water. Neither of us had ever seen swimming snakes before, let alone so many of them together. There were scads, as I recall, stretching across the moving waters of the river and fast approaching where we stood.

We moved into action! And with far greater haste than we'd entered, we scrambled out of the river and onto its nearest bank. Alas, those beautiful bathing suits never saw water again. But, they did come in handy later on as we covered ourselves with baby oil and lay sun tanning on a blanket in the prairie sun. As for swimming, I think the desire must have been scared right out of me by those snakes! Regrettably, my courageous attempt to swim had ended in down-right failure, no doubt about that.

Much later on as an adult, I revived my hopes of learning to swim and took lessons at the Edmonton Recreational Centre near where we lived at that time. But to no avail! My body simply would not be taught to swim. And even at present, although numerous family members have tried to impart their 'how-to-swim' wisdom to me, I still remain a non-swimmer! But I am so glad to know the young students of today are offered swim lessons as part of their Elementary School education. How very wonderful! Such privileges were not the case in my school days.

And along with swimming and other activities, I hear sex education is now given to all students at the grade five levels. Not so in my school days during the 1940's! Then, there was no sex education at any level. And to my chagrin, Mother, who was reserved by nature, totally ignored discussing the subject with me. And so it was Hazel who came to my rescue. She knew I needed to know about the physical changes going on in my body as I went through my adolescent years. Being those six years older, Hazel helped me out by answering all my questions. I think girls without big sisters and with unforthcoming mothers must have really suffered in those bygone days of my youth and beyond.

15. Brother Bud

I loved my younger brother Buddy, although he was a constant worry to me in our growing-up years. At times though, I was so busy growing up myself I didn't notice he was no longer the little Buddy who got baptized with me. For instance, he didn't want to be called Buddy anymore.

"Just call me Bud," he insisted. And so we did. And Bud's choice of friends left a lot to be desired, at least to my way of thinking! They were a gang of older boys who hung out late at night on the downtown streets just looking for trouble. But despite Bud's late hours, Mother never applied any rules to his behavior. It seemed Bud could do no wrong as far as Mother was concerned. I used to wonder about that sometimes and concluded that it was because he was the baby of the family. But I could see plainly it wasn't helping him become a very nice person.

One night when Laurene and I were walking home from a movie, we saw Bud and his gang on the street. They were 'smoking up a storm,' as we used say. When I challenged Bud the next morning he firmly denied he smoked at all. I knew he was lying to me as I'd seen him as plain as day and besides, he always reeked of tobacco smoke. I waited and watched and sure enough, when he used the outhouse in the backyard, I had my evidence. There were great clouds of cigarette smoke pouring out of every crack and cranny of that old wooden structure we called 'the toilet.' Bud smoked alright and was lying to me about it.

I began to wonder where Bud was getting the money to buy cigarettes and I started to think he might have become dishonest in other ways. Sure enough, when I asked Bud he couldn't resist bragging. He told me his gang was good at stealing stuff they could sell for cash and the money paid for their cigarettes. Then, he even went so far as to boast about stealing money from Mother. This really upset me! I told him I couldn't believe he'd be so mean as to do that. To prove to me he could do it, Bud showed off his thievery in front of me. He walked over and took a ten dollar bill right out of Mother's purse when her back was turned. Now I was mad. I threatened to tell Mother on him. He only laughed and dared me to go ahead.

"She won't believe you, anyway," he said. And he was right! Mother insisted I must have been mistaken. Once again, I realized there was nothing I could do to put an end to the dysfunction in my family. It made me so sad! However, the worst episode concerning my brother Bud was yet to come.

Late one night, he finally overstepped the mark and stole a parked car on a dark street and took it for what he called a 'joy ride.' I didn't even know Bud could drive! Being barely twelve years old, he must have barely been able to see over the radiator of the car. Remember how huge those cars were back in those far-off days? Anyway, Bud did manage to keep the stolen car on the road and headed out of town on Highway #2 where he continued northward. He got as far as Claresholm, a distance of sixty miles from Cardston, before the R.C.M.P. finally put an end to his escapade. They brought him back to our house in a police car and there was a very grave warning given to Mother. Any further illegal behaviour by Buddy and he would be sent to Reform School. I was so embarrassed for him, but he acted as if he'd been clever and pulled off something smart. I hardly even knew my kid brother anymore.

16. Mother's House

The war years gave Mother some much needed help financially due to the fact that my two older brothers had left ranching and joined the United States Marines when the US entered the Second World War. As their Mother she qualified to receive part of their monthly pay allowance and it didn't matter that she lived in Canada. By now, she was tired of being poor so she wisely invested most of Uncle Sam's money into purchasing a small city lot in Cardston. A prudent choice! However, due to her private nature, Bud and I only became aware of this when she hired Curtis to build a house for her on the lot. This part of her plan was an unfortunate mistake on Mother's part. At least I thought so!

Curtis knew how to plaster the walls of a house, as his Dad had done before him, but he was not a builder. Mother had great confidence in him, nonetheless and purchased a load of cinder-bricks to get him started. Curtis spent months forming the above-ground basement walls with those bricks, but it was hard work for him. The bricks were made of gray cement, big and heavy, the type with three good-sized holes down the middle of each one. Bud and I went after school sometimes to watch the progress of Mother's house as she was working full time at the laundry and couldn't keep an eye on things. The cinder bricks were being cemented into place by Curtis and he explained to us two kids, how the house he was building was very unique.

"What's unique about it?" we asked him and he proudly told us. He was filling the three-holed bricks of the wall with empty glass bottles. How he loved to boast! So we watched the house's uniqueness taking place daily after that. As Curtis worked he also drank and his choice of drink was lemon or vanilla extract, a flavoring loaded with alcohol at that time. And like he boasted, he was filling the holes in the bricks with the empty extract bottles. We watched him!

Remember, ours was a Mormon town and no liquor stores were allowed there, not even one, just as none exist there today. But we did have bootleggers and they thrived by selling liquor at exorbitant prices. Curtis couldn't afford the high prices and had resorted to drinking the extracts as they were sold cheaply at the grocery store, despite the fact that they were generously laden with alcohol. And Curtis bought them by the case, which consisted of twenty-four small bottles. Extracts were meant to be used to flavour cakes and other baked goods then, just as they are today. Yet today and for many, many years now, extracts have been made differently and contain no alcohol at all. Thank goodness!

The whole idea of anyone sinking to the level of drinking that stuff disgusted me! My young mind wondered why the owner of the grocery store didn't question the buying of such large quantities of the extracts. Of course, that never happened. Instead, Curtis showed off to Bud and I, just how he could drink a complete bottle of extract in a matter of seconds and then ceremoniously drop the empty bottle into a hole in one of the bricks. This was repeated as the wall of the basement grew higher, brick after brick. But, as time went by, the hours of work Curtis put in, slackened off due to his drinking and so consequently the building of Mother's house got far behind schedule. By the end of summer, when the house should have been finished, there was only a basement with a framed-in main floor on top. Hardly a home ready to be moved into!

And there was more bad news to come, just as the tree leaves began changing to autumn colours, Curtis made an announcement so typical of him. He was moving away. He was going to Creston B.C. with Hazel to take another job, working in construction there. I was seriously upset, not about Curtis leaving, but because Hazel would be departing. I would no longer have her close in my life. The very thought of her going away made me feel down and dejected! It seemed too unbearable for words! But, regardless it came to pass and I had to bear it.

And as if matters weren't bad enough, after they left another frightening disaster struck our family. We had a roof-fire in that awful old house we lived in and it scared me half to death! How did the fire start? Well, I suppose it came about because Bud and I were always complaining to Mother about being bitten by the bed bugs. At this particular time, surprising enough, Mother decided to do something about our grumbling. She rolled up a wad of old newspapers and lit them on fire. We didn't know what she was going to do with that burning torch? But we dully followed her upstairs and watched her climb up on a chair in order to reach the attic entry in the ceiling. Then she pushed her fiery torch up into the attic opening and made every effort to burn the bugs out of the space above where we slept. Bud and I were mesmerized! We couldn't believe our eyes.

Unfortunately, right then the cobwebs in the attic caught fire and the flames quickly spread out of control. The roofing itself started to quickly burn and in the end, a fire truck had to be summoned to extinguish the resulting roof fire. I remember standing on the lawn crying and thinking our entire house was going to burn down and we would be left homeless. Of course that didn't happen, but it did cause a flurry of activity to get Mother's house finished and ready to move into. And so, at long last, we were planning to vacate the horrible old condemned house. We sure weren't going to miss it, for now it reeked of smoke which made it even more deplorable. But believe it or not, the bed bugs were finally gone. Burned out, every one! Bud and I couldn't help giving a great big hooray for that!

17. More Changes

At this point in time, while we waited to move into our house and without the bed bugs to worry about, I started to worry about Mother. She'd always complained she had a lot of things in her life to be bitter about, like it was an excuse for her to turn to drink or something worse. It all troubled me so much. Was she resentful about having to raise Bud and me by herself, too? For years I'd seen through Mother's smoke screen of excuses and knew it had been her choice to break up her marriage and in a sense, suffer the loss of two sons by sending them away. It was all such a sad state of affairs!

And I was tired of hearing her speak so hatefully about my Dad, too, as it cut me somewhere deeply inside. She claimed he had deserted her, but I knew that wasn't true! But, admittedly though, I was your typical teenager, oftentimes arguing with Mother because of my own frustration about the things I couldn't change. All the while, what I really wanted was to be loved and to find a place for myself in this changeable world. I knew life for most people was not a smooth road, but I felt mine was more than bumpy, it was atrocious!

44

Did I say Mother was turning to drink? Well, she didn't drink alone! Frequently her 'gentlemen friends,' as she called them, came by at night and brought whiskey with them. It was a familiar pattern. Neither of us kids had a curfew, so when Bud or I returned home late at night we'd often find the house in darkness. Of course, both of us knew what to expect! As soon as we opened the door Mother's voice would speak to us from the dark room inside.

"Go upstairs to bed. You can brush your teeth in the morning," she'd say. You have to understand, in that house the only sink was in the kitchen and we wouldn't be allowed to turn on the lights. We'd know then, Mother was entertaining a 'gentleman friend' in the shadowy darkness of the front room. And, both Bud and I learned early on to identify the sour odor of whiskey hanging in the air.

In my innocence, I was glad we were eventually going to move away from that house and the sooner the better. Though it was childish thinking on my part, I hoped that then, all of Mother's appalling 'gentlemen friends' would not be able to find where she had moved to. But before anything like that could take place, my whole world as I knew it was suddenly, as if by sleight of hand, turned upside down.

A letter arrived in the mail which changed my life completely! The letter was from my beloved sister Hazel, asking Mother if I could come and live with her in Creston B.C. Why? Because Hazel's husband, Curtis, had been caught stealing and sentenced to six months in the jail at the prison in Nelson B.C. In the letter, Hazel stressed she was feeling lonely and really needed me to come and be with her for company.

Mother, as usual said, "Do as you please." She was leaving it up to me whether I went to Creston or not. Well, I certainly didn't have any doubts in my mind! I knew it was the chance of a lifetime for me to escape my boring, small town life and I definitely wanted to go and be with her. Without wasting a moment of time, I immediately began packing my things into the only suitcase we owned.

It was hard for me to say goodbye to Laurene after our three wonderful years of friendship. But she was happy for me and wished me well. We had often imagined how marvelous it would be to leave our small town-roots behind and now I was about to do just that! Mother even bought me a few new clothes to take away with me. I remember them in detail. There was a gold three-quarter length coat with a matching gold cloche hat, a pleated skirt and a neat red blazer jacket with plaid sleeves. Nothing short of the very latest style! I'd never had so many new clothes in all my life and I was most grateful to Mother.

At times I felt like this opportunity was a dream and if I pinched myself I'd wake up and find it wasn't really happening to me. But it was! And very soon I was on my way to Fort McLeod where I'd board the train travelling westward to the beautiful Province of British Columbia.

Funny about the things you remember! When saying goodbye, I noticed Mother didn't display any emotion or mention anything about me coming back in six months. There had been a definite cloud of discord between us over the last few years. Perhaps she was even happy I was leaving? On the other hand, I was tired of her make-believe world and I wanted to gain a sense of realism in my own life. As my thoughts drift backwards in time now, I understand my mother suffered from an undiagnosed and untreated type of mental illness. I believe it could have been caused by the burden of bitterness she carried for so many years towards my Dad. It was like a root buried deep inside her, making her hang on to a victim complex. Over the years, it had swallowed up any chance of a happy, normal life and left her with a fantasy world of her own making, which was terribly sad.

Yet my heart couldn't help singing as I got ready to leave. I was happy about the break from home. My future beckoned me. And I earnestly desired everything it might offer me. I'd been given a new chance in life, or at least that's how I viewed my going to live with Hazel. The very thought of it filled me with happiness and the promise of newfound hope. Absolutely nothing could stop me now. I was moving forward into the unchartered waters of my future and a popular song of the day began breaking out in my heart. It was called *Dream*, one of Frank Sinatra's hit songs. I felt like some of the lines were written just for me.

> Dream when you're feeling blue...
> Dream that's the thing to do
> Dream and they might come true...
> Dream, dream, dream...

And so I did.

18. Creston

I travelled to Creston by train and it was the very first train ride of my life. Unfortunately, it took place in the overnight darkness and I missed the spectacular scenery of the Rocky Mountains I'd admired from afar all my growing up years in Cardston. During my train trip, the noisy clacking sound of the train wheels on the track spun around in my head hour by hour until finally, from sheer exhaustion, I nodded off despite my sitting up position. I recall thinking as I dozed off that it would be good to sleep for a while even though inside, I was revved-up and excited to take the next step into my future. This journey was bringing many chapters of my life to an end and I really needed to rest for the undiscovered adventure that lay ahead. In all my fifteen years, I'd never ventured so far from my hometown. But I was ready, as well as eager, to begin a brand new life in Creston.

Arriving at the train station early the next morning, I climbed down the flight of iron stairs from the day-coach and looked around the platform. It was as if the entire town of Creston was fast asleep under the heavy clouds of that overcast day in December 1944. Still, in my heart I could feel the sun shining on the new path leading me forward into my unknown future. I had Hazel's address in my hand and I started walking even though I didn't know exactly which way I should go. I found myself on Main Street and entered the Creston Hotel for directions. When I was told it was only a few blocks straight north, I felt relieved, as by now my one suitcase containing all my worldly goods was feeling heavy. Not aware that my sense of direction was compromised, I proceeded to walk north, or where I perceived north to be, until the gentle hill I climbed came to a dead-end. I had actually been walking westward and so now I had to retrace my footsteps to the Hotel, feeling faint with fatigue. There, I turned the only other direction that seemed possible and found the address a half a block away.

It was a small, one-roomed motel cabin nestled in a bunch of trees, and Hazel, still in her pajamas, opened the door in answer to my persistent knocking. It was a joyful reunion, but by now I was very weary from my long and quite sleepless journey. I pulled off my clothes, donned my nightwear and joined Hazel in her double bed. We talked for a while, reminiscing, before I turned over to surrender to sleep. Hazel slipped her arm around my waist and I felt a peaceful glow wash over me from head to toe. I felt like I'd come home. A phrase I remembered, from an ancient hymn, lulled me off to sleep, "and to my listening ears, all nature sings and round me rings, the music of the spheres."

During the following days, Hazel acquainted me with the downtown area of Creston and helped me enroll as a student at the Creston Valley High School. It was all very exhilarating attending C.V.H.S. and I enjoyed the experience of being the new girl in town. Right away, I got to know a girl my own age named Marg whose family also lived in one of the motel cabins like we did. We hung out as friends and would sometimes walk to school together. Marg was shy like me.

Hazel was so delighted I'd come to live with her and those six years between us in age, in a lot of ways didn't seem to exist. She loved music and dancing just as I did and even her job in the local music store on

Marg and Me in front of C.V.H.S.

Main Street was perfect. I went there most days after school and listened to the latest Hit Parade songs on the vinyl recordings that Hazel was hired to sell. We were both crazy about the popular swing-music of the era and playing the records was free for us, as it allowed the customers to hear the current tunes which encouraged them to buy. It wasn't long before Hazel and I found out there were big country dances held every Saturday night in and around the Creston area. We started to go to them and had fun dancing with various partners at the dance, as was the standard tradition then. At the end, when the band played *Auld Lang Syne*, Hazel and I would walk home together.

Sometimes the dances were held out at Erikson, Wynndel or Lister, which were Creston's neighbouring towns and we were offered a ride there by Marg's older brother Clarence. Then, as time progressed, instead of joining up at the end of the dance, Hazel sometimes would disappear before the final waltz. I assumed she'd found someone she wanted to spend time with, but it meant I had to go home alone.

Whenever that happened, Clarence offered me a ride in the closed-in back of his truck with others from the dance. That's how I met Ron, who was a couple of years older than I was and no longer a student. He had dropped out of school to work. Ron was a good dancer and taught me the latest jitter-bug steps right in the middle of the dance floor. You might say he was my very first boyfriend as I'd never had one before in Cardston. But to me, Ron was just a friend to 'hang out' with, much like I did with Marg and her brother Clarence and others from the Saturday dances.

But then, one night something happened! Ron walked me to the door of our cabin and gave me my first kiss. It was not as thrilling as I had imagined a first time kiss would be and I thought it was because I didn't have any romantic feelings towards him. Was that what it was? Then, to my complete surprise, Ron got the idea I was 'his' girl and it did not sit well with me. Ron insisted I ought to tell him why I was saying no to a more permanent relationship. So I did, but to be kind, I didn't tell him I wasn't attracted to him, I just told him my other reason, which was his drinking.

At the dances, Ron often went outside to have a drink of liquor right out of a bottle, like a lot of the guys in those days did. I could smell the awful odor on him afterwards and it disgusted me! So I told him I could never be serious about anyone who drank. I was glad he accepted my explanation and didn't try to change my point of view. The two of us did remain friends and continued to be dance partners whenever we met at dances. And I never regretted my decision of not going steady with him.

Clarence, me, Marg, Ron & two friends.

19. High School and My Friend Al

I enjoyed attending Creston Valley High School and began making new friends there at once. I was glad some of my embarrassing shyness, that had dogged me for years, was very slowly beginning to disappear. I felt well-dressed too, with all the new clothes Mother had bought for me in Cardston.

The Creston high school was a huge building, so finding all my classrooms was a bit of a challenge for me at first. But my classwork seemed easy enough and I thought it must have something to do with moving from Alberta to B.C. There was only one class I wasn't doing well in, and was starting to dread attending. That was Home Economics. Everything about kitchen stuff was foreign to me and definitely not something I was familiar with. My Mother had not been an example to me, having lost all interest in cooking years ago. Bud and I had usually just lived on what we could scrounge up for ourselves. However, now that I was with Hazel, I could see she loved to cook and wanted to do the cooking for the both of us. So any attempts at cooking myself, appeared to be my downfall. Fortunately for me, I met this friendly girl in my Home Economics class by the name of Al.

Al, my new friend.

Feeling good in some new clothes. My red jacket (left) and my gold coat (right).

Al more or less took me under her wing, you might say, as she was very confident about cooking. Even so, one particular day in class still haunts me! We were all following a recipe to make an individual biscuit and Al whispered to me, "Do what I do and you'll be fine." Of course I wanted to do well, so I diligently tried to follow her example. Without looking at the recipe, I attempted to keep up with Al as she combined all her ingredients together forming a ball of biscuit dough. Then we were told to flatten the ball into an individual biscuit and put our initials on top. Mine was nice and round and the initials were easy to do, so I put them on top very ceremoniously! All the biscuits went into the oven at the same time and we waited impatiently for the timer to tell us when the baking time was up and they were ready to eat.

The timer finally buzzed and the pans of biscuits came out of the oven looking raised up and beautiful, all of them with the exception of one. To my shame, it was MINE! No mistaken identity either, for the flat, pitiful looking biscuit was emblazoned with the initials M.P. for Marie Posing. I felt like I died a thousand deaths in that moment.

Then Al uttered to me, under her breathe, "I think you must have left out the baking powder." She was right. I had indeed omitted my Baking Powder Biscuit's main ingredient. I must have blinked and missed it when Al added that rising agent to her dough. Could I ever to live down my failure to make such a simple and easy biscuit in my cooking class?

Al and I often walked part of the way home together, and whenever we did, she was constantly talking about her older brother who was eighteen and in grade twelve. She raved about his distinction as a great athlete and conveyed all his winning statistics to me. He was a starter on the high school basketball team as well as an accomplished track and field star, both as a runner and a high jumper. Oh dear, the list was endless when it came to this hero of a brother she had. She insisted I'd have to meet him. Little did she know, I was steadily getting tired of hearing her brag on and on about her famous brother. I had no intention of ever letting that introduction happen.

But then, it happened and I remember it like it was yesterday. I was walking with Al towards the town-center after school one day and suddenly she started to get excited. She'd caught a glimpse of her brother up ahead and began shouting out very loudly to him, "Wait up, Jim!" I was embarrassed and wanted to die! I saw this guy ahead of us turn around and wait for us to catch up. Good grief, I thought to myself, there was absolutely nothing I could do to avoid the inevitable meeting with Al's renowned brother. I would just have to grin and bear it!

To this day, Jim says he remembers the exact spot where we met in Creston for the first time, on that day in March. As for me, I remember how flustered I became as Al and I drew closer to him. Without doubt, my mind started to backtrack very quickly and I found I was changing my opinion about Al's brother. The nearer we got, I could see that he was a pretty cool looking guy. He was not only tall and good looking, but his eyes were drinking me in the closer we got to him. He was observing me with interest. How very nice! But right then, to my horror, I felt my old shyness kick in. Redness crept up my face and I could feel heat as I involuntarily blushed. How embarrassing! Why is it that some of life's most significant moments arrive by surprise and we are not able to cope with them and stay composed?

I opened my mouth and stammered my hello to him as Al introduced us. But inside I was feeling awkward and tongue-tied. The whole conversation that took place between us became a blur as the three of us walked on together. I was being hounded by the fact I'd made a fool of myself by blushing like that? Such a terrible first impression I'd made. I felt devastated!

Later, when I was alone, I questioned why I judged myself so harshly? I wouldn't do that to anyone else, would I? It was time to change and have more self-esteem. From now on, I was genuinely going to give it my best efforts. After all, being self-confident couldn't be that hard. And besides, I could become anyone I wanted to be on this fresh new page of my life.

The second time Jim and I met was the following week when we passed each other on the Main Street downtown. This time, I was walking with Hazel and when I saw him coming toward me, I gave him a big smile, even though inside my heart was pounding uncontrollably.

"Hello beautiful," he said in a whisper meant for my ears alone. I immediately received his compliment, but I was still thankful he didn't see my red face. I'd blushed helplessly once again, just as we passed by each other. I still had work to do on controlling that blush, didn't I?

This scene, or a version of it repeated itself a few more times and I knew there was definitely something happening between Jim and I. Yes, I felt it! Or was it spring fever? I really didn't think so, but I then began to ponder, when was Jim and I was ever going to actually spend some time together? My fervent hope was it would be soon.

20. Jim

And then, it was springtime in Creston! It began in early April, flooding the valley with all its magnificent fresh paint palette of colours. Even a type of misty-green fell on the trees and the white blossoms hung thick on the fruit trees. I was undergoing a fullness of springtime in my heart as well. An explosion of joy that I couldn't explain was taking place there! It centered on this fellow named Jim, even though I hadn't even had a meaningful conversation with him yet.

Then April turned into May and the annual May Blossom Festival appeared on the horizon. It was the 'talk of the town' in Creston. At last, my starry-eyed dream materialized, when Jim stopped me as we passed in the hallway at school and asked a question.

"Are you planning on going to the Blossom Festival?" he inquired. When I answered yes, he smiled and asked if he could walk me home when it was over. Wonder of wonders! Time together at last! Just saying yes had started my heart doing flip-flops and the bubble of joy inside me seemed about to burst. I could hardly contain all my happiness.

In the days that followed, I recalled a quote from *Anne of Green Gable's book*. It said, "Looking forward to things is half the pleasure." However it did not work that way for me! I begrudgingly counted the slow-moving days until the Victoria Day weekend and the arrival of the Blossom Festival. Hazel understood my impatience as I had confided my dream concerning Jim which was about to come true. I sensed she understood how I felt as she seemed to have found some kind of happiness herself that she wasn't yet, sharing with me. I didn't press for the details, as she deserved some privacy and joy in her life. And besides I was caught up in my own tale of promising romance.

The day of the Blossom Festival finally did arrive and Hazel accompanied me to the Civic Centre grounds, promising to wait until Jim made his appearance. The festivities were well under way when he suddenly appeared, towering over me, smiling and talking like we'd been friends forever. Hazel gave me a wink of her eye and excused herself and disappeared. Jim and I were alone at last.

We enjoyed the merriment together and had a fun-filled evening until the very end. Our walk homeward was a continuation of the meaningful conversation between us and was filled with lots of laughter and sharing. I was feeling so very comfortable and relaxed with Jim, as if we had indeed known each other for a long time. I was overflowing with happiness beyond measure.

At my doorstep our conversation wound down and came to an end and Jim pulled me close and our lips met. I somehow knew it was the first kiss of millions-to-come and the orchestra inside me exploded into a symphony of music. Our first kiss was that exquisite moment I'd dreamed of and would treasure forever and it told me, I was in love!

From that time onward, Jim and I were a twosome and indeed only had eyes for each other. It seemed incredible to me that our love at first sight could actually take substance and be lived out in real life, But yet, our hearts told us it was so. We were intoxicated with love for each other and spent every possible moment together. I was learning so many things about him, his dreams of his future beyond high school and, thankfully, that he was too young to be called to serve in the war. He did look handsome in a uniform though, as he was a captain in the Creston Cadet Corps.

Jim in his cadet uniform.

I recall once seeing him as he marched proudly down Main Street in a parade, leading his troop and looking ever so somberly composed. However, I knew how very tender-hearted and affectionate he was with me and it made me smile as I waved fondly to him, despite his eyes being riveted straight ahead, just as a good soldier's eyes should be.

Time flew by with great speed, as it has a habit of doing when we're happy. The month of May turned into June and Jim's Grade Twelve Graduation ceremony at C.V.H.S. was upon us. It was a very special time for me, as I watched him walk across the stage and receive his Graduation

Certificate. I knew his heart belonged to me alone. We loved each other so deeply and planned to spend the rest of our lives together. We talked endlessly about our special day, the day when we would get married and live the rest of our lives together. We had nicknamed that indefinite day, 'our day' and we hoped it would be in the not too distant future.

At the big Celebration Dance that night, held in honour of the many Grade Twelve graduates, I was Jim's escort and everything was so perfect, like a dream come true. Then, about half way through, one of Jim's classmates strolled by where we were sitting on the sidelines and spoke directly to Jim.

"Come on," she said, "how about dancing with some of the grade twelve girls?" I felt terribly excluded by that remark, but Jim paid no attention to her or any other girl and danced only with me. It made me feel very special. We both knew we were sweethearts in the truest sense of the word and only wanted to spend time together. The world around us seemed dimly out of focus.

By now, I had been invited to Jim's home for dinner and although I was nervous at first, it all went very well. Jim's Dad, Thomas, was away with the Army and stationed in Edmonton, so I was greeted by his Mom, who welcomed me with open arms, and of course his sister, Al, who I already knew from school. Their house was on a five acre fruit farm and I felt right at home and greatly enjoyed my visit. Jim's older sister Irene, three years his senior, was now married to Ted Walker and they lived across the road from the Rolfe's fruit farm.

I saw and admired a portrait displayed on the living room wall. It had been taken when Jim's Dad was home on leave from the army.

I learned Jim's parents had come from Lancashire, England following their marriage and settled in the small Saskatchewan town of Waseca on a farm. Their immigration was sponsored by an uncle who was already farming in that area.

Those were grim years when all farmers were going through great difficulties leading up to the great Depression. Thomas and Alice Rolfe suffered economically along with many others, trying to work the land and provide for their family. They had four children who were all born in the hospital in Lashburn. Their eldest child, Ethel, contracted pneumonia at the young age of fourteen and sadly died. She was buried near Waseca in the Forest Bank Cemetery. Irene was the second born and two years later, Jim came along, followed by Alice.

As a family, they moved away from the Prairies and settled in Creston for a brief period at which time Jim's Dad joined the Army. When he received his posting in the vicinity of the lower mainland, the family moved there, first to Langley and then to Surrey. But as time went by, and Thomas was moved around to various places, the family returned to Creston and settled on the fruit farm where they now lived. Jim was in grade ten at the time of their move back.

Front row: Jim's Dad, his Mom and Jim. Back row: Irene, Ted and Al .

21. The Summer of 1946

Oh, if life only came with an instruction book so we knew what to expect and how to handle it. It doesn't work that way though, does it? Both Hazel and I had forgotten the six month anniversary of my arrival was coming to an end soon and that it would definitely mean a big change in our lives. Curtis would be getting out of jail and returning to Creston and there was nothing we could do about it. But before that could happen, Hazel and I had an unexpected visit from some members of our family we hardly knew.

Our Dad arrived and brought with him our two older brothers, Harold and Floyd. Dad's car was pulling a small house trailer, in which they all stayed. Hazel remembered them only faintly from her childhood and I was just a youngster of four when Dad left Alberta, so of course they were more or less strangers to us both. Still, it was a very happy surprise for us and we sincerely welcomed them. The Second World War was over now and Harold and Floyd had been officially discharged from the United States Marine Corps.

Both my brothers had served in major battles in the South Pacific. They had been stationed in Iwo Jima, Okinawa and Saipan and took part in other key invasions as well. They had come safely through those terrible war years and we gave thanks for that. Floyd did get wounded in the hand in one battle, although not seriously, but still he received the Purple Heart for his bravery in action.

Dad had suggested the trip to Canada before our brothers started to look for civilian jobs, as he felt it was time for us all to get reacquainted. It seemed strange meeting them and knowing we were all part of the same family, but without much family history together given the great distances that had separated us. I instantly liked Dad, the father I grew up never knowing. He was outgoing and friendly and I saw where I had inherited his brown eyes and dark hair as well as his common sense and level-headedness. Harold and I definitely favoured Dad's side of the family with our darker colouring, whereas Floyd with his red hair and Hazel's reddish-brown hair lined up with Mother's side of the family. All of us reminisced by the hour and never tired of sharing story after story.

Hazel, Harold, me, Floyd & Dad.

We picnicked by the river in Creston and explored the countryside, simply enjoying each other's company. I remember it was in the month of June and I was preparing to write my Provincial Final exams, so I did my studying outside under the coolness of the trees. I didn't want to miss any of our family time together. And remarkably, I did well on those exams, too!

Eventually, it was time for our visitors to leave and it was difficult to say goodbye, as we didn't know when we'd see each other again. They had taken time out of their busy lives to come and spend it with us, so we were thankful they had. We said our goodbyes and promised to write each other and keep in touch.

Saluting my family.

Once Hazel and I were alone again, the inevitable happened. Curtis arrived at the doorstep, fresh out of jail and still as cocky as ever. He proudly bragged about how he'd learned a lot from his cellmates behind bars. I remember feeling like life's joy had slipped away that day and I started to worry about my future again.

Now that I knew Jim, the true love of my life, I didn't want to leave Creston and return to Alberta. Hazel didn't want me to do that either! On the other hand, to share the motel's single bedroom with her and Curtis was an unbearable thought! At once, I started to feel despondent! I was going to be right back in my dysfunctional life again. What was I to do? Hazel was quick to come up with an idea and told me I wasn't to worry about leaving.

She said, "We will just have to make the best of the circumstances." And with that, she located a cot for me to sleep on in the corner of the motel room. It was the best she could do and she insisted it would work. Thankfully, the motel room was large enough in size to accommodate the little bed in the corner, so I accepted her plan. Beggars can't be choosers.

During the days and weeks of the summer holidays, Jim and I spent as much time as possible together. We listened to his collection of jazz records by the hour and discovered Hoagie Carmichael's great song *Star-*

dust and claimed it as 'our' song, which it remains to this day. In the heat of the summer, we went to the riverside and Jim tried to show me how to swim. But regrettably, I just couldn't relax and learn in the cold river water, even with Jim there to protect me from swimming snakes! He was so patient with me. I was in love with him and that love was greatly reciprocated. Never before had my world looked so wonderful.

The hot sun brought a bountiful fruit harvest in the Creston valley that year and Jim spent weeks picking fruit on his family's farm as well as on other neighbouring farms. He also had a part-time job working at the Creston Review newspaper office. While he was busy working, I spent time lending a hand to Hazel at the music store. But whether we were together or apart, nothing hindered Jim's love for me and my love for him. It just seemed to only get deeper and stronger over time.

When I wasn't needed at the store and Jim was working, I'd take long hikes up Goat Mountain which was not far from where I lived in the motel. I loved to climb that well-worn trail as it twisted and turned and ascended forever skyward. The path was bordered with evergreen trees and the rich pine smell seemed to nourish my soul in a wholesome way. It helped soothe my inner thoughts and took my anxiety away. I enjoyed the quiet atmosphere, broken only by birds chirping overhead and the occasional distant train whistle. Up there my mind was freed from the uneasiness of what was in store for me in the future yet to come.

In October of that year, Jim's sister, Irene, gave birth to twins and named them David and Donald. Jim took me to visit them at their house soon after Irene came home from the hospital. Both Irene and Ted were so friendly towards me and I liked them immediately. They proudly showed me their tiny little twin sons. I don't think I'd ever seen newborn babies before and they seemed ever so small and helpless.

When Donald was just four months old, tragedy struck. He died of a chest infection and once again, if only penicillin had been available then, the doctors may have been able to cure him. It was such a sad time, not only for Irene and Ted, but Jim's entire family. And all I could do was ask, why God? I didn't understand why a little twin boy had to die.

I was loving high school and had happily settled into the five day routine of the classroom as the second month of school passed by. I didn't find going to school monotonous or dull, but instead I actually liked having my days structured. It gave my life order and purpose. However, as much as I enjoyed the everyday sameness of life, a big change was right around the corner waiting for me.

22. Kimberley

To our surprise, Curtis took a job in the town of Kimberley B.C. which is located high in the Purcell Mountains about 150 kilometers from Creston. It was terrible news for me. However, Curtis had already reserved a hotel room there for us and I was told we'd be traveling there immediately. I was very unhappy about it for several reasons. There was the distance it put between Jim and I, which would be so terribly hard on both of us, and also the fact we'd be going from our cabin to a busy downtown hotel room in Kimberly. To top it off, there was the challenge of starting over again at another high school mid-term! All in all, it was not welcome news, but somehow I managed to trudge ahead through all the changes needed, but not in a happy frame of mind. My life felt intolerable!

The three of us drove to Kimberley and I was enrolled at the high school and nothing about it was easy. I was embarrassed when I had to give my home address as that of the local hotel. I remember the raised eyebrow of the school secretary as she peered at me over her glasses. Little did she know the worst of it! There was no cot available in that hotel. What could I to do? I did what I was forced to do. I slept next to the wall in our only bed, which wasn't a queen or a king either, as all beds were doubles in those far away days of yesteryear.

The kids at my new school were different than my former class-mates in Creston. Or was it that I somehow got involved with the wrong crowd? I was looking for a friendly face and this girl smiled and greeted me in a friendly way the very first day. However, she turned out to be a kind of 'ring leader' and an all-round bad girl of the school.

After class one afternoon she invited me and a couple of other girls to go for a walk with her up into the hills surrounding the school. Once we got up there, she produced a pack of cigarettes and gave us all one to smoke. It was all new to me, and the tobacco tasted awful in my mouth. Yes, totally yucky! Then again, I had watched the movie stars smoking for years on the movie screen, so I pretended it was cool and tried to avoid coughing.

The ring leader was also a 'mouthy' girl that used some pretty foul language, some of which I hadn't even heard Curtis or his brother use. I inwardly questioned myself. What was I doing getting involved with this bunch of girls? Right then and there I decided I'd find myself some new friends who would be more compatible to my way of thinking and living.

My 'home life,' if you could call it that, since we lived in a hotel, was a repeat of the highly dysfunctional life from before. The three of us in one small cramped bedroom did not work well. When Curtis's working hours ended he spent time, as was his habit, in the beer parlour and he insisted Hazel accompany him there. Of course his drinking sprees led to continuous fights between them. Curtis had a very jealous nature and it became a big issue. If any man so much as looked at Hazel, his anger would flair up and sparks would fly.

At the end of one of those nightmare evenings, when he was exploding in a fit of rage, he took his cigarette lighter and started to burn Hazel's clothes that were hanging in the hotel's tiny closet.

"It's your clothes that make you so attractive to other men," he uttered accusingly. The flames in the closet were extinguished by Hazel so they didn't spread, but even so, most of her things were a mess and couldn't be saved.

During this display of rage that took place in front of me, I felt terrified, not for myself, but for Hazel. What more would this wretched man do to her? Fortunately though, Curtis's flood of anger was over quickly and then he told us the bad news. He'd lost his job that day and another move was coming. His past history was repeating itself. You can be sure none of us got much sleep that night.

The only source of security I seemed to possess at that time was Jim. And we kept our relationship alive by letter-writing. I couldn't talk to him by long-distance telephone, as it was far too expensive, making it out of the question in those days. So I put my pen to paper. And writing also helped me vent my feelings. I didn't tell Jim all the negative news concerning Hazel and I, since it would only worry him, but kept it upbeat as much as I could. Both of us were finding our separation hard enough, so filling my letters with reassurances of my unending love actually helped pull me out of my pit of gloominess as well. We'd often tell each other about our dreams of the future when we'd be married at last. It relieved the loneliness we were both experiencing, which at times was unbearable.

Then, very unexpectedly, my life changed around completely, one more time. Hazel and Curtis had returned to Creston for a few weeks, leaving me alone in the hotel and now Hazel surprised me by arriving back by train. She told me she'd come to fetch me back to Creston, and so my days in Kimberley were brought to an abrupt end. Hazel hugged me with a smile on her lips and that 'twinkle' in her eye she so often had.

"I've got a special surprise for you," she declared. And her surprise was Jim! He had traveled on the train with her to accompany me back. For us to be reunited was ever so heart-satisfying for both of us. We thrilled at the very nearness of each other all over again. My heart soared skyward and I felt life was beautiful once again. Well, at least for the moment, anyway!

Despite the joy of our reunion, the question still remained concerning my future. I'd left my Kimberley education behind me now, but was I to start school in Creston for the second time in that semester? Even the thought of doing that made me feel foolish and embarrassed! Christmas break was coming up soon, so I decided to wait until the holidays were over to make my new plans about school. I was hoping by the start-up of school in January that whatever path my life was taking would be made clear to me. No wonder I sometimes felt like my life was a ship without a rudder!

Jim gave me such a wonderful gift for my sixteenth birthday that December of 1946. It was an album of six records of the Big-Band music era. We both loved that kind of music so very much. Jim had personally illustrated the cover of the album with my name and many neat, black ink drawings. He had worked on it while we were apart all those months. I've kept that album among my treasured things to this day.

Also at Christmas that same year, he gave me one of the most special gifts I'd ever received. It was a large oval, satin-lined box of *Evening in Paris* cologne, perfume and dusting powder. That particular scent was absolutely the rage everywhere in the world at that time and was known as 'the most famous fragrance in the world.' It was such a very extravagant gift for me to receive and it made me feel cherished beyond words by my sweetheart, Jim. We were more in love than ever.

23. The Cabin

By the time we welcomed in the new year of 1947, Creston's gray wintery days were starting to close in around me in a suffocating manner. You see, I was not going to school and was most depressed about it. Curtis was still unemployed and kept insisting he had some contacts in Vancouver coming his way and we'd be moving there very soon. I felt I was playing 'hooky' from school, having not started back in January. It was all so upsetting to me! Yet, how in the world could I start school again and then quit a second time, when we moved? Was I to believe we were moving at all? It was so indefinite and I was full of gloom and heart-broken about missing out on my education.

Since our return to Creston the three of us, Hazel and Curtis and I, had been living in a small one-room fruit picker's cabin. It was all we could afford, but it was appalling. It had no electricity or heat, so it wasn't very suitable to call home especially in the cold wintertime temperatures of Creston. Hazel had been rehired at the music store on Main Street, but her wages were meager and didn't meet many of our living expenses.

Occasionally a letter came from Mother with a five dollar bill in it and Hazel and I would stock up on food and necessities. It always amazed us how many groceries that one bill would buy in those days. Sometimes we even had two quarters left over and we'd splurge and have a piece of Boston cream pie at the local café. Even so, our moments of feeling on top of things were fleeting. The months of January and February with their dreary weather seemed to drag on and on. As usual, Curtis was using his customary way of coping with his miserable state of affairs by frequenting the local beer parlour to drown his sorrows. So what else was new!

I hated living in that dreadful cabin, but even so I never imagined I'd experience the most horrifying night of my entire life within those four walls. It started out badly when I arrived home late to find the cabin door locked and everything in darkness. I located the skeleton key on the nail where it was kept and opened the door. I knew where Curtis would be at this hour of the night, but where was Hazel?

With no electricity in the cabin, I fumbled in the pitch darkness of the room for the box of matches we kept on a shelf near the door. I intended to light the candle we kept on the small table just below the one and only window. But to my horror, the match ignited the entire top of the table into a mass of rising flames! And it was no wonder. The table had piles of melted wax on its surface from all the former candles melted there. They had all merged into a mountain of wax just waiting to be ignited!

The frightening flames leapt high in the air directly in front of the small window looking out to the street. Immediately, I heard distant voices crying, "Fire, fire!" I grabbed a towel and smothered the flames as quickly as I could. And my hands did not go unscathed from the hot melted wax either, but then again, I was oblivious to the pain. Once the fire was out, I saw in the dim darkness through the window, a couple of people running up the long path toward our cabin. They must have been passing by on the street. My heart began beating double time as someone reached the door and began pounding on it loudly. What could I do? I pulled the door open.

"Is everything alright, we saw flames?" a man's voice inquired from the darkness outside. I felt my body trembling, but I forced my voice to be calm. "The fire is out and I'm not hurt," I replied.

Then the shadowy person outside the door stepped back and turned away to join some others waiting on the dirt path. After a brief discussion, they turned back towards the street and disappeared down the pathway out of view.

I shuddered, noticing the footpath was ice-frosted by our early winter temperatures. And I stepped quickly back into the cabin closing the door. I was trembling with the cold now, so I got undressed hurriedly in the room's inky blackness and climbed across our one-and-only bed and lay shivering against the wall. The warmth of the heavy quilt over me finally spread its heat throughout my body and I relaxed and fell asleep.

Just how long I slept, I had no way of knowing, but suddenly, my eyes flew open and I was instantly awake! Something had drawn me out of a deep sleep and all my instincts were instantly on alert. I didn't move. I waited, holding my breath. A cold feeling ran up my spine. Then I heard the other shoe drop and I caught the faint smell of stale beer.

Curtis was undressing at the side of the bed. But where was Hazel? She still was not beside me in the bed as always. My mouth went dry and I swallowed. A shallow breath caught in my throat and I tried desperately to think. There was no use screaming. Who would hear? Our cabin was isolated without any close neighbour's nearby.

Then his rough hand reached for me and I knew what I had to do. I had to fight! I had to be the stronger one. An uncanny strength seemed to flow into my body right then and with it a great deal of self-determination. I pulled myself out of his clutches and headed for the door. I didn't make it! My energy began to ebb. I was no match for his muscled strength. Nonetheless, I stubbornly willed not to give up and to keep on aggressive fighting!

My body took a beating as I was slammed against things and smashed onto the floor several times, but I just kept on fighting and fighting. Then, in my struggle, though I was pinned down, I managed to free my knee and forced it upward against his body. At last, my battle was over! Both of us collapsed onto the bare wooden floor in sheer exhaustion.

I had won the battle, but I didn't feel like a winner. I felt nauseated by what I'd gone through. Then I heard his remorseful voice close beside me.

"If I had a knife, I'd kill myself." I knew where the butcher knife was kept and it was directly above my head on the kitchen counter. Swallowing angry tears, I reached up and took hold of the bladed weapon, and held it in front of his face. In the dim darkness of the room he reached out and took it from me.

There was a prolonged eerie silence when it seemed like time stood still. And then he broke down crying. And I didn't care! I wished he would use the knife! Agonizingly, I felt an actual pain in my hard heart. Both of us laid there motionless on the cold hard floor, still breathing heavily and equally drained of strength. Finally I pulled myself together and stood up.

"I'm going to bed," I said. Then as I moved away, I heard Curtis say in a low, but sober voice, "We leave for Vancouver tomorrow morning." And then in a mere whisper, he added the words. "This won't happen again."

I climbed into the bed facing the wall and closed my eyes, but my body had no intention of going to sleep. I was terribly upset, but I knew crying wouldn't help! I hated Curtis so much! I would never forgive him! He sat smoking a cigarette by the door until it opened and Hazel came in. I expected a violent fight to flare up between them, but only a quiet discussion took place. My mind continued to churn with nerve-racking thoughts and my head throbbed with pain. After a while, my aching body finally demanded rest and I once again drifted into a deep sleep.

The next morning I awoke stiff and sore with numerous bruises and sore spots on my body. Thankfully, they were all hidden by my clothing. I wouldn't have wanted Hazel asking questions of me. In my mind, I had a mission to accomplish before we left Creston. Absolutely nothing could stop me from saying goodbye to Jim.

I went to the school and had Jim released from class. We stood in the cold, empty hallway saying our goodbyes. It was extremely agonizing for both of us. We embraced and declared our love for each other over and over again. Would we be able to overcome another separation and keep our love alive? I genuinely hoped so, but at the moment it seemed like a downright impossibility. Our hearts were broken. Why was life turning out like this? What did the future hold for us? There were so many unanswered questions. I gave Jim one last kiss and wiped away my woeful tears as I let myself out of the school.

24. Vancouver

Almost immediately, the three of us were crammed into the car Curtis owned and we started out on our long road trip to Vancouver. It was painful for me to see the town of Creston fading away out the back window. My life was so wretched and I could do nothing but moan to myself. My heart felt shattered into a million pieces and I hated watching the miles add up as we drove forward toward our destination. It meant the distance between Jim and I was growing greater by the minute. I sank into the cramped backseat, surrounded by my personal stuff and my tears began to flow freely. I felt so dejected. My sixteen year old heart had so much to cry about now.

After a while, I closed my swollen eyes and slept. When I woke up from my nap, I noticed through the car window the colourful, spring-like scenery that was whizzing by. In place of March's receding snow banks in Creston, I could now see dazzling shades of green and brilliant flowers along the roadside outside the car window. It seemed like we were moving into spring as we travelled following the sun toward the west coast. It was a very nice change of scenery and almost cheered me up. When we finally did arrive at our Vancouver destination I was in for a surprise! It turned out to be very different than I would have imagined.

We pulled up to a lovely home on an upscale street in the rich and exclusive neighbourhood of Vancouver's Dunbar district. How Curtis knew this family and why they opened their home to us, will always be a mystery to me. Nonetheless, they had invited us to stay with them until the work Curtis had been hired to do was ready to start and we could find a place to live.

That first evening we were all so weary from our terribly long car trip that we retired to bed early. When I sank into the soft and luxurious bed provided just for me, it felt too wonderful for words. What incredible luxury! No confined quarters either. I had a bedroom to myself down the hall from Hazel and Curtis. The last thing I did before falling asleep was whisper Jim's name. He seemed so far away and I already missed him so terribly.

For the next two days we were treated like royalty and shown, in every way, a genuine level of extravagance. There is no other way to explain it! Each meal served at the dining room table was delicious and nothing short of gourmet. I thought I'd died and gone to heaven! Why would we be treated so wonderfully kind by these rich people? They just had to be angels!

The man of the house went to work and his wife cooked and cared for us and their preschool twin daughters. For the first time in my life I caught a glimpse of what a true family looked like and it was an eye-opener! Still, somehow I just knew our life in paradise wouldn't last. My past told me all good things come to an end and so they did the very next day.

Curtis returned from the city late and said he'd found a place for us to live. We would be leaving the next morning. It made me sad! At breakfast, the lady of the house pointed out a high school situated very close by and we saw lots of young people walking in the direction of the school. Later, when I was alone in the bedroom gathering my things to go, this kind and concerned woman came to me with a proposal. If I wanted to stay there and live with them, I could attend the high school and in return help her care for their little twin girls. I was totally surprised by her invitation.

My mind tried to make a decision on what I was being offered, but I couldn't think of my life apart from Hazel. It sounded like a different sort of life and the unknown part of it scared me! I was too immature to fully see the opportunity I was being offered.

"Thank you, kindly," I said, "but I have to go with my sister." A decision I would live to regret in the future.

25. The Other Marie and Hazel's Escape

Our move took us to Richard Street in the downtown part of Vancouver. Was it a nice place? No, it was a dump! Not only that, we moved in with Curtis's older sister, Marie, who didn't have room for us at all. She had two daughters who were younger than me and their family was already overcrowded in their small, rented rooms. The father of the girls had long-since deserted them.

I hated the fact that Marie shared the same name as I did and I disliked her right from the very start. Why? She looked so tough and 'rough around the edges,' at least to me. She was a woman past her prime, with dyed red hair and lots of makeup. And Marie's two daughters didn't seem overly happy about us arriving on their doorstep either. Then I got it! They already shared a bedroom and now all three of us would be sleeping in that room. The whole situation disturbed me and I blamed Curtis entirely. This was an ill-chosen move on his part.

It was nearly suppertime by the time we settled in and we were all very hungry. That's when I found out more about Marie than I wanted to know!

"My cupboards are bare," she announced to us and it was true! She had absolutely nothing for us to eat. "Don't worry," she added, "I'll go out and rustle up some food, but I'll need an hour to turn a trick first." A trick! Was that what she called it? I was shocked! She was a prostitute and ever so blatant about it too! I couldn't believe my ears! But true to her word, an hour or so later, we were all around the table, gorging ourselves on mounds of bread smothered in peanut butter and jam. Across the table I heard Curtis snicker. He thought it was humorous! What kind of a place had he brought us to, anyway?

I sure couldn't relate to Curtis's sister and her so-called way of existence. I didn't envy her two young daughters either, as they were caught up in the middle of it all. Doreen, the oldest girl, appeared normal enough to me, but Gloria, the younger sister, was a sulky and depressed girl. I heroically tried to cheer her up, but was told by her older sister, she had good reason to feel the way she did. This raised my curiosity! Yet after I found out what Gloria's difficulty was, I could only feel extremely sorry for her.

Marie had told her daughter years ago, that she was an unwanted child. In fact, Marie gave Gloria all the nasty details. When Marie got pregnant a second time she gave herself an extremely hot bath and drank a full bottle of gin hoping to abort her child. It didn't work though. Obviously, Gloria was born. I was horrified at this tale! Any mother who could be so harsh and unloving, in my estimation, had to be sick in her mind. I couldn't wait to get away from such a malicious person as Gloria's mother and her atrocious lifestyle as well.

Our days dragged on and on until it appeared there was little hope of ever breaking out of there and moving. Curtis was drinking heavily again after work and Hazel started going along with Marie to what she called her 'night-time' job. Together they cleaned out several empty movie theatres on Granville Street after closing hours. But I'd heard some of the stories Marie told of inviting service men inside the theatre for company. That idea made my hair stand on end. I was against Hazel going along on that job. So much to worry about! It was like we were caught up in a web of futility and despair.

It was at times like this when life appeared hopeless and I couldn't see any light at the end of the tunnel. I tried to get a job as an usherette in one of the movie theatres, but they said I was too young and I couldn't find any other prospects around. I was so miserable and unhappy. Nonetheless, I tried my best to keep my letters to Jim up-beat and optimistic. My connection to him was the only link I had of escaping my dismal surroundings. Often, my thoughts returned to the kind lady with the twins and in retrospect, thought what a bad choice I'd made. Yet I realized all choices have their consequences and I had to live with mine now.

It seemed as if things were going from bad to worse and Curtis's fiery temper continually led him into fits of jealousy. They surfaced more and more as time went on. And then it all came to a head late one evening when everyone else was out except Hazel and I. Curtis arrived back that night in a drunken state and the whole scene turned ugly. He was argumentative and full of suspicion regarding Hazel and cornered her with every intention of hurting her. He had his open pocket knife in his hand and was trying to slash her with it. I panicked!

In his drunken state, he was threatening to fix Hazel so that no other man would ever look at her again. Hatred for him, once again flared up in my own heart and I knew very clearly why I was still with Hazel and not somewhere else! I had to convince Hazel to leave him, to come away with me before she became a police statistic. I'd never seen my sister as full of fear as she was that night.

Despite being only 16, I took the upper hand in the situation, even though I was petrified with fear myself. I put a protective arm around Hazel's shoulders, pulling her out of his reach. It broke the hostility of the moment, for this time anyway. But, with his threating actions towards Hazel surfacing more and more, I knew we had to get away and somehow lose ourselves in the city of Vancouver. Somewhere he couldn't find us! And I sensed instinctively it would only happen if it was all planned extremely well.

Thankfully, the next day when Hazel and I could talk, she agreed with me and we set about preparing for our escape. I was glad Hazel was not showing any reluctance about leaving her abusive husband. Fear had made her see the truth of the situation. But we both agreed it had to be done in absolute secret!

Subsequently, as soon as Curtis left for work one morning, only days later, Hazel and I gathered our few belongings together and quietly left. We vanished without telling a soul! We only had enough money to pay a month's rent on a place and beyond that our future was unclear. But one thing we knew for sure, wherever we went, it had to be as far away from Richards Street as we could get.

26. Jobs

A fresh new start for Hazel and I began that very day! It was a definite turning of a page to a new chapter for both of us. I felt it! We mutually experienced a feeling of light-heartedness, as we travelled on the street-car, to a different part of the city that was unfamiliar to us. We found ourselves in the inner-city part of Vancouver that was given-over to row after row of rooming houses. They were the original, old two-story homes formerly lived in by the Vancouver's elite, but now, showing the scars of their age. Still, they looked good to us!

We trudged along the sidewalks looking for a rental, weighted down by our suitcases which held all our earthly belongings. It seemed hundreds of people lived in this area and that made it feel safe to us. We even began enjoying the smiles of strangers and started to reciprocate by smiling back. We both felt free at last and we weren't worried about our future.

When we reached the nine hundred block of Hornby Street, there was a 'For Rent' sign on one of the old houses. We knocked confidently on the front door and were told it was a bedroom for rent which would be small for the two of us. We took it anyway. Size didn't matter to us and we were used to sleeping together anyway. It was certainly a step up from Richards Street. The landlady told us there was a larger suite around the back coming vacant soon and she promised it to us. And so with that in mind, we signed on the dotted line to rent the bedroom. We both slept well that night

The first thing on our agenda was to find some type of work for both of us. Hazel wanted to try working in a factory, so we inquired at the unemployment office. Hazel got hired at the Hobbs Glass Company and loved it. I took a job at the Economy Sausage Company and hated it. During the years of the war, the media had made factory work sound glamorous because so many of the females 'left behind' had to take those jobs. But there wasn't any amount of glitz or glamor at all, in working in a factory from what I could see!

Every day I joined a group of five girls around a long metal table, linking sausages. I disliked everything about my job from the beginning. Standing for eight long hours, while I pinched and twisted the long, slippery snake-like coils of meat into sausage lengths was boring and also back-breaking. Not only that, the place was cold and for some reason, the metal floor where we stood was flooded with water, daily. This made wearing rubber boots a necessity. I'd return home after a day of work, weary and chilled to the bone and ready for bed. Hazel liked the fact that I could bring home sausages and hamburger for mere pennies a pound, but I had no appetite to eat them. We were strapped for money so I kept that job and day-dreamed of a different line of work, something I could actually enjoy.

Meanwhile in Creston, Jim was about to finish his senior matric year of grade thirteen and was facing a decision in his life. In our letters going back and forth we had regularly shared about this big decision that was coming soon. His Mom and Al were moving to Edmonton to join his Dad, who was still stationed with the Army there. And Jim had to decide whether to go with his family to Edmonton or come to Vancouver? It was no surprise to me when he chose to move to Vancouver, where I was. Our affection for one another was still very strong and knowing we'd be living in the same city again made our reunion that much sweeter.

Jim thought he would like to work for a newspaper, as he had gained experience from his part-time job at the Creston Review. However, that didn't work out. Instead he was hired by the Canadian Bank of Commerce and sent to their 41st and Victoria branch, as a teller. The next step for him was to find a place to live. And he found one! It was a two-bedroom suite in a nearby rooming-house which he would share with a fellow by the name of Al Black. They became fast friends and Jim liked it there, although the smell that wafted through the rooms from the land-lady's habit of frying kippers for breakfast became somewhat tiresome.

Meanwhile, I had given into my dislike of factory work and gone back to the unemployment office. I asked for another job, only this time in a retail store. I got one! I was hired to work in Woodward's Toyland department and though it was a temporary position, it would last through the Christmas season. It was a start and a real break for me. What I really wanted now was to gain some retail experience so I could fulfill my dream of working in Vancouver's fashion world. I trusted that retail experience would open that special door for me.

27. My Fashion Dream Comes True

On the first day of my new job, I walked the ten blocks to the Woodward's store with 'a spring in my step.' I was astonished how my attitude towards work had changed overnight. I was thrilled to be a Woodward's employee! As the days of December marched along, my job became a very busy one. I assisted the little children when they climbed up on Santa's knee and had their pictures taken. It was very enjoyable work! I loved kids and I was happy that I didn't have to dress up in some weird costume either, as my satin name-tag with the words TOYLAND identified me as Santa's helper.

My work days sped by and before I knew it, the last photo with Santa was taken and the 1947 Christmas season ended. It all happened so fast, it was 'like a magical snapping of your fingers' and I was back to seeking a new job in retail. And my hopes were sky high! This time the unemployment office seriously viewed my retail experience and sent me to a ladies ready-to-wear store called Anne Maloney Limited on Georgia Street. And I was hired!

When it came to lady's fashions, the Anne Maloney store was rich in distinction and status in Vancouver at the time and I was happy to carry out my position as a junior member of their staff. My job meant filling in wherever I was needed, in the office, on the sales floor or wrapping purchases as well as doing shopping for the alteration ladies. I must have bought a hundred spools of thread at the nearby Hudson's Bay to match the colour of the scores of dresses altered by our 'fitting room ladies.' I liked the happy atmosphere in the store and was never bored! I felt almost cherished by the staff there, too. They treated me like a kind of 'mascot!' Mostly, I think, because I was so much younger than the other members of the staff and they wanted to 'mother' me. I was barely seventeen years old.

It wasn't long before I discovered what I called my favorite responsibility of the job. It was working behind the scenes alongside the store manager, Mrs. Steele. She was a lovely widowed lady, tall and thin and up in years, and the sole owner of the store. She never blinked an eye at marking the fashions from eastern Canada up two hundred percent above the cost price she had paid for them. Toronto and Montreal were the centers of fashions in the 1940's. Imports from New York or the European cities didn't exist back then. It was all Canadian.

As I unpacked the smart-looking feminine clothing from their boxes and Mrs. Steele tagged them with prices, we had time for some long, interesting, as well as fascinating, conversations. I learned so much from her years of experience and expertise in the fashion world. I admired her and felt she was a mentor to me. And I was no slouch at work either, I tried to always look smart, often wearing my fashionable black suit. Looking back to those years of the 1940's, anyone serving the public in the retail field had to abide by a colour code of wearing dark clothing only. It was an unwritten rule of conduct that all of us followed. A far cry from what we see in today's world, wouldn't you agree?

Anne Maloney's store was ideally located to sell women's high-end clothes. We were right across the street from the elite Hotel Vancouver and next door to the Hotel Georgia, both of which were Vancouver's hotels of distinction back then. We were a well-staffed store that had mature sales ladies with eons of retail experience. As I said, I was young in comparison to them. They admired my youthful energy and treated me so wonderfully well, calling me 'dearie' with great affection. I felt surrounded by their love.

The clothes we sold were very expensive garments and I'd wrap them carefully in tissue paper and place them in a box, always with a smile. I loved our customers and would add a few cheerful words to my smile as well. It all flowed directly from my heart, for I couldn't help showing how much I enjoyed working for Mrs. Steele in her store.

Attaining my 'dream job' motivated me to give my very best effort every day. So, at times when a special order item had a rush on it, I'd personally deliver it to the hotel or take it by streetcar to the home where the buyer lived. Most of the time, our customers were from the wealthy part of town, like Point Grey or Dunbar. I remember the first time I set out to deliver a dress to a lady in Dunbar, I got on a bus going the wrong direction. Suffice to say, my sense of direction had not improved much since I left Cardston! However, I did learn to force myself to ask for directions later on.

Some of the clientele buying our expensive fashion creations were influential women, as well as Vancouver's richest women. On a few occasions, a big-name 'star' would make it really exciting to work there and I'd have the privilege of meeting a famous personality.

In the springtime of 1948, while I was working at the job I loved so much, Jim was transferred by the Bank of Commerce to the town of Grand Forks in the interior of B.C. That upset both of our worlds! We had already survived two separations in our time of knowing each other, so why did our love keep being tested, I questioned? Jim got ready to leave and again we were forced to say our unhappy goodbyes. Of course, we renewed our promises to keep our love alive by vowing to write faithfully. Nonetheless, once I was alone again I felt overcome with sadness and my heart told me I was going to have a lot more difficulty battling loneliness this time.

28. Friends

My sister Hazel and I were still very close, but her new found freedom had allowed room in her life for new friends. And so I got to know Margo, a girl my same age who lived in a nearby rooming house on Hornby Street. We found we had a lot in common and started going to the movies and dances together and once we even double-dated, after Jim gave me permission by letter, of course. Still, I wanted so much for Jim and I to be united again. His letters, even though they came often, almost daily, weren't a very good substitute for his presence and his loving embrace.

As time moved ahead, Margo introduced me to a friend of hers that was a bit older than either of us, by the name of Dennis. Why Dennis liked me so much, even at the start, I never fully understood. I tried not to encourage him, but he insisted that we could just be friends, like he was with Margo. He worked for Finning Tractor and eventually asked me to be his escort at their annual fall dinner and dance. I thought it would be harmless to do so, and after sharing it with Jim by letter, it was agreed I should go.

Dennis bought me a corsage of pink roses for that evening, which looked beautiful on my dark green wool dress. The dress was an extravagance, even at cost price from Anne Maloney's store. Despite looking forward to a 'dreamy type' of evening with good food and dancing, it all turned out to be more of a nightmare for me!

Right from the start, the work-buddies of Dennis plied him with drink after drink, which he seemed to take willingly. All the while, I sat nursing a *Coca Cola*. Not surprisingly, Dennis got drunk and then, to top it off, got sick in the washroom and left me sitting alone wondering where he was.

As the night proceeded, all he could do is stay seated and suffer the consequences of his drinking. I was angry and then I became indignant.

He wasn't my friend and I regretted saying yes to his invitation. I'd set boundaries in my life and shared them with him, so he was without excuse. He was well aware I hated drinking and even though I may have seemed too straitlaced to him, my morals stuck to me 'like gum sticks to the sole of your shoe.' So, as far as I was concerned, it was a wretched evening and the sooner it came to an end, the better.

Driving home in the taxi, I was more than mad at him, I was infuriated! I never wanted to see him again and told him so. I wanted our friendship to be over. He felt really bad and wanted to make it up to me and began waiting outside Anne Maloney's for me after work, always with a bag of chocolates or cashews, knowing they were favorites of mine. He even tried to get me to go and talk it over with him at a small coffee shop we had sometimes visited. I stubbornly refused to go! By now, I was starting to realize that his feelings for me went beyond friendship and it was not what I wanted at all. I had to bring it to an end!

Time proved me right when instead of nuts and chocolates Dennis brought me a gift. It was a beautiful gold compact engraved with 'All my love, Dennis' on it. Breaking up was turning out to be more difficult than I had imagined. Dennis insisted we should go on seeing each other. I firmly disagreed! In due course I did get my way, but Dennis still hoped I'd change my mind. He told me he'd wait at 'our' coffee shop every evening for me to join him. I never did go there. Not even once! I felt cruel, but it seemed the least painful way to put an end to a situation we'd both entered into quite innocently.

Years later we passed each other on the street and neither of us said hello. We both just avoided looking the other one in the eye, you know what I mean? It was very sad! I really did hope Dennis had found a special 'someone' in his life to receive his love and return it. And maybe he did. I'll never know!

Meanwhile, Jim seemed very far away as he worked at his job as a teller in Grand Forks. By now, he had learned the bad news that the bank had plans to transfer him to a new location every six months. This precipitated the discussion of how hard it was to be separated and how we might be able to make some changes. We mutually decided that Jim should quit his job at the bank and return to Vancouver and find some new line of work. He was very optimistic he could find meaningful employment somewhere in the big city of Vancouver and I agreed.

Just the thought of us both living in the same location again filled my heart with melodious joy. Did you know that sometimes you can almost taste joy, it's so intense? I was overwhelmed with thankfulness that Jim was coming to Vancouver to live. In my time there, I'd come to love Vancouver and I wanted Jim to love it, too!

It was not the city it is today. No, back in those days of simplicity and unsophistication, Vancouver was trouble-free and only one-third as large as it is these days. The numerous rooming house rentals brought a great many people to live in the city's downtown area. People not only worked there, but lived there by choice because they loved it. We knew our neighbours as well as our neighbourhoods!

Few people in the downtown owned a car, for we were happy to use our transportation system which was streetcars running on tracks down the paved streets, buses or taxi-cabs. There were no street-people living in the back lanes or alleys with no place to call home. Our skyline was that of a township, rather than a city. No high-rise structures either, only the grandiose Marine Building which was our tallest building, standing proudly alone. I loved the small-town feeling of Vancouver in those post-war years and couldn't get enough of its immense beauty and appeal, not just to us Vancouverites, but traveling strangers from afar, as well.

I was excited about our upcoming reunion and began counting off the days on the 1948 calendar until the November date of Jim's arrival. We had written and dreamed about this wonderful event for so long. I was wide-eyed in awe of it all. Then, incredibly, it did unfold and became an everyday reality. Who says dreams don't come true?

29. Extraordinary Events

As for selecting a new career, Jim soon conquered that challenge once he arrived in Vancouver. He was hired to work in the office of Metals Limited, a wholesale plumbing and heating company located on Beatty Street. And it was mind-boggling how a place for Jim to live came about! My sister, Hazel, who still worked at Hobbs Glass, had started dating a special guy from work named Eddie. He was new in town and looking for a place to live as well. The two of them, Jim and Eddie, teamed up to share a two bedroom suite.

Their rooming house was only a couple of blocks from where Hazel and I lived on Hornby. And remember how Hazel and I had hoped for a bigger place to live? We now had the suite at the back of 967 Hornby and it gave us much more space, allowing us to have Jim and Eddie over for dinner. Hazel still loved to cook and we all certainly enjoyed her delicious home-cooked meals.

As the two guys, Jim and Eddie, got to know each other better, they soon learned they were both born in the same small town of Lashburn in the northwestern part of Saskatchewan. What an extraordinary coincidence! A bond was immediately created between them, making them more like brothers than merely friends. And the four of us grew close like family and began enjoying the benefits and pleasures of living our lives in the wonderful postwar city of Vancouver.

A fresh feeling of peace in Vancouver had followed the war years. People were adjusting back to living their ordinary lives, trying their best to forget the chaos of the Second World War. Eddie had spent an extended time overseas in the Canadian Air force and was happy to be a civilian again. He hoped to eventually return to his family and farming in Saskatchewan.

It was obvious that Hazel and Eddie were falling in love, but of course, Hazel was not free to marry. We had no idea what had happened to Curtis, or where he was now. This 'storm cloud' hung heavily over Hazel's life, as divorce at that time was only granted on the grounds of adultery. Hazel and Eddie's future together as a married couple appeared hopeless, yet they enjoyed the love they could share in the moment. What else could they do?

Jim and I enjoyed having special friends in our life and one couple we saw often was Stewart Black and his girlfriend Diane. Jim had known Stewart ever since joining Metals, as Stewart also worked there as a salesman. We all liked the same type of music which was the Jazz and Swing popular at that time. And we were fortunate to be able to attend the live performances of a few of those great performing bands that were all the rage back then. Stan Kenton, the Ames Brothers and Louis 'Satchmo' Armstrong were a few of the headliners we saw when they made personal appearances in Vancouver. We weren't 'bobbysoxers' anymore but we lined up and got autographs with the other enthusiastic fans just the same. Life was good!

Yes, we were music-rich in those days even if money-poor, but we did splurge sometimes and occasionally enjoyed an evening at 'Theatre-

Under-the-Stars' in Stanley Park. That is, when it wasn't raining! I say that because we tried so many times to attend performances there and got rained out! As I recall, we did make it once with Stewart and Diane. They were always a pleasure to spend time with, although they were considerably younger than we were. They became engaged and began making plans to be married which made us happy. And they eventually did marry and we were there at their wedding. I love weddings

Having very little extra money, Jim and I found a lot of things to experience and appreciate that were free. On Sundays, we'd frequent some of our favorite spots like English Bay or Spanish Banks, where the beaches were wide-open stretches of sand, unlike the over-crowded places they've become today. Stanley Park's Hollow Tree, Brockton Point and the Zoo were worth a leisurely afternoon stroll to visit and appreciate. We were energetic and loved to walk, so we hiked everywhere on foot, even sometimes across the Burrard Street Bridge just for the exercise.

Walking across Burrard Street Bridge.

I marvel at how all those truly special times seem to crowd together as I look back to those distant years. A street photographer by the name of Foncie captured little snippets of that unique period in his random photos taken of unsuspecting Vancouverites. During those years, ordinary people didn't carry cameras around like they do today. Only the tourists did. However, Foncie had his camera set up daily on Granville or Hastings Street and captured many of us on film, time and time again. Foncie was a true legend of his time. He made his living by taking spontaneous street-photos of the people in the city he loved! His biography, published after his death, revealed that he snapped thousands of pictures a day. What an extraordinary guy!

Me and Hazel.

Most of us walking along the street were unaware of his camera until there was a flash and we were handed a card to retrieve our photo from his archives the next day. There must be scores of people today who have bundles of his photographs stashed away, that summarize cherished moments in time of their loved-ones back then. We've kept our share of those 'spur of the moment' photographs and we think they're priceless. They help us recall sweet memories of the past.

I was still employed at Anne Maloney's store on Georgia Street and relishing each day at the work because I enjoyed it so much. Therefore, I was not anticipating anything out of the ordinary to happen. I recall that day in question very clearly. It began like any other, but it ended up invading my mind with a tremendous fear of losing all the happiness I'd finally found in life. I can describe what occurred that day in detail...

I had set out on my lunch-break from Anne Maloney's store to walk down Granville Street, as was a habit of mine. I loved to window-shop and stretching my legs after eating my bag lunch. On this particular day, I was enjoying my outing and nibbling on some nougat candy from Purdie's when my gaze took in the street scene ahead of me. I could see far ahead and something or rather 'someone' instantly caught my eye. I was definitely not mistaken! I saw Curtis walking toward me, but he was still over a block away and not aware of me, as he advanced in my direction. Not as yet, anyway.

Me and Jim.

Abruptly, I came to a stop and whirled around completely! I started walking with giant strides in the opposite way as quickly as I could. It was an uphill grade so my heart began hammering ferociously in my chest, but I continued my fast pace regardless. Not until I turned the corner at Georgia Street and saw Anne Maloney's store ahead, did I slow down my rapid rate of speed. Had he seen me? Was he following me? I did not dare look back to see!

Only when I was safe inside the security of the familiar store could I quit trembling, relax and breathe normally again. It was a close call and the shaking inside me wouldn't go away, but lingered for a long time. Yet, in spite of this near encounter, it was to be the only time I would ever lay eyes on the person I hated so much again. Just that glimpse of him was more than enough to convey terror to my heart and soul.

30. Planning Our Future

What stands out in my mind about the year 1949 is how Jim and I started to seriously think about getting married. We talked endlessly about our future and began to make some preparations. I'd spotted a gorgeous white gabardine suit in a store window on Granville Street and had inquired as to its price. I loved nice clothes, but had purposely denied myself as I wasn't able to afford expensive things. The suit was tagged at one hundred dollars which was a literal fortune to me at that time! But I surprised myself and decided to buy it anyway, despite its outrageous price. What happened to my frugality? Well you see, there existed for us poorer people in those days, something called an installment plan. It meant I could pay money down on the suit and have it laid-away until the final payment was made. And that is how the magnificent white suit became mine!

By the time May rolled around, low and behold I was wearing an engagement ring and had only one payment left before the white suit was mine. Most exciting of all, our wedding date was set for June twenty-seventh and I was so excited. I had always wanted to be a June bride.

Finding a place for us to live after we were married was something Jim and I had procrastinated about. In the end, it all came together nice and easy. One of the sales ladies at Anne Maloney's was vacating the small suite she rented on Napier Street and was moving to Victoria. She asked if we would like to reserve it for our home after our honeymoon. Indeed we did! The landlord and landlady turned out to be wonderful people by the name of Arne and Winnie and they immediately agreed with our plan and treated us like we were family.

Our second floor suite ran across the front of the well-kept heritage-style home and we loved it from the start. Even today, that regal old structure stands as elegant as ever on the lovely tree-lined Napier Street. The suite was small, but met our needs at the time. It consisted of a bed-sitting room with a closet and a small kitchen with a gas stove. I was scared to death of that stove, I remember, perhaps because gas smelled like rotten eggs back then. Otherwise, our new place was great and best of all, it was low in rent. Just a pittance compared to today's prices.

We had fun buying a new chesterfield, our old-fashioned name for what you call a sofa today. It had to be unique, in that it would make down flat to be our bed at night. Our other piece of furniture was a wine overstuffed rocking chair. With just two new pieces of furniture, we were set to move in to our first home together.

I told Mrs. Steele at the store I would be quitting my job when I got married and of course when word got around, those on staff jumped to the conclusion that Jim and I were going to start a family right away. I didn't set them straight, but what I intended to do was find another sales position in order to earn more money than the thirty dollars a week I was paid there. Jim and I wanted to save money towards buying our own house someday. I also felt very confident I could find a higher paying job with all my experience in retail. I treasured my time at Anne Maloney's store, but I felt it was time to move on.

My final days of working there went by quickly and the office ladies put on a 'surprise' bridal shower for me in early June. I was thrilled and most grateful. Jim and I would be starting out with nothing much to speak of, so receiving their gifts made us very thankful.

We were not church-goers, so Jim and I gathered up our courage and made inquiries at Christ Church Cathedral, an old stone building on Georgia Street. We had walked by that massive church hundreds of times and felt at ease asking to use the chapel downstairs. Our wedding was to be small in size anyway. Jim, you recall, was raised Anglican and felt comfortable getting married in that tradition with the prayer book service. I hadn't attended church since my Mormon days back in Cardston, and had no other suggestions. So Anglican it was going to be.

31. Our Wedding

There wasn't going to be anything very elaborate about our wedding, as we'd carefully planned it so as not to go into debt. Even our short honeymoon had to be within our budget. Jim went to the Union Steamship Company at the foot of Carroll Street and made preparations for us to go to Bowen Island for a few days after our ceremony in June. It was what we could afford! Yet, to have a honeymoon at all was exciting and 'over the top' for both of us!

Back then there was no such thing as receiving pre-marriage counselling, so the order of service was all we talked about with the Priest before the actual day of the wedding. The custom at that time was to have your 'bands,' which were your intentions of being married, read out in advance for three Sundays in a row. And we thought it was best to attend church for those three Sunday services and we did. During the first week, the prayer book made me feel a little uncomfortable, as the language in it was foreign to me. But I did manage to struggle my way through. Before another Sunday arrived, I solved my problem by asking Jim to share one prayer book between us. Being raised Anglican, he naturally knew his way through the turning of many pages in the prayer book and I felt more relaxed.

The twenty-seventh of June fell on a Monday the year of 1949 and it was a Civic Holiday. That meant statutory holiday rules were in effect, meaning all government places of business were closed. No wine could be purchased and the toast to the bride would have to be made with fruit juice. This was a minor detail to me, but it seemed to upset Eddie, making him nervous. Jim had asked Eddie to be his best-man and Eddie took it all very seriously, especially the offering of a toast on my behalf. Hazel was my matron-of-honour and my only attendant! She seemed relaxed and happy that Jim and I were finally getting married. "They threw away the mold when they made Jim," she always said, meaning she thought the world of him. I totally agreed!

Our wedding day turned out to be a typical late June day in Vancouver, rainy and wet. I recall thinking the curl in my hair was going to suffer as I made my way to the chapel door and entered. Showing how changeable a young girl's mind can be, I had chosen not to wear my white suit after all, but a dress of pale rose taffeta, with the bodice overlaid in lace. A corsage of pink rosebuds was pinned to the shoulder of my dress.

Eddie was waiting for me inside the chapel door. It was planned, he would walk me down the aisle in place of my Father. I'm sure I was beaming with happiness, as I'd waited a long time for this 'dream' day to come true. As a result I felt calm and composed. I linked my arm through Eddie's, and at once realized Eddie was shaking like a leaf. I didn't know if he was nervous for me or himself, but we proceeded down the aisle together. And there was Jim, my wonderful knight-in-shining-armour, waiting for me in front of the altar.

Jim committed himself to me in the traditional vows straight out of the prayer book. Then it was my turn! The priest asked me, "Wilt thou have this man to thy wedded husband, to live together after God's ordinance in the holy estate of Matrimony? Wilt thou obey him, and serve him, love, honour, and keep him, in sickness and in health; and, forsaking all others, keep thee only unto him, so long as ye both shall live?" I responded with "I will."

Then Jim pledged his troth (or promise) to me saying, "Marie, I take you to my wedded wife, to have and to hold from this day forward, for better for worse, for richer, for poorer, in sickness and health, to love and to cherish, till death do us part, according to God's holy ordinance; and thereto I give thee my troth." Then, as coached by the Priest, I responded on cue with the same words of intention to my beloved Jim.

When we arrived at the ring part of the ceremony, Jim said to me, "With this ring I thee wed, with my body I thee honour and with all my worldly goods I thee endow, in the name of the Father, the Son, and the Holy Ghost, Amen." The groom didn't get a wedding ring back then, it was a one ring ceremony! So at that point, Jim and I kissed and the wedding service was over. Our smiling faces hid our sighs of relief, that we were now a married couple, and heavenly joy flooded our hearts.

Our reception took place in our two-roomed apartment on Napier Street and Eddie did well with his 'toast to the bride,' despite his nerves. Our group was small, consisting of Jim's Mom, his Dad and his sister Al, along with Hazel and Eddie and Arne and Winnie, our landlords. And we were most grateful Winnie had made and decorated a simple, yet lovely wedding cake for us, and we proceeded to enjoy it with a cup of tea. Jim and I felt we were the most fortunate couple on the face of the earth to have finally accomplished our goal, by reaching 'our day.' And a little later, we waved our good-byes to one and all and left for our island honeymoon. I was wearing my instalment-plan white suit.

Our wedding photo.

Bowen Island turned out to be a paradise of beauty, beyond anything either of us had experienced before. It made the rainy, wet launch ride and hour long ferry trip all the more worthwhile. The old, but nevertheless elegant, Bowen Island Inn, where we stayed, was a superb choice on our part. It was filled with quaint antique furniture which we so admired. And our second floor bedroom was luxurious and comfortable too. Our window was hemmed in by a massive climbing vine that teemed with flowers that were coming into bloom. Such beauty everywhere we looked, all arranged beautifully in the midst of a quiet tranquil setting. A perfect place for us to unwind and enjoy our first days of married life. We tried to slow the passing days and savour each one to the fullest, but regardless, they flew by altogether too quickly. And so regrettably, we were soon being ushered back aboard the motor launch to return home.

32. Famous Limited

Once we returned to Vancouver and settled into our ordinary lives again, I went looking for a new job. Though I was just eighteen years old, my retail experience opened the door for me into my fashion dream-world once again. A retail store on Hastings Street by the name of Famous Limited hired me and said I would be trained by one of their managers. Trained for what? They didn't explain.

Under my manager Mr. Argue's tutelage, I began working at the cash register in the children's department of the store. I liked the job and I was greatly impressed with Mr. Argue as well. He was an older man with a fatherly way about him and I found him easy to work for and to be around, although I did notice he kept a watchful eye on me at all times. Why, I had no idea at the time, but would discover many weeks later. I liked working in the downstairs department with the children and their parents. The store had installed an early type of X-ray machine that customers could stand in and see their feet inside their shoes. And people used it over and over in selecting shoes for their children. Thinking back now, it probably did more harm than good.

My job was running smoothly when something happened that created a bad outcome for me! At one of my busiest times at the cashier's desk, Mr. Argue sent me to fetch a pink paper he said was lying on his desk in his upper-floor office. And I blew it! I could not find a paper of that colour anywhere, though I looked high and low! And so, in desperation, I grabbed a different shade of coloured paper and hurried back.

My boss was not pleased and I said to myself, "I do hope that wasn't a test of some kind?" However, it didn't turn out to be.

Shortly afterwards, it was announced that a brand new Famous Store was to be opened beside The Hudson's Bay Store on Granville Street, and Mr. Argue had recommended me for the position of Head Cashier! How did that happen? I guess he forgave me my colour-blindness! Anyway I was thunderstruck with joy and could hardly believe my good fortune. I felt nothing short of amazement! Looking back, I still do consider that it was a big accomplishment! The store must have had other people more qualified for the new store's job, wouldn't you think? But I got it. Yes, imperfect me! So I secretly shouted, hooray!

The new Famous Limited sold ladies' ready-to-wear exclusively and being next door to The Bay was an asset, for it more or less guaranteed lots of customers walking by our door. I remember that new store so well, with its funneled entrance between two angled windows, in which we displayed our lovely array of feminine clothing on make-believe models.

I was entrusted with the keys to open the store each morning and relied upon to set the alarm at night when I locked up. I was again on 'cloud nine' so to speak, with all these good things happening to me and I vowed to do my utmost to live up to everyone's expectations as I continued to live my dream life!

The Jewish gentleman who owned the store came in every day just before closing-time with a purpose. He wanted to read the total amount of our sales for the day on our cash register. I suppose maybe he was checking to see if he'd made a good investment? I became a little nervous with his daily visits, only because he was a very aloof person and never said a word to me or anyone else. I was happy that our days were busy with customers and even brisk at times, regardless of the owner's continued nonverbal visits. I decided to learn to live with that.

As a result of the new store's successful start, Head Office hired two part-time ladies to work daily with me. One was Margie Maier, who had newly arrived from England and was about my age. I liked her immediately and she was an excellent sales lady. The other part-timer was Ellie, who was not a happy sort of person and appeared to me to be a bit depressed. Sure enough, it wasn't any time before she confided in me about having marital problems at home. She had a wayward husband, she said! Hearing her problems raised a red-flag for me. Dysfunction always spelled trouble. And who knew a great deal about dysfunction? Right you are. Me!

It wasn't long before I noticed the odor of alcohol on Ellie's breath when she came to work, so now this was escalating into a real concern to me! Yet, what could I do about it? I hadn't hired her. I started keeping an eye on her when she was dealing with customers and handling money at the till. There was nothing to worry about as yet, for up to now the cash register had balanced accurately each night. Still, I was apprehensive!

From time to time, Mr. Argue, my friend and former boss, would drop into the new store and ask me how everything was going. I knew he would be there for me if I ever needed to share any concerns. Yet I didn't want to get Ellie into trouble, as she'd told me she really needed her job. Then, on one of his visits I noticed Mr. Argue watching Ellie closely, just as I recalled he'd once watched me. I was relieved. I knew I could trust him to spot the problem and take care of it. And indeed he did!

It was handled without any involvement from me at all. Ellie must have been spoken to privately. But I recognized the change in her immediately. She no longer showed evidence of drinking during her daytime hours. I was so glad my kind and fatherly mentor-boss hadn't just fired her, but had given her a second chance.

I must admit, I discovered something about myself when that episode transpired. I am a person who doesn't like to confront people and their behavior. Perhaps it stems from my experiences growing up or it is just a shortcoming in my character. On the other hand, it has been confirmed to me many times over in my lifetime. Now, I accept that about myself! It is always good to discover new depths to your individual personality, even if sometimes they are minuses.

33. Holidays

One year after our wedding, when we both had a two week holiday away from our jobs, Jim and I decided to make a journey back to Creston by taking the Greyhound Bus. You may recall we still didn't own a car. During the first week, we visited with Jim's sister Al, who was holidaying at Irene and Ted's place in Creston. And it was at this time, Al underwent a name change and became known ever afterwards as 'Auntie How.' This came about because Irene and Ted's three year old son, David, couldn't pronounce 'Auntie Al' and it came out sounding like 'Auntie How.' The nick-name at once became carved in stone, you might say.

So, ever since then, every member of our family and some of her friends have addressed her by the name of Auntie How. And I think the pet name stuck to Jim's sister, because she wanted it to. The name made her feel special, as she never married or had a family of her own, yet she endeared herself to all of us, in a specific way as Auntie How.

Our second week in Creston was spent at Sanca Park Resort located on Kootenay Lake not far from Creston. The Wilson family had owned and operated Sanca for many years as a fishing location for vacationers and it had also been like a second home to Jim when he was growing-up. He had been a friend and close fishing-buddy with the Wilson's son Earl and they happily recalled those past years and the many fishing trips they'd enjoyed together. And of course, now that I was in the picture,

Auntie How & nephew David.

the two of them welcomed me to join them on a fishing trip the first day we were there. I bravely stepped into the boat and had a lot of fun trying my hand at the art of fishing. I had a lot to learn to be sure!

Earl's Mom and Dad had readied a cabin for Jim and I at the lake's edge and I felt welcomed along with Jim. We basked in the sunshine of the great outdoors all week, reminiscing with Earl and his family of former days at the resort. It was a vacation we'd remember for a long time as it was a great change of pace from being Vancouver 'city-slickers,' as they liked to call us back then. We joined into the fun with the entire Wilson family, little knowing this was to be only the first of many such visits to Sanca in the years to come.

Us fishing on Kootenay Lake.

All too soon, we had to return home by bus again to our little suite on Napier Street. And we were just in time to find a marvelous change had taken place. The suite next door to us, on the same floor, had become vacant. Hazel and a girlfriend Lou, from Hobbs Glass were moving in. I was thrilled to have Hazel and Lou as next-door neighbours. Eddie was still in Hazel's life, in fact very much so! The two of them were very much in love still, but the fact that Hazel was married continued to hang over them like a heavy storm cloud. It was so sad! But then, quite amazingly, the storm cloud was swept away for good.

This is what happened. Lou asked Hazel and Eddie to double-date with her and a guy she knew from Smithers, B.C., named Bob. When the four of them met that evening, Bob brought up the subject of Hazel's last name. He said it was a very familiar name to him as he knew a Curtis by that name in Smithers. Hazel was shocked to hear this and decided then and there to share with Bob her desperate situation. After giving him a brief history of her marriage to Curtis, she explained she was hoping to discover grounds for a divorce from him.

Jim and Marie at Sanca, BC.

It was then Bob revealed he was a member of the Royal Canadian Mounted Police Force stationed in Smithers. In that capacity, he told Hazel, he had crossed paths many times with the unscrupulous Curtis. And he knew that he currently was living with a native woman and had fathered more than one child with her. Bob said he was willing to provide a witness for Hazel, if she would arrange for the divorce proceedings in a court of law. All it would cost her was a return airline ticket for a witness to appear in court and sign the affidavit or sworn statement of Curtis's adultery. This plan would take some time to be put into effect, but Hazel was overjoyed with the prospect of gaining her freedom. It was so close now and seemed too good to be true after so many years.

34. Our First Home

Later that year, Jim's Mom and Dad came from Edmonton for a holiday and we talked to them about our hopes of buying our first home. Mom's motto was 'buy a house as soon as possible,' as renting to her was like throwing your money away. She wanted us to talk to a real estate agent right away and begin looking for a house in order to put an end to our rental payments. And best of all, they were going to help us with a down-payment. Such generosity! So, we went out, the four of us together, to look at what was available on the real estate market.

As often happens, the first house we were shown was a great three year old, two-bedroom bungalow listed for $6,750. Imagine a house with a price like that available in the Vancouver of today! We looked no further and purchased it straightaway. The house was located at 3463 East 4th Avenue and the monthly mortgage payment was within our budget. It was all so exciting and literally happened overnight! Jim and I had moved up in the world. Imagine, we were now homeowners and would pay taxes!

We didn't realize until we moved into our house that it was almost in Burnaby, or at least, I hadn't realized that! Still, we loved the house and living in the suburbs was fine, even if it was a fair distance to Vancouver's downtown where we both worked. Our only means of transportation, without a car, was a tram that we caught several blocks up the hill from our house. In those days, a tram was a double street-car train which travelled at relatively high speeds. We found this out the first time we went to work. The tram did a lot of swinging and swaying from side to side as it reached its peak traveling speed. Our commute, five days a week, took us thirty-five to forty minutes each way! But, we were young and took it all in stride as we were so thankful to have a home, even if it was a bit remote.

Our three-year old home had a real fireplace that burned wood, hardwood floors and a big tiled kitchen. It was a no-basement home with a utility room and a sawdust-burning furnace. That furnace was somewhat of a test and a trial during the winter months, at least for me. At times, the damp sawdust would stick in the hopper and then fall in a huge lump, quenching the flames. Then there would be an explosion when the fire ignited the sawdust once again. It was scary and created some unwanted smoke, too.

In spite of this, we were happy living there and realized every house has its imperfections. We were happy to be situated on a friendly street with good neighbours on either side. And before long I was catching a ride to work with Frank, who lived next-door to us. This was a great help to me! Frank's wife, Marg, was a 'stay at home' Mom with a young girl called Rhonda and theirs was such a nice family. I appreciated the drive into work, as I was very conscientious about being on time, having the keys to open up the Famous Limited at 9:00 o'clock sharp, six days a week. And, I always did!

35. Being Pregnant

As time moved forward, my friend and co-worker Margie announced she was pregnant and both her and her husband were deliriously happy as they'd been trying to get pregnant for some time. Her news got me thinking! Up to now, I hadn't even given a second thought to having a family. But now I did and Jim and I began discussing the subject at length. I didn't know much about motherhood, yet I did know I'd want to plan my pregnancy. No surprises for me! As Jim and I talked further on the subject, we agreed it would be good to have our blessed event happen in September of the following year of 1952.

And it happened just as we planned it! Within a month of conceiving, I knew I was pregnant, but kept it a secret at my workplace. Why? I'm not sure, except I was conscious of Marge reveling in her pregnancy and I didn't want to take the 'spot light' away from her. Having not yet turned twenty-one years of age and feeling exceptionally healthy, I felt I could continue working through the early stages of my pregnancy. I didn't 'show,' as we used to say and so I went on working until my fifth month. That was when the incident on the tram happened!

On my way to work one Saturday morning, I passed out on the tram with its swinging and swaying back and forth. My neighbour Frank didn't work on Saturday, so I had to catch the tram on that one day of the week. That episode scared me even though I was seated and my fainting spell was all over in a brief span of seconds. To my knowledge, not even one person on the fast moving train noticed anything amiss. Still, it scared me! I felt only a bit light-headed and a slight feeling of nausea, as well. Still I made a visit to the bathroom thinking I was going to be sick when I arrived at work! But I wasn't. Yet, it was the closest I'd come to throwing-up in my entire pregnancy. Isn't that amazing! Just the same, that affair on the tram started the wheels in motion towards choosing to end my working career. It was time! So I handed in my resignation.

I had achieved one of my big goals in life by attained my dream-job! The store would hire someone new to take my place and go right on serving the public and I'd be forgotten. Even so, I was so pleased Mr. Argue made a point to say I was going to be greatly missed. I think he genuinely liked me and thought of me with pride, as one of his protégés. Some very wonderful people exist in this world and it was my privilege to meet one of them.

From then on, I took pleasure in being a 'soon to be' Mom and felt excited to begin this new chapter in my life. The winter season passed by quickly and in March we had word from Irene, Jim's sister, and husband Ted, who were living in Hamilton Ontario. They were now parents to a little baby girl, a sister for David. They named her Deborah Ann. The Rolfe family was certainly growing in numbers.

My friend Margie and I were spending a lot of time together now that the bright days of summer were making their appearance. Both of us being pregnant gave us so much in common to talk about and share. Her baby was due only a matter of weeks earlier than mine, so we shared the expectations we had of our future years of motherhood. We shopped for baby clothes at Woodward's and met at a beach to take in the benefit of the sun. That was long before sunscreen had even been thought of, so we lounged on the sand covered in baby oil.

I remember one time looking back as we walked away from our sandy spot at English Bay and getting the giggles. It looked for all the world like two big walruses had spent the afternoon there from the look of the huge impressions we'd left behind us in the sand.

Now that Jim and I were living in the distant suburbs and were without a car, I had a question? Who would take me to the hospital downtown if our baby decided to be born on a weekday when Jim was at work? So we looked to our other next-door neighbours. Would they drive me, if need be? They were a retired older couple, but ever so friendly and, of course they said yes. There was only one thing that made me apprehensive about their willingness. Mr. Thompson was the sole-driver of their car, as most men were in those days, and he had a wooden left leg, which I hoped wouldn't interfere with his driving. On the other hand, Mrs. Thompson was a former nurse and that seemed to balance it out, making it safer at least to my way of thinking, anyway. I was to call on them whenever I needed transportation to the hospital.

Waiting out the months of pregnancy was hard for me, especially as in 1952, the heat seemed to really be intensified as we moved into the summer months of July and early August. It was about this time, a call came from Margie's husband to tell us they were the proud parents of a healthy baby girl by the name of Gail. I was so happy for them. This started me wondering whether Jim and I would have a girl or a boy. My family doctor, Dr. Sockowski, would only say my pregnancy was normal and going well. There was no such thing as ultrasound technology to determine the sex of babies in the far away years of the 1950's. We just had to wait for the outcome, meantime speculating as the time drew near, whether we would have a boy or a girl.

36. Motherhood

My due date was the fourth of September and so it was a big surprise to me when I woke up at five thirty on Thursday morning, August the 28th, feeling some slight cramps. Were they signaling the beginning of labor? Jim was concerned for me, but I sent him off to work as usual, telling him that labor could take hours and hours, maybe even days. That's what people had told me! However, that was not what happened to me! By nine-thirty sharp, I was in my neighbour's car, whizzing past the clock on the corner of Birks and Sons, at Granville and Georgia Street and heading for St. Paul's Hospital.

I was in the back seat and having labor-pains about five minutes apart. Mrs. Thompson was trying to keep me calm by speaking kindly from the passenger seat in the front and Mr. Thompson was driving fine, despite his wooden leg. Personally, I wouldn't have cared if he had broken the city speed limit, as I sure didn't want to have my baby in their car.

At the hospital entrance, I was bustled inside and a nurse propelled me down a hallway so fast, I couldn't even say a proper thank-you to my kind neighbours. I sure wished Jim could have been with me through all that was happening, but he would have been turned away at the door. Perspective fathers were excluded from accompanying their wives inside the maternity ward then. Imagine such a thing! They were told to go home and wait to be called by phone and that phone call would only happen after their baby was born. How things have changed in today's world! Now, of course, fathers participate throughout the entire birthing process. Hooray, for change.

Our baby daughter arrived precisely at 10:47 am, that day, on the 28th day of August, weighing 7lbs. 4oz. and measuring 20 and 1/2 inches long. When Jim finally was allowed in to see me, I told him I was so happy we had a sweet little girl as I didn't want to go through childbirth ever again. That was my instant response when the details of the birth were still so vivid in my mind.

Why would I say such a thing? Because the delivery procedures were extremely flawed and barbaric in those days, at least I thought so. Without any prenatal information or instructions, those of us giving birth to a first baby, were fearful as we didn't know what to expect. The barbaric side was that I was strapped down in the delivery room as I went through the anguish of labor pains. Throughout the entire process, one of my arms was secured to a board attached to the side of the bed. I felt like a prisoner! And I couldn't help wondering if they thought I was going to try and get up and leave? Was that the reason I was tied down?

Thankfully, there was a wonderful nurse to coach me during my labor. She instructed me about the breathing technique of birthing and told me to take hold of her hand with my free one. I gripped hers so hard at times, it must have really hurt her, but I suppose she was used to that! A few moments before the actual birth, I saw a nurse approaching with forceps in her hands. I had never seen forceps before and they had a menacing look about them. It scared me!

Right then a final contraction swept through my body and I felt like I was literally being torn in half. Amid that pain, I seemed to zoom headlong into a tunnel of light and was propelled rapidly forward at a high rate of speed. Or was that all in my imagination? Subsequently, the bright lights of the tunnel grew dim and dimmer and I plummeted into unconsciousness.

When I awoke, a smiling nurse presented me with my tiny baby daughter wrapped up in a blanket. I was surprised that she had a lot of feathery black hair that fell across her forehead and she had high colouring with rosy cheeks. My baby looked just like a little Eskimo baby, I thought! It was difficult to grasp the fact that she was really mine, having not been conscious at her birth. Yet that was just the way it was, back in those days! I learned I had stitches following the birthing process, but my elbow was the most painful of all. It had been rubbed raw during my time of labor!

Jim and I took turns holding our precious little girl and telling each other how great it was to be a family of three. We had not selected a girl's name ahead of time, although I did have a preference for Susan. But in the end, Jim suggested the name Leslie and I agreed. For her middle name we chose Diane, after our dear friend at that time, Diane Black.

Having a baby at that time meant a full week of confinement in the hospital, not only for me, but for all mothers. St. Paul's Hospital, at that time, was staffed by Roman Catholic nuns and they took their orders from their Mother Superior. And she was the epitome of strictness, which I soon found out.

The ward I was placed in had three other new Moms in it. They were young like me and we had a good time together. We even giggled and acted like teenagers a lot of the time. It was only natural, as we were bed-ridden for so many days and bored out of our minds. We had been given strict orders by Mother Superior to lie on our tummies all the time, except when breastfeeding our babies. She said it would make our inner organs return to their normal places. Of course, the four of us were disobedient, only flipping over into that position when we heard the Mother Superior, or any other nurse, coming down the hall.

The days passed slowly and the nuns gave us daily instructions on how to care for our babies as well as how to nurse them. In that area, I wasn't too confident. And even by the time I was released to go home, I was still struggling with the nursing aspect. How I wished I'd had someone at home to help me, like Jim's Mom who was so maternal and would encourage me and spur me on. But, Jim's parents and Auntie How were still living in Edmonton, so I'd just have to work it out on my own! A baby was certainly a big responsibility, I decided.

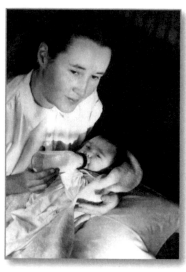

Left: Arriving home.
Above: Me and my baby.

Arriving home with my tiny baby Leslie, I had only one thing to assist me in my new role of motherhood. It was a popular baby book at the time, written by Dr. Benjamin Spock. And he advised on every aspect of child care that a new mother might encounter. I studied the pages of his paperback book by day and sometimes well into the night. Still, I couldn't find the answers I needed, especially on the subject of colic, which seemed to be what caused our wee one to cry every day at the same time for an hour or two. She was not nursing well and her colicky cry made me frantic! So, by the time Leslie was five weeks old and was still struggling for enough nourishment, I returned to my family doctor, with my nerves frazzled.

He recommended bottle feeding her with a formula of canned milk, water and sugar. I felt very upset and could barely hold back my tears in the doctor's office. I felt I had failed at being a Mom, for sure. I wanted so much to nurse my baby, but being inexperienced with infants and far from being a relaxed mother, it hadn't worked. So from now on she would be bottle fed.

Baby Leslie & Daddy.

Making up the formula only added to my workload of washing cloth diapers, drying them on an outside clothesline and taking care of the house, as well as cooking. Motherhood, it seemed, did not come easy for me.

One thing that did come naturally though, was giving my baby unlimited amounts of love and affection. Having a lack of love in my childhood memories made me more keen to show Leslie how very much she was loved and wanted.

From my own experience of being a 'latch-door' kid, I'd always planned to be at home with my children. And I was thankful that I could be. Jim and I were doing well and I'd fulfilled my dream of a career in what I called the 'fashion world,' so from now on I wanted only to be an 'at home mom.' We were financially secure, too, although some changes had taken place where Jim worked. Metals Limited had been bought-out by a company called EMCO, the Empire Brass Company, and Jim found them great to work for. He still maintained his office position and enjoyed his nine till five job, which gave him time for other things in his life. We were ready to settle down to a family way of life.

37. Our Vancouver Family Grows

We were a happy family of three in our little bungalow and content to have such a nice environment to raise our daughter in. Our home had two nice green lawns in the front and a spacious garden area in the back. Jim loved to grow and tend a garden and it was then that he developed his 'green-thumb' reputation! He grew loads of vegetables for us to eat and planted the rest of the yard full of beautiful flowers. Of the numerous flowers Jim grew at that time, my favorite was the deep-rooted, long-stemmed sweet peas, dressed in their delicate shades of pastel colours. I'd bring a big bouquet of them into the house to fill it with their 'out of this world,' heavenly smell.

Our Vancouver family started to grow in numbers again when Mother and my brother Bud arrived, unannounced, to make their home in our city. Bud was driving a newer car, which he said belonged to Mother. She had traded her mortgaged house in Cardston for the car, even though she did not drive! I was inclined to think it happened because she got behind in her mortgage payments, but I didn't dare ask. I sounded like an unfair swap to me, but at least it forced them to leave Cardston and the lifestyle they were living there. I hoped it would result in a fresh start for both of them.

We put a single bed in with Leslie's crib for Mother, but Bud, being the independent person he was, said he'd find a place for himself and drove off. This notion of Mother sharing Leslie's bedroom was a bit of wishful thinking on my part, but I wanted to help her out. I soon discovered Mother had not changed much since I'd seen her last. She still continued to go out and drink with Bud several evenings a week.

One night, it all came to a head when I woke up and heard Mother's key in the front door lock. It was very late! This had happened before, but on this particular night, Mother disturbed Leslie in the room they shared. She began to cry and I was quick to go to her. I found Mother bending over her crib, struggling to lift Leslie up and out. I realized instantly Mother reeked of alcohol and was unsteady on her feet. I snatched Leslie from her arms and said the first thing that came to my mind. "Don't ever pick up the baby when you've been drinking!" Perhaps those were harsh words to say to my own Mother, but I felt like a mother-bear protecting her little cub. A difficult situation all round, for sure.

Shortly after that incident, Mother moved out and got a small apartment just off Commercial Drive for her and Bud. It was a positive move and sort of a new beginning for them. But even so, I didn't feel too optimistic. I could not see much change in their ways and I doubted they would regularly make their rental payments, if Mother's past was any indicator. As a kid, it seemed we always behind in paying the rent, even in that condemned house. Yes, we still had to pay rent to live there! Mother justified her lack of paying by saying it was too high-priced or the landlord was rich anyway and didn't need the money. Still, I had hopes for a better life for them and wished them well in their new location.

Our family in Vancouver grew larger in number once again, when Jim's Dad and Mom decided to move from Edmonton to our city. Jim's Dad, Thomas, was still in the army and had asked for a transfer to the army base at Jericho Beach. He had retirement from the army in mind and wanted to be at the coast where the climate was milder, for health reasons. His legs and knees were beginning to bother him from the years he spent standing in the cold, wet trenches during the First World War. Auntie How, who was unmarried and lived at home with them, was able to transfer to the Canadian Imperial Bank of Commerce's main office in downtown Vancouver.

So the Rolfe family came and bought a small, no-basement house in the 2700 block on East 5th Avenue. Jim's Mom, or Granny as we now called her, was delighted to leave Alberta's cold winters behind and call British Columbia home again. I remember how she would travel by bus to the public library and get bags of books to read and they were mostly books about Canada. They helped her to learn more about B.C. and its history as well as the country of Canada as a nation. Granny and Grandpa Rolfe had emigrated from England in 1919, right after they were married and became naturalized citizens of Canada as soon as they possibly could. They were very proud to be Canadians and felt it was a privilege to live in our beautiful country. I was impressed, as I had always taken my own citizenship very much for granted, having been born in Canada.

38. Baptism and Family Reunion

Before very long, the subject of baby's baptism came up due to Granny and Grandpa Rolfe having a background in the faith of the Anglican Church. Granny suggested we have Leslie baptized while she was still a small baby, so we made plans for this to happen when Leslie would be four months old. We inquired at Christ Church Cathedral, where Jim and I had been married. They had a Sunday afternoon service for Baptisms coming up after Christmas, so we made arrangements for Leslie's baptism then.

In the tradition of the Anglican Church, we were to choose two godmothers for our daughter and one godfather. We asked Auntie

At Christmastime.

104

How to be Leslie's Godmother along with inviting our friends, Diane and Stewart Black, to be godparents. After all, Leslie shared Diane's name!

We celebrated Leslie's baptism as planned, with the Rev. Cecil Swanson officiating. I dressed Leslie in her long white christening gown which was a gift for the occasion from her Granny and Grandpa and Auntie How. She also wore the gift of a gold locket from Diane and Stewart Black. It was a very special day and an affair to remember for everyone in the family.

Leslie's babyhood stages seemed to zoom by so very fast, it is hard to remember all the details. When she was ready for a highchair we bought her a Baby-tenda instead. It was a unique little child-sized seat suspended in the center of a low square table. I don't think they exist anymore, but it was ideal for her. Leslie loved sitting inside her little table and playing with her stuffed toys as well as enjoying eating her meals there.

Leslie walked just before her first birthday and I recall baking and decorating a birthday cake for her with one candle on it. I had no memories of birthday cakes in my own growing up years, either bought or homemade. It made me want to do all those extra things for my daughter that I had not experienced myself. And I enjoyed it all with her.

Leslie no longer a baby.

My Dad and two brothers came to see Hazel and me once again in 1953, following Leslie's first birthday. It turned out to be a family-reunion and we made a point of posing together as siblings, for a family photograph. It was taken in Hazel's suite on Napier Street and it is still a very special picture to me, as never before had we posed as a family altogether. Looking back now, it seems to me the five of us were so young. In the photo, Harold was 33, Floyd was 32, Hazel was 29, I was 22 and Bud the youngest, was just 20 years of age. We were brothers and sisters who had grown up apart from each other, but united at long last. I cherish the picture with all of my heart, as it turned out to be the only one ever taken of the five of us together.

For me, it was also interesting to see my Mother and Dad meeting after having not seen each other for well over fifteen years. They had brought the five of us children into this world and yet were almost total strangers to one another. Mother acknowledged my Dad by nodding towards him and saying, in a very formal way, "How are you, Mr. Posing?" It was a surreal moment in time to witness that encounter between them.

Floyd, Hazel, Harold, Me & Bud.

39. Happy News and Wedding Bells

After such a long wait, as is customary with court cases, Hazel received her divorce notification from the B.C. court system. She was given just one week to appear at the Divorce Court proceedings, which was more than enough time for us to 'stew over it.' We had dreamt of this day for what seemed like forever, but it still came as a thunderbolt out of the blue. Hazel wanted me to accompany her to the courthouse on the day of her divorce-trial just in case a character witness for her defense was needed. Of course I said I'd go, but I was scared! Why? Because so very much depended on the judge's verdict to set Hazel free.

Eddie and Hazel.

When the day we dreaded finally arrived, Hazel and I were both literally sick to our stomachs with worry and nervousness. Yet, if we'd only known, our fears were for naught! The judge, after hearing the evidence presented by the Smithers witness, made his announcement in a loud, clear voice. "Divorce is granted." This was followed by a loud bang of his judge's gavel in dismissal.

It was over and done with! We'd both been feeling so tense, fearing the worst and now we were ecstatically happy. What an emotional roller-coaster ride! I felt like jumping up and down for joy personally, at the tremendously positive outcome. Hazel was at last

107

free from her past and could marry Eddie. It was happy news, indeed!

Right after that, in November of 1953, Hazel and Eddie were married in the parlour of the nearby United Church Rectory on Napier Street. It was a simple, straight forward service and Jim and I were their two attendants.

Once they were married, as expected, Hazel and Eddie were soon saying their goodbyes to us, ready to begin their eastward journey to Saskatchewan and a totally different way of life. Farming was a big part of who Eddie was and now he wanted to return to his place of birth and work alongside his father and his brother, Ivor. Together they'd be rais-

ing crops of grain on the two sections of land the family owned outside the small town of Lashburn. With a willing heart, Hazel was helping Eddie fulfill his dream, even though her own future held many unknowns yet to be discovered. I was going to miss my sister a lot, but I could only hope she'd find the happy, secure life she so richly deserved.

The four of us at Hazel and Eddie's wedding.

40. Our Young Family

Jim and I were finding life good and we were happy and content now in our role as parents to little Leslie. Life was running smoothly and even though Jim worked fulltime, he was an excellent 'handyman' around the house and greatly enjoyed keeping up the yard work, too.

In the summer of 1954, he built a large wooden sandbox for our backyard so Leslie, now two years old, could spend countless hours playing by herself or with her friends. Sometimes Margie brought little Gail over by street-car and our two girls had a great time in the sand with their rubber pails and shovels. They were so close in age and temperament it was almost like they were twins. Margie and I would have a cup of tea and share our ongoing experiences as new mothers.

Not many of us women had cars back then either. Most families had only one car and it was used for the dad's transportation back and forth from work. I didn't even have a driver's license myself! Like other women of that time, I thought nothing of travelling downtown to shop or across the city using the street-car system. Woodward's had only one store back then, located on Hastings Street in the downtown area. They were noted for their $1.49 Day Sale every month and, whenever possible, I would go in order to buy their marvelous bargains. At that low price they were still of good quality and worth the trip on the streetcar. Sometimes Granny Rolfe would babysit Leslie or else she would go shopping for me and get their $1.49 children's clothes. We took Leslie with us many times before her kindergarten days, too. I remember one time Granny lost her there! Of course, she was found soon enough among the round racks of clothes and I forget if Granny had to have it announced over the store intercom system or not. It was a common occurrence back then for a child's description to be broadcast because they were lost.

Leslie was a very bright little girl who loved her many books and knew the stories off by heart, repeating them from memory even in her second year. She was very close to her Granny, who came to see her often, but didn't always warm up to my mother or Bud, as they were infrequent visitors. Leslie could be very shy around those she didn't know well. I remember how she would sometimes hide in the folds of my skirts when feeling extra shy.

We heard once again from my American side of the family. A letter from my Dad came saying my brother Floyd had met and married a wonderful girl while working in Glacier National Park that borders Montana and Alberta. The girl's name was Gigi and she'd come to the Glacier Resort with her Grandpa Budd, who was a man of great wealth. Floyd was at the resort as a backcountry guide to take the guests horseback riding. Gigi was crazy about horses, which sounded like just the girl for Floyd, a lover of horses himself.

The two of them fell in love and decided to get married right away and her Grandpa agreed. He even bought them an extravagant wedding gift of a ranch on many acres of land with a lovely home on it. He also gave them a house-trailer so they could travel. Mr. Budd had gained his wealth by investing in one of the prosperous American railways in his younger days and he loved to spoil his granddaughter Gigi, giving her whatever she wanted. And Gigi wanted Floyd and so nothing was allowed to stand in their way. I was happy for my brother Floyd.

And as early as 1955, when Leslie was two and a half years old, Jim and I started thinking about having another baby but I didn't get pregnant right away as expected. We were disappointed and realized it wasn't going to be as easy as we'd thought it would be. We'd have to have patience. In a lot of ways, the waiting process only made us more desirous of adding another baby to the family.

Time passed by and we had saved enough money to purchase our first television set. It was an RCA model with a twenty-one inch screen that cost $299.50, which was a high price back then. We were excited about owning our very own T.V. and right away it gave us more visitors, as television watching was something new and not everyone could afford a set. Not like today. Even Mother and Bud came out without much coaxing. In some ways, television sets drew families together.

As adults, we watched the *I Love Lucy Show*, *The Millionaire*, *Gunsmoke* and the Sunday evening *Ed Sullivan Show*. Leslie, at three years of age, enjoyed many of the children's programs of the time such as *Howdy-Doody*, *Captain Kangaroo*, *Lassie*, *Leave it to Beaver* and also *Father Knows Best*.

Leslie in front of our first T.V.

41. More Changes for our Family

Finally, in July of 1955, I excitedly discovered I was pregnant. We were ever so happy knowing our second child would be joining our family in the spring of the coming year. It seemed like our wait had been eons of time, but miraculously, all my fears of giving birth had disappeared. I was looking forward to another baby and having our family grow in size. We didn't want Leslie to grow up as an only child.

As the first time around I had excellent health during my months of pregnancy. I had no 'morning sickness' or nausea. Did it make a difference that I was young, not yet twenty-five year old? Maybe! In any case, it certainly helped me enjoy my pregnancy.

And, it was as I was sailing through my second pregnancy, that we acquired a black cocker spaniel named Gypsy. Irene and Ted told us they were giving us their dog before they left to go overseas to Germany. Ted was to be stationed there for two years with the Airforce. They drove Gypsy all the way out to Vancouver from Ontario.

I recall Irene telling us how they travelled with both of them driving night and day and all sleeping in the car. Gypsy slept in the back on the floor, nine year old David across the backseat and three year old Debbie's bed was up in the back window of the car. Who would have thought that would work? But for them it did! Their visit was short, mostly planned to say goodbye to Granny, Grandpa and Auntie How, as well as us. Then they were off, departing for overseas by air.

Gypsy was both a lovable and a trying young female dog. She was very good with children and three year old Leslie took to her at once, but she loved to bark endlessly at the mailman every single day. There seemed to be no way to break her of the habit. I must admit, there were times when I lost my patience with her and her constant barking.

And it was during this time, in the final months of my pregnancy that our family underwent another major change. We moved! But the move to a different house in the month of January of 1956 was not at all difficult. Why? Lots of people helped us, both family and friends and I was especially careful not to overdo it myself physically. I had continued to feel very well and in the end, only gained twenty pound just the same as during my first pregnancy.

42. Chrissy Makes Her Appearance

My due date was April 4th, but as I had learned previously, that was only Dr. Sockowski's estimated date, so I kept hoping my baby would come earlier. And my wish did come true! On Sunday evening, March 28th things started to happen. I had cooked a roast beef dinner and my brother Bud had come out to share the meal with us.

We had no more finished eating and Bud was about to leave in his car, than I had a sure sign my baby was getting ready to be born. While in the bathroom, my water broke! I still wasn't very knowledgeable about having a baby, but my common sense told me it was time to make haste to the hospital, especially since this was my second baby. Both Jim and Bud agreed and away we went in Bud's car to St. Paul's hospital with me in labor once more in the backseat.

The three of us and Gypsy.

The rules at St. Paul's Hospital had not changed much and yet my experience was quite different and very much better than it was three years and seven months earlier. My doctor was not yet at the hospital, so the intern on duty set me up to have a spinal injection. This meant I would be numb in the lower half of my body. It worked wonderfully well for me. I was also given a type of oxygen mask that I could self-administer when labour grew intense. Everything moved along at high-speed and my baby girl was born just after midnight, making her date of birth the 29th of March.

She was adorable with her sandy-coloured hair. She weighed 7 lbs. 7oz. and measured 21 inches, which is a long length for a baby, so I was told. My own doctor arrived after I had given birth and when I told him how fast and easy my little daughter had been born, he muttered under his breath that I wouldn't have had a spinal if he'd been there. But, as for me, I was glad it happened like it did. I felt great and even wanted to go home. Why not? I didn't even have stitches!

Jim came the next morning and we excitedly fussed over our tiny, precious infant and felt thankful for our perfect little girl. A wee sister for our Leslie! At first we were without a name for our newborn, but it didn't take long before Jim suggested the name of Christine and I liked it immediately. Of course, because she was such a petite little girl, we shortened her name to Chrissy! As for her middle name, we decided it would be Ann, after her Granny Alice Ann Rolfe, as well as my Grandmother and her Great-Granny, Elizabeth

Chrissy with Daddy.

Ann Sanders. Now that she was named, I was ready to take my little baby girl home and show her off to her big sister. But, as was still the custom, my hospital bed care continued on for a full week.

Those seven days were very taxing for me as I not only missed Jim, but now my little treasure, Leslie also. I had a photograph of her to look at periodically, which helped. Learning baby care from the nuns had not changed at all since my last stay at St. Paul's Maternity Ward. However this time I surprised myself and did extremely well at nursing my baby! I was very proud of myself. Being a relaxed Mom this time, caused my wee baby to be contented too. Jim was such a happy new Daddy and on his visits said Leslie missed me a lot as he did as well. When my stay was

Chrissy, Granny and Leslie.

Chrissy in her Baby-Tenda at Christmas.

up and I could bring baby Chrissy home, I remember I laid her on the chesterfield, so Leslie could look at her up close. She was just amazed at how small her sister was.

At home, I was given a lot of support and encouragement from Granny who knew so much about nursing, having nursed all four of her children. Her good advice helped me so much and if I had questions, she was more than ready to help me find the answers. I hardly opened Dr. Spock's book anymore. I felt experienced at being a Mother now and was so much more at ease taking care of my tiny infant, Chrissy.

Leslie seemed so big and grownup to me after I got home. She had been well taken care of and had lots of attention while I was in the hospital. Jim had hidden an Easter basket for her behind the heavy curtains in the front room, which she found in no time. And Granny Rolfe had shared lots of new stories with her from her books and she recited them for me. I gave her a listening ear as it was clear she had missed me as much as I'd missed her. She lovingly accepted her tiny baby sister, with lots of kisses and hugs and I was glad there wouldn't be any sibling rivalry to worry about. Granny's heart had more than enough room to love both of them.

Our marvelous new addition to the family became known to all of us by her pet-name, Chrissy, a name she retained throughout all her preschool years. Christine just seemed too formal for such a sweet wee girl. And from the very start, Chrissy was outgoing in nature and loved having people around her. We put our Baby-Tenda to good use once again and propped her up in it before she could sit well on her own. As the months went by, it was her favorite seat in the house and she enjoyed being the center of attention there. It was where she ate her meals and continually enjoyed a circle of toys around her, just as her sister Leslie had before her.

In December of 1956, after Christmas, we decided to have Chrissy baptized like her sister was before her. She was nine months of age. Auntie How and Auntie Hazel were chosen as her two Godmothers and

Chrissy's baptism day with her loved ones.

Uncle Eddie as her Godfather. It was such a family affair! Chrissy wore the same lovely white christening dress that Leslie had worn a few years previously.

Hazel and Eddie had flown from Saskatchewan to be there for the baptism and to visit with us over Christmastime. Such a delightful time! I could see they were happy. I learned farming was going well for Eddie and Hazel was now working in Lashburn as a telephone operator. And it was so wonderful having Hazel and Eddie to share life with us again. Their Christening gift was an adorable locket and Chrissy wore it during her baptismal ceremony. She was a happy baby, bubbling over with smiles for everyone.

On the day of Chrissy's baptism, after the ceremony at church, everyone who had attended gathered together at our house for a celebratory tea. A picture was taken of us with Granny and Grandpa Rolfe, Auntie How, as well as my Mother, Hazel and Eddie and Granny's friend, Mrs. Rumsey.

43. Our Neighbourhood

The house we were now living in at 2657 East Fifth Avenue was so much more to our liking. Granny and Grandpa lived only a block away from us, over the hill. This new house was more spacious and best of all, it had a basement. Hooray for basements! Children love to play in basements, especially during the rainy winter months in Vancouver. Or, at least ours did! Our move to this house gave Leslie, and now Chrissy, a lovely street to grow up on and lots of neighbourhood kids to play with.

There was a special family we became friends with just four houses down the hill from us. Their last name was Peters, Jim and Lois, and they had two boys the same age as our two girls, which worked out nicely. Johnny was their eldest, Leslie's age and Harry was exactly Chrissy's age. Lois and I liked each other from the start and became friends and what I recall most about her was her endless energy and very soft-spoken voice. The Peters also had a younger third son we called Jim-Jim and eventually Lois would have an additional two children, both girls, named Angela and April.

Despite the noisy mayhem always happening at their house, our girls liked to play at the Peter's home. I knew Lois kept a watchful eye and she had a great deal of patience in every situation, more than most moms did! I thought of myself as a patient person, but I was never able to be as unruffled as Lois was, even though their family had more than their share of daily upsets to face.

Among the other little girls who lived on our street, a favorite was Nikki. She was the young granddaughter of our Italian neighbour, Mrs. Sardoni. Both of Nikki's parents worked and this, as I've said before, was most unusual in those days. Nikki's Grandma loved to serve up hot Italian dishes for lunch to tempt her granddaughter's poor appetite. And to Leslie's joy, she would often be invited to come along and eat lunch at the Grandma's house, as well.

But, Nikki was not only a 'picky' eater, but to the shame of her Grandma, didn't like Italian food. She would loudly protest at the sight of it. Nonetheless, with a lot of coaxing, Mrs. Sardoni would get her little Nikki to finally eat her plate of meatballs and spaghetti, or chicken with spaghetti, or pork-chops with spaghetti. Leslie loved food of all kinds and would greatly enjoy those Italian meals and I think she also had a persuading effect on her friend's appetite, too

Right next door to us on our street was our young and sometimes 'crazy' neighbours, Stan and Barb. They were always trying to get the best of one another and fought their battles publicly. For example, Stan loved to fly kites from his backyard porch. If he was slow coming inside for his supper after repeatedly being called, he was in big trouble! Out the door Barb would march with her scissors in hand. Quick as could be, she'd cut the string of Stan's highflying kite, with him yelling loudly in protest. He would be really upset and jump into his car and roar away chasing his precious kite. Sometimes Stan lost his kite and other times he retrieved it, but it always made for pandemonium on our street.

At other times, Stan would have the upper hand in their dispute and we'd watch him chasing Barb all over their backyard with the garden hose spraying her, full-bore with cold water. Being fully clothed, she would be completely soaked and mad as 'a wet hen,' so the saying went. She would finally escape by running inside and locking all the doors. Then Stan took exception and complained loudly at the top of his voice for all the neighbours to hear

Their antics were always in fun and we personally liked Stan and Barb a lot. They always kept our block lively with their entertaining pranks, followed naturally by their making up, too. Our houses were so close together that our bedroom windows were only separated by the width of the fence in between us. With no air-conditioning away back then, we'd all have our windows wide open in the boiling heat of the summer nights and it was then, we'd hear Stan's voice call out, "Goodnight Jim!" It would make us both chuckle in our bed.

And I must add, they did settle down after their first child named Cindy joined them. They chose her by adoption and she was a sweet little girl all of us on the street loved very much.

Later on, a new neighbour moved into the house on the other side of Stan and Barb. They were a Dutch family, and their oldest daughter was Freda, a nice girl, around the age of our two girls. What was unique about Mrs. Schipper was that she sang in their Dutch Reform church choir and exercised her singing voice, daily while hanging out her laundry. What made it unusual was that she sang Christmas carols all year around. Her powerful soprano voice could be heard throughout the entire neighbourhood singing, *Silent Night* or *O Come All Ye Faithful* and the whole repertoire of Christmas choruses, such as, *Let It Snow, Let It Snow, Let It Snow*. Meantime, all of us were perspiring in the heat of the Vancouver summertime.

Mrs. Schipper had a big audience too, even if hidden from her sight by all our backyard trees. We all hung our laundry out on our backyard clothes lines, daily as well. Without any other means but a clothesline and the sunshine, us moms, had to dry our wet wash outside. It was an endless and nonstop task .Up to that point in time, electric clothes dryers didn't exist, but perhaps, the exceedingly rich families, might have owned such a luxury item. But it was rare!

And now, as I recall that backyard scene in my mind, I wish I had relaxed a little more and appreciated the free operatic entertainment of my neighbour's outstanding soprano voice. She offered it so freely. I might even have thought to applaud her once in a while, too.

And I mustn't forget little Ronnie on our street, either. He lived with his elderly Grandpa most of the time. And, we couldn't figure out whether Ronnie was bad or just liked to tease his Grandpa. Every day before mealtime, the Grandpa, who was of considerable years, would be out searching for Ronnie. We knew what would happen next. Once found, the Grandpa would bribe Ronnie with cookies and treats just to get him to come home for lunch. Later on, the whole performance was repeated. I remember thinking it must have been difficult for Ronnie's Grandpa. It was all so hard on him! Why was an elderly man raising his grandson? Where were the boy's parents? Alas, my questions were never answered.

Left: A family party. Right: Chrissy walks on her 1st birthday.

44. Life's Changes and the Saw

The next few years held a lot of changes for us as a family. Our Chrissy was growing up fast and no longer a little baby. She took her first steps the day before her first birthday and I baked and decorated a special birthday cake for her, bearing one candle.

Chrissy was a happy, good natured little girl and was near and dear to her Granny and Grandpa Rolfe. I can picture with fondness the November 11th Armistice Day, when Grandpa came by to show our two girls the metals he always wore to the services commemorating that special holiday. He had been given those medals for his wartime service in the First and Second World Wars and we were all so proud of him.

Tea with Grandpa.

Chrissy also loved to be rocked and sung to by her Granny, who happily obliged. She cuddled her and sang many of the old nursery rhymes she recalled from her English childhood and now loved to share with her little granddaughters. A favorite was *Hear the Pennies Dropping*, which stemmed from her Sunday school days of dropping pennies onto the offering plate as a child in England.

> Hear the pennies dropping; listen while they fall,
> Everyone for Jesus, He shall have them all.
> Dropping, dropping, dropping, dropping;
> hear the pennies fall.
> Everyone for Jesus, He shall have them all.

Leslie had a great imagination and even at a young age liked to play make-believe school with Chrissy. She would set up a school room in which she was the teacher and Chrissy was her pupil. The 'teaching' part was always the role Leslie took, but Chrissy rarely complained. Even though a lot of the school work was beyond her age-level at first, Chrissy was an avid learner and would soon catch up to whatever was asked of her. She was smart and had a desire to learn from the start.

In 1959, the famous Barbie doll was 'born,' or should I say, made her appearance. The two sisters switched back and forth between playing school and playing with their Barbie dolls, having great fun and enjoying both. Especially when Vancouver's rainy weather kept them from going outside. I was more than busy keeping those Barbie's well dressed with homemade doll clothes, but I did it! I put the trusty little portable Singer sewing machine to good use and sewed by the hour, if not to make clothes for the girls themselves, then for their dolls. As their Mom, my heart always rejoiced to see the two of them having fun and playing together. Friends were fine but family bonds were so precious to me.

Around this time, we saw a lot of Bud as he decided to buy a Shop Smith saw on the installment plan and asked us if it could be set up in our single car garage. Naturally, we said yes to his request and he came out to our place to use it whenever he could. I was relieved that Bud now had a job. He was a longshoreman and for once was spending his money on something useful. At his previous job in a furniture factory, Bud had learned how to construct furniture and now he wanted to make some of his own, with Jim lending a hand, of course. The two of them always got on well together and worked side by side at the saw for hours on the weekends.

Bud took pleasure in being around our two girls as well and that was nice for him and for them, too. I think Bud's sense of humour made him a dear Uncle to our daughters and he enjoyed them as he'd never married and didn't have friends with children either.

Bud and Jim's first project was a long, low bookcase for our front room. It turned out to be just beautiful when it was all varnished in a light golden brown. Next, the two of them made bedroom night tables with three deep drawers in each and also a headboard for our bed. All the pieces were made so sturdy they're still in use today, over sixty years later.

Jim enjoyed Bud's expertise and fellowship, but before long and true-to-form, Bud lost his job and got behind in his payments on the saw and lost interest in building furniture as well. The store where Bud had purchased the saw started threatening him with repossession if he didn't make his monthly payments. This was the story of Bud's life repeating itself over again. Who knows how many other things he'd lost that way!

This time though, Jim came to his rescue and took over the payments on the saw. Jim urged Bud to continue to come out and share in the use of the saw and Bud said he would, but he never did. This was typical of Bud and his behavior. Sometimes I almost wanted to give up trying to understand my brother.

Jim had a list of things he wanted to build with the saw and he went ahead and made them. It became a fulltime hobby for him. Our spacious sundeck over our single garage needed rails, so he made them first. He seemed to find endless energy for what was now his hobby. He constructed four large outdoor pieces of wood furniture for our sundeck and I surprised myself by sewing their sling-back seats out of some colourful, striped canvas material. They looked great on our deck and the canvas seats were very comfortable to sit in.

Next, Jim designed and made a wooden rocking-horse for the girls to ride on and a teeter-totter, such fun items to play on in our downstairs basement. As well, when the girls needed a large table to operate their small electric train on, Jim supplied that, too. His very biggest project though, by far, was the backyard slide he constructed. It stood between five and six feet high, a junior version of the giant slide we had taken the girls to enjoy in the recreational park, but ours was every bit as nice.

When the slide was finished and set up in our backyard on the lawn, a crowd of neighbourhood kids gathered. All of us were excited about Jim's latest creation. He had produced a real professional looking slide. The girls and I were so proud of him. Jim and I stood there watching as a long line of kids formed to climb the four ladder-type steps to the top and have a turn. It was breathtaking to watch them come squishing down the slick sanded slide surface. Jim had polished it so it was as smooth as glass. What fun the kids had! The slide was greatly used and appreciated by Leslie and Chrissy and their friends and they enjoyed it over and over to their heart's content. I don't recall ever trying it myself, but now all these years later I wish I had.

45. Kindergarten and Changes

In those years when our children were young and active, the years flew by quickly and before we knew it, Leslie was turning five years of age and I was enrolling her in afternoon kindergarten classes. They were held at Laura Secord Elementary School located on Broadway by Lakewood Drive. It was a ways away and you had to cross the busy streets of Broadway and Nanaimo to get there. We had an elementary school nearer to us called Chief Maquinna, but it was newly built and didn't provide kindergarten classes as yet. Lois Peters was also registering her Johnny in the same kindergarten class.

We all walked together with our five-year-olds on the first day of school, but after that they'd be walking the eight blocks to the school by themselves. It was common in those days for kids as young as kindergarten age to walk to school in pairs. Lois and I both had little ones at home taking naps in the afternoon, and back then it seemed very natural for Leslie and Johnny to be that responsible and independent.

The kindergarten classes were held three times every week and Lois and I cautioned Leslie and Johnny of the dangers they might encounter on their long walks to school. Our greatest concern was the set of lights at the busy Broadway and Nanaimo intersection. They both agreed to be extra careful and it seemed to go well or at least as far as we knew.

Later on we did learn there was one scary incident at that intersection with the traffic-lights. Johnny had held up the bumper-to-bumper traffic on Broadway when he stopped, just half way across and knelt down on one knee to carefully re-tie his shoelace. And Leslie, of course, stayed right at his side. The traffic-lights changed and the cars patiently waited for them to exit the intersection before they began moving through again. Later on, as they innocently shared what happened, Lois and I were struck with alarm at the thought of that petrifying scene and yet we had to be sympathetic with their child-like actions. At their tender age, tying a shoelace was of prime importance!

Leslie recounted to me, well after the fact, that one afternoon on the way home, she and Johnny had a bit of a fight and he had stomped on ahead of her, leaving her crying on the sidewalk. Thankfully, help was quick to come as a kindly lady stepped out onto her front porch and called Johnny back saying, "You take that nice girl home with you!" And all was well!

Around this time our family experienced another change. At EMCO, Jim was asked to go on the road as a salesman. It was a big surprise to us all, including Jim! Immediately, he had to get tested for a driver's license because he'd never owned or driven a car in his life. He took a few lessons and passed his driving test easily.

It was an exciting day when he was given his very first car, a brand new 1957 company-owned Chevrolet. Jim could use it for his work as a salesman and for our private family use and all expenses were paid. Hurray! It surely was a step up in life for us as a family and we felt privileged, too. Not every family had a car in those days.

Not long after that, we purchased a small tent and began doing some camping on weekends, traveling short distances out of Vancouver. We drove to some of the lakes and spent an overnight in our tent. I remember trips to Alice Lake and Alouette Lake, as well as other places not very far away from Vancouver.

I wasn't a big fan of camping, or 'roughing it' as I called it, but our two girls loved everything about it, even the chores that had to be done. Watching their Dad chop wood for the bonfire and eating outside at a picnic table pleased them no end. They liked discovering the various creepy, crawly things found in the campsites and they loved sleeping in our four-man tent. But we had a firm family rule about where Daddy slept in the tent and he had to abide by it. We insisted that he sleep in front of the doorway flap, just in case an unwelcome bear showed up in the overnight hours. He was our protector and as long as he was sleeping at the door guarding us, the girls and I felt safe in the outdoors.

A car made all the difference in the world to us as a family as it gave us a new sense of freedom and took us to new places we'd never been able to see before. And Jim enjoyed being a salesman. The only drawback was he had to travel to Vancouver Island for a few days every month to make sales calls. We soon got used to those trips and I remember the girls and I always missed him so much. When he was away, I always cooked my special creamed salmon over rice dinner. The girls and I liked that rice dish, but Jim wasn't too fond of rice in any way, shape or form.

46. Church

Chrissy was growing up quickly and was soon celebrating her second birthday in March of 1958. It was decided to have a joint birthday party with Granny as her birthday was just two days earlier than Chrissy on the 27th day of March. In celebration of the dual birthdays, I planned a tea-party with the usual fare, strawberry jello with ice-cream and my homemade decorated birthday cake.

This year the Walker family joined us. Ted and Irene with Debbie and David had returned to Vancouver after Ted had completed his two years overseas duty as a member of the Air Force in France and Germany. They had found a house close to Granny and Grandpa and Auntie How, who were now living at 2182 East 5th Ave. Granny and Grandpa, had sold their little house over the hill a block away from us and moved further the other way on 5th Ave. But they were still just five city blocks from us. Now, all of us were within a few blocks of each other! Ted found work as a car salesman and Irene was clerking in a shoe store, so Granny helped with looking after their kids. Debbie often came to our house to spend time with her cousins. Leslie and Debbie were the same age.

I remember it was around this time that Granny, with her Anglican Church background, was attending St. David's church near Hastings and Nanaimo. Grandpa didn't go regularly with her, but Auntie How got involved in leading a girl's youth program there. Granny asked Jim to drive them to church and pick them up afterwards, as he was the only one in the family with a car. Once Jim became their driver, Auntie How offered to take Leslie to church with them so she could attend the Sunday School. Leslie loved going and it was the beginning of her church life.

Jim and I were not attending church at all anymore as we'd quit going to the downtown Cathedral. It was hard to feel connected to such a large, inner-city church and besides, I was not too keen on the Anglican Church for myself anyway. The structured prayer book still seemed foreign to me and yet I had no other church ties, my Mormon days being far behind me.

The only link I had left with that religion was my friend Laurene and that friendship had dwindled to exchanging birthday and Christmas cards. She had married a local Mormon boy, moved away from Cardston and was now living in Lethbridge where her husband had become a dentist. She was also the mother of two children and would eventually have four in total. Their family lived under the strict and staunch rule of Mormonism. I didn't feel I had much in common with her or the Mormon religion anymore.

Three months drifted by before Jim and I decided to attend a church service at St. David's church, although Granny had encouraged us to join them from the beginning. Eventually, we did! Leslie was really enjoying the Sunday school classes, as she had a great desire to learn. Soon our young Chrissy joined the younger age group in the Sunday school classes, too. So it was decided! We would all go to church and it felt good to me to be together there as a family.

By the following summer, we had even signed up for our very first Sunday school church picnic and it was held at the Peace Arch Park near the U.S. border-crossing. It turned out to be a day of fun for all of us with our girls taking part in the games and races provided for them there. Jim and I had made a few friends in the St. David's congregation on a social level too. Yet, as for me really going to church and enjoying it, that was still a far off reality!

Church had its rituals to follow. For us females, hats and gloves were a necessary part of our attire, and a suit and tie for men. Children were taught to be 'seen and not heard,' something I remember so well. I would whisper quietly to them when they joined us before the final hymn. "Sit quietly now and wait for the conclusion of the service." Looking back, I don't think going to church was much fun for children in those days. Or, as a matter of fact, for any of us! It felt more like a duty than a joy.

47. Sightseeing

Owning a car was still very exciting to us as a family and nearly every Sunday we drove to see some interesting place. We'd cross over Lion's Gate Bridge to explore the Northshore and experience the thrill of walking across the Capilano Suspension Bridge. Other times we'd drive out to Horseshoe Bay and back just to enjoy the scenery. There was always one more place we hadn't seen and captured on camera. We loved our beautiful city and were motivated to uncover all the fascinating and out of the ordinary corners we could possibly find.

The Second Narrows Bridge was being built at that time and we kept track of the different stages as the work on it advanced. We visited the site just about every week just to view their progress. Thinking of that bridge triggers a memory that I treasure to this day. A major accident happened while that huge bridge was being constructed. After many weeks of positioning the steel girders out over the water, the heavy beams, for some reason, broke apart and fell into the waters of Burrard Inlet. The collapse of the bridge was photographed and the picture hit the front page of our newspaper, the Vancouver Sun.

It was the current topic of discussion for days on end, so as a family, we drove to see the accident with our own eyes. It was a sight to behold alright! We were shocked as we sat there in our car viewing the disastrous spill of iron into the water below. Then, all of a sudden, we heard Chrissy's voice from the backseat announce confidently, "Daddy fix!"

There was no question in her young mind that her Daddy could fix anything that was broken. I suppose he had proved that to her many times in her young life. And I would be amiss to forget a special childhood memory like that.

Once the Second Narrows Bridge was repaired and completed we used it often to drive up Grouse Mountain or Mt. Seymour on our Sunday excursions. Our family did not ski, but we enjoyed ascending to the top of those Northshore Mountains by means of the ski-lifts, just so we could marvel at the city spread out below.

We also drove out into the countryside around Langley, where Jim had lived as a youngster before moving to Creston. We often talked about buying some acreage out there. We were thinking ahead. We always thought we'd live in our beloved Vancouver for the rest of our lives. Yet, little did we know what the future would bring.

Granny and Grandpa Rolfe came on our Sunday car trips much of the time, as they enjoyed seeing all the sights of the city they'd chosen to live in. With no seat belt restrictions in those days, we could often squeeze three in the front seat and four people in the back of the car. It always made me happy whenever my mother and Bud came with us, too, but they often made excuses not to. It disappointed me, as having family members around us was important to me. On our travels we appreciated the natural charm of our city and like the tourists, we relished the boundless beauty that extended in every direction as far as our eyes could see.

Before we knew it, it was September of 1958, and Leslie turned six years old and entered grade one at Chief Maquinna, our neighbourhood elementary school. Leslie's friend, Johnny joined her there and would call on her so they could go together. They now had only a short distance to walk and that was a relief for them. And for Lois and me, too!

Chrissy was feeling a little left-behind with Leslie going to school fulltime, but her outgoing personality soon helped her adjust. There were still lots of kids on our street for her to play with and that included Harry Peters down the street, who was her same age and a great pal. And Lois and I were still very close friends so again, there were friendship bonds between our two families.

When Leslie returned home from school, or on a rainy weekend day she'd still offer to be the teacher and play school with her younger sister. I think she felt she had more to pass on to Chrissy now she was actually in school. In fact, I remember she'd try to teach everything she'd learned that day to Chrissy! And it was to Chrissy's advantage too, increasing her ability to listen and absorb at a very young age.

When Leslie was in the first grade, we acquired a cat. Granny had suggested it, saying it would make sure no mice would ever creep into our house. Our new cat was an orange tabby. I wanted to call him Ginger, given his colouring, but Leslie insisted on the name, Puff, from her readers at school. So Puff it was. The girls loved him and he was a good pet for us now that Gypsy was no longer alive. Puff had a unique tail, in that he had absolutely no feeling in it whatsoever. It just hung down lifelessly. Sometimes, we'd see him walking along the top of the back fence and falling off because he didn't have such good balance with that poor tail!

48. Happy Times and Sad Times

In June of 1959, we had a wonderful surprise when the closing ceremonies drew near at Chief Maquinna School. The teachers had been asked to choose a grade one student for the honour of presenting, on stage, a flower bouquet to the wife of the President of the School Board. Leslie was the student they chose! As her parents, we felt both pleased and grateful she had been privileged in this way. And of course, I wanted her to look her prettiest, so I got busy and sewed a new dress for her to wear. Remember, clothes were always important to me.

The dress I made was of a deep rosy-pink sheer, trimmed with black velvet ribbon and we got her new shoes in the latest style of white patent leather with a single strap over the top. Jim even went so far as to sandpaper the bottom of those shoes so she wouldn't slip when crossing the stage with the flowers. We tried to make it happen without a hitch and it did! Leslie rose to the occasion and did it beautifully, and with a smile on her face. We were likely the proudest parents in the entire world that evening.

Leslie's big moment.

When fall arrived that year, we had yet another visit from my Dad and my brother Harold from the United States. Lots had happened since their last trip north to see us. Harold, now in his forties, had married Glenys and we were excited to meet her for the first time. She seemed to fit right into our family and took a real liking to Leslie and Chrissy.

In their time with us, Glenys shared how she loved children, but would never be able to have any of her own due to an operation she'd undergone in her youth. However, not being able to have children had directly resulted in them excepting the role of Den Parents in their Denver Baptist Church Youth Group. She said their rumpus-room was always full of teenagers and that brought them sheer delight and gave them a real sense of family life.

During their visit, we had several get-togethers for the family at our house. Mother came out to join us but Bud purposely stayed away. He told me he had no wish to see his Dad again. I knew he still bore a grudge against his father for not being there in his growing-up years, but I felt differently. Bud believed all the terrible things Mother had chalked up against Dad in the past but I wanted to accept Dad for who he was now. I instinctively knew there were always two sides to every story.

There was always an awkward moment when my Mother and Dad came face to face in the same room. Yet, I think no one noticed except me! I couldn't help thinking how sad it was their marriage hadn't survived, as neither of them had re-married and both had spent over twenty long years alone and most likely lonely. How sad life turns out for some people!

After our family members returned to the United States, there was a period of time when I lost touch with Mother and Bud. They had moved with no forwarding address. In the past, I'd often invited them out to our place for a Sunday dinner, even though they were frequently reluctant to come. I had learned not to give up trying as I wanted them both to be a part of our lives, especially for the sake of our two daughters. In the back of my mind I also worried about whether they were safe and if they ate well enough. They were both such very independent people, not wanting anyone's help. This all troubled me.

Mother finally did call to say they didn't have the car anymore, for reasons that were never explained, and they'd decided to move down town. What did she mean downtown? When I pressed for information, she was hesitant. She finally told me they were in a hotel on Cordova Street, and told me that she didn't have a phone in her room and it was awkward to use the front desk phone. Well, at least they were alright and I felt relieved to know where they were. What had happened to their nice rental suite on nearby Commercial Drive? I thought the worst! They probably got behind in their rent and were asked to vacate. But, that information was never forthcoming, so all I could do was be happy I knew where they were and let the rest go.

Yet as time passed, my curiosity got the best of me and I decided to go and visit Mother on a week day, while Leslie was at school. I took Chrissy with me on the streetcar to Hastings and Cordova and the hotel was not hard to find. It was an awful old dump-of-a-place, situated in the heart of Vancouver's skid-row area. I didn't feel safe on the street even though it was daytime. I couldn't help feeling embarrassed that I had family living in such a place, but I went in with Chrissy by the hand and asked the desk clerk for Mother's room number.

I believe Mother was uncomfortable that the two of us had come, but made room for us to sit on the bed. When I offered her some money to help her find a better place to live, she definitely wasn't interested. She said this hotel was just fine with her and Bud. She said they liked their location close to the stores. To me, it was an awful place to live, as it was quite obvious the hotel housed people who were addicted to drugs or alcohol, or both. I struggled with the whole picture, but what could I do? Mother didn't seem to care, or want me to either.

Returning home I felt very sad and helpless that they had made the choice to live in such a dreadful place. Nonetheless, I had to face the fact, there was nothing I could do about it. But, I couldn't bring myself to go there again although I continued to urge Bud and Mother to come out for Sunday meals and join us in car rides. They were my family and I didn't want to lose touch with them. On the Sundays when they did visit us, they always enjoyed seeing the girls and Bud especially took pleasure in showing them the slight-of-hand tricks he could do. He was an uncle that was a lot of fun to be around, joking with them and making them laugh.

Bud with the girls on a rare snow day.

49. Vacations

In July of 1960, Jim and I and our two girls took another holiday, this time to Saskatchewan to visit Hazel and Eddie, who were new parents. And surprisingly, I was able to talk Mother into coming along with us. I was so surprised that she decided to come, but I think she truly missed seeing Hazel, just as I did. It was a two-day car trip from Vancouver to Lashburn, so we booked into a motel the first night and Jim and I looked after Mother, paying all the expenses.

Hazel and Eddie were such proud parents of their first child, a baby girl just three months old. She was named Arlowa Marie, after Eddie's younger sister Arlowa, and after me, of course! It was such an honour to me and I was especially elated when I learned she would be called by her second name, Marie. I was so happy to have a precious little niece as my very own namesake! And I noticed how radiant Hazel looked too, as a new Mom, appearing much younger than her 36 years of age. She was bubbling over with joy at being a mother at long last and I couldn't have been happier for her.

There wasn't much to do or see in the small town of Lashburn, but we enjoyed being there all the same. On one of the hottest days of our stay, Hazel organized a wonderful wiener-roast down by the river where it was cool in the shade of the tall trees along the riverbank. We took baby Marie in a net-covered basket and my mother appeared to take great pleasure in sitting beside her new little granddaughter and watching over her.

We had a wonderful time and the days slipped by very fast. When the time arrived to leave for home, both Hazel and I hugged and said our goodbyes tearfully, as usual. It was always the same, as we never knew when we'd see each other again. Fortunately though, this initial trip to Lashburn was only the first of many visits we'd make over the years ahead. Nonetheless, for both Hazel and I, saying goodbye put an ache in our hearts. I guess it was a wrenching throw-back to our past life.

The following year of 1961 was crammed full of events for our family of four. As a starter, we had our very first official time spent away from home that wasn't a visit to see family members. It was a big deal to us! We'd made arrangements to go to a cottage in Parksville on Vancouver Island. It was fun right from the beginning, when we took the long ferry ride over to Vancouver Island and felt the fresh ocean breeze on all of our faces. Leslie was nine years old and Chrissy five on this special holiday.

The small town of Parksville was a great place to visit, and so was the neighbouring town of Qualicum Beach. Our little rented cottage in Parksville was located close to the ocean and we were delighted about that. Going to sleep listening to the tide-waters washing up against the shore at night was something Jim and I found irresistible and soothing.

During the long and hot days, all of us enjoyed the gigantic sandy beach that extended out for miles at low-tide and we relaxed in the summer sun. Jim especially needed to have this time away from the tension of the daily grind of his work and the girls found pleasure in the simplest things. They built countless castles in the sand and looked for hidden treasures on the beach or in the nearby forested area. It was one of our best family holidays we ever had.

Us four at Parksville.

50. Piano Lessons and the World's Fair

It was in the autumn of 1961, after Leslie's ninth birthday, that we bought a piano. We wanted her to begin taking piano-lessons. The gift of music was always something I wanted to give our children. Chrissy was also keen to learn but we felt she was too young for lessons at five years of age. The piano we bought was not a new one, but an older, upright model that was second-hand.

A lady in the neighbourhood gave Leslie music lessons to begin with but before long, Auntie How suggested we ask her friend, Elaine Jan, to teach her. Elaine was studying advanced music at the University of B.C. and although she was not a music teacher per se, as a favour to our family, she began teaching Leslie the Toronto Conservatory preparation program. Leslie was a good student, practiced daily and loved learning under Elaine's inspiring tutelage. Elaine Jan would become a special friend to our family.

In that same year of 1961, we enrolled Chrissy in the new Kindergarten Class at Chief Maquinna. We were glad she wouldn't have a long walk to kindergarten like her older sister had. Chrissy's friend, Harry Peters was also in her class of five-year-olds beginning kindergarten that year.

Both Leslie and Johnny were still at Chief Maquinna too, in the fourth grade. I found it hard to believe, although it was true, that I was now the mother of two children registered in the Vancouver school system. I was a thirty years old.

Shortly after school started, my neighbour Lois and I were talking over coffee and discussed whether we should join the Parent Teacher Association at Chief Maquinna. We thought it might possibly be a good way to keep ourselves informed and to support our children's attendance there. The organization seemed like a good place to give of my time and perhaps make new friends. After all, as moms we shared so much in common concerning the education of our young children. I decided I would definitely think about volunteering my time. The PTA was to be the first women's group I ever joined.

It was Christmas 1961 when we received some wonderful news by long-distance telephone from Hazel and Eddie. They were expecting a second child by harvest time of 1962 and indeed, later on in September of that year, a baby boy was born to them. They now had a little brother for his two year-old sister, Marie. They gave their son the name of John Edward, but he's always been called by the nickname of Jack by everyone who has known him. Hazel was so happy to be a mom for the second time and Eddie was overjoyed to have a son. We made a promise we would make another visit to see them the following summer.

Time raced ahead of us and 1962 arrived before we knew it. That year, Jim and I realized we had planned the very same vacation destination as a zillion other people. Where was that? Attending the Seattle World's fair. It was a huge event and on everyone's agenda to attend sometime between April and October. Leslie and her cousin Debbie were thrilled when their Auntie How offered to take them to Seattle with her to explore the fair and what it had to offer. Such excitement! It would be an experience of a lifetime for the two ten year olds.

Seattle had undergone a major makeover for the fair with a unique Space Needle constructed to dazzle everyone with its height and the view of the entire city from its revolving top floor. As well, a new monorail was built and designed expressly to move the crowds of people around more quickly. And there was also a new Pacific Science Centre opened to the public. This was of great interest to Leslie, as she loved science at that early age. Both girls enjoyed their very special adventure with their Auntie How and, even today, have lasting memories of that trip, I'm sure.

Statistics state that ten million people from around the world flooded into Seattle for that fair and Jim and I were among them. Looking back, we realize we made a mistake in not including Chrissy with us in our plans. We thought she was too young at six to gain much from it, but we know now that young children can absorb much that we think is over their heads.

That same year held something in store that delighted Chrissy. She began taking piano lessons with Miss Jan, too, and she was a natural at it! Her creative ability with music by that time had led her to play the piano by ear, just by listening to Leslie practice. So we were not surprised when she advanced very quickly in reading the musical notes and proved to be an apt and capable student of the piano.

Chrissy at six.

51. My Confirmation

As fall turned into winter and we were regularly attending the Anglican Church as a family, I started to think about being confirmed myself. I had a reason! In those days, only those who had gone through the sacrament of confirmation could take the communion, that is, the bread and the wine on Sundays. I felt left out when Jim would go forward to receive communion with the rest of his family. For you see, Jim was baptized and confirmed at an early age and now I realized our two daughters would be able to receive communion when they reached the age of twelve. And I'd still be sitting back alone and unable to participate. Action was needed and so I signed up for the communion training course offered in the evening during that winter.

At the first meeting, I discovered I was in a class filled with the current twelve year olds of the parish. Being over thirty years of age at the time, I felt somewhat out of place, but I was determined to take this step. I was there for every class and, unlike most of the younger kids, I was serious about learning all I could.

I found it interesting when we learned the history of the laying-on-of-hands which was another name for the sacrament of confirmation. The teacher showed us in the Book of Acts in the Bible where the laying-on-of-hands promised to be a spiritual infilling of God's Spirit. This intrigued me, even though I didn't understand what it meant. And, of course, I didn't want to embarrass myself by asking questions. Still, I hoped it would be an experience to help me understand more about the God I'd left behind in Cardston.

On the appointed day of June 16th in 1963, the members of our confirmation class gathered at the Anglican Church where the Bishop of the Diocese would be confirming us. We were all excited and dressed for the occasion, the guys in suits and us females in white dresses. I remember, too, how there was a lot of nervous giggling around me by the twelve year old candidates.

Once the service started, we waited anxiously for the appropriate time to stand and go forward to the Bishop. We had been told he would confirm each one of us individually. When the time finally arrived, we filed up one by one, each kneeling before the Bishop for our personal laying-on-of-hands and prayer.

My own special moment arrived and I felt the Bishop's hands lightly on my head and I leaned closer to hear the brief words he was saying over me. "May this servant daily increase in thy Holy Spirit more and more," he said, "until she comes into Thy everlasting kingdom." That was it! Over and done with! I felt a mixture of relief and then immediate disappointment. I had expected an encounter of some sort with the God of the Universe. Wasn't he able to touch me in some overpowering way? I wondered. Had I expected too much?

I automatically moved slowly back to my place with the other young candidates, my mind contemplating what had just taken place. I told myself it was only natural to have some let-down feelings and I needed to concentrate on the positive side of my Confirmation and try to be thankful. One good thing, I could now go forward at church with Jim and the family and receive the bread and a sip of wine like I had watched them do. Even so, my disappointment about God lay hidden there inside me and all I could do was push it deeper and bury it. I had reached out to God in my Confirmation, but He simply wasn't there for me.

52. Mumu Dresses

Even though I didn't work outside the home, as a Mom, I was busy. Our two girls were constantly growing out of their dresses, so I continued sewing dresses for them and though I'd never had lessons or any instruction, I learned and got better by trial and error.

My mother had given me one of her prized possessions, a portable Singer sewing machine that she had bought on the lay-away plan back in Cardston years before. I recall making many items of clothing and getting more professional at sewing as time passed by. After Mother settled in Vancouver the machine had been shipped out to Mother, along with several beautiful tablecloths and other linen pieces she had decorated by hand in needlepoint and cross-stitch. There was also a Royal Albert six-piece tea set in the Petit Point design. These were things I knew Mother held very dear and they reminded me of her great love of fancy dishes and producing beautiful handwork. As a young woman, before marriage Mother had learned the fine art of embroidery and cross-stitch along with all five of her sisters, just as every young lady of that time did.

When the box of her things arrived, we were still in our no-basement home didn't have space to store them. Mother didn't either and the box ended up in Granny Rolfe's basement. And, unfortunately, their basement was flooded by a sump-pump problem and some of Mother's unique things were water-damaged and thrown away. A number of the pieces from Mother's past, such as the tea set, a few of the linens, and the sewing machine came to me. I've used and valued them ever since. They remind me of the wholesome past my mother came from when she was a young girl surrounded by her nine siblings and influenced by her pioneer mother and father.

I wasn't surprised to discover I had inherited Mother's love of beautiful things. And I felt it helped me in my attempt to create attractive clothes on the sewing machine for the girls and me. Sewing was both fun and frustrating, as most sewers soon find out. And in those years, when our girls were young and we had little money, I always managed to buy some yard goods to be sewn into clothes. And the girls never complained about having homemade dresses.

When Auntie How returned from a vacation in Hawaii with beautiful material for us as gifts, I was delighted. There were lengths of Hawaiian print for each of the girls and a length of print for myself. I sewed dresses for the girls in the 'mumu' style that was a popular style then, a red print for Chrissy, and a brown print for Leslie. I also made a red shift style dress for myself that I really liked, because it turned out to be the best dress I ever did sew for myself and I wore it for years to come.

Those Hawaiian mumus were the first things the girls packed for our second road trip to Saskatchewan, in the summer of 1963. We were eager to see Hazel and Eddie again, as well as their little Marie, and their new young son, Jack. Now he was no longer a baby, but a fair-haired little fellow nearly a year old and walking. Naturally, he was the center of interest, especially around his sister and his two older cousins. All three girls playfully fought over the 'right' to hold him and Jack, naturally reveled in all the attention coming his way.

We enjoyed every moment of being together as family once again. Hazel served us her scrumptious home-made meals, always accompanied by her fantastic homemade white buns that were as light as a feather and our all-time favorite. I must say, they disappeared as if by magic. Our gratifying visit galloped by so swiftly, it was time once again to say goodbye before we knew it. So, again with tears and hugs, we left to make our way home to Vancouver, both Hazel and I hiding the dull ache we felt in our hearts. Would there be another time?

Marie, Leslie, Jack & Chrissy.

53. The P.T.A.

The fall-term of school in 1963 held a surprise for me, when I was asked to let my name stand to be a member of the executive of Chief Maquinna's Parent Teacher Association. Remember, I had previously given it some thought and I was flattered to be asked. Still, I was somewhat apprehensive about taking on the position and of its expectations of me. In spite of that, I did become an executive board member! However, I truly wasn't prepared for the negative outcome that was the result of that decision. We really never know what is ahead of us in life, do we? And it's simply based on the choices we make today.

I became the Program Convenor on the P.T.A. executive board and this called for me to work closely with Mr. Crossen, the school's principal. I enjoyed being in discussions with him as I respected him and found him comfortable to talk with. The president of our executive was my good friend Helen, a nearby neighbour and a great leader and encourager. It was a group of really nice women with only one exception, a lady by the name of Lila. What was wrong with Lila? Of all things, she seemed just too friendly to me! I'll explain what I mean by that!

At first I felt complimented with Lila's flattery and desire to be a very close friend of mine. That is until she started bombarding me with phone calls every day that began to wear me out and infringe on my sense of privacy. With no urging from me, she shared the most personal and intimate details of her married life with me on a daily basis. I was embarrassed hearing how her husband didn't love her anymore and that she suspected him of being unfaithful and having an affair. I wasn't a counsellor! I didn't know how to respond to her and the entire friendship was having a smothering effect on me.

Still, I didn't want to hurt her feelings. I knew she needed help, but when I suggested counselling, she wept on the phone and said she only wanted to confide in me. Couldn't I give her my support? So I continued to be her sounding-board, allowing her to call me relentlessly. The suffocating friendship started putting a lot of pressure on me and I didn't know what to do. I genuinely felt sorry for Lila, but I had a family to care for. Finally I just plain wanted out of the situation! Ah! Easier said than done! I was held captive by her friendship and her persistent daily calls.

Something had to give and it did! One evening, when several of us on the P.T.A. board were leaving the school after our executive meeting, Lila's name came up. She'd not been at the meeting that night and the other women were saying they felt Lila's focus was elsewhere and her time on the executive should end. I felt the shock of those words! I was very aware how important Lila's position on the board was to her. She'd told me it was the only place in her life where she felt needed and found satisfaction. Her sorrowful voice and the voices around me whirled in my head. I felt like a hypocrite wanting to agree with my friends and yet feeling such empathy for Lila. Shouldn't I be defending her?

It was at that precise moment, something snapped inside me and my response was a flood of sudden and unexpected tears. It was so unlike me!

The emotions inside me were like a dam that had collapsed! As those hot tears slid down my face, I felt arms go around me and gentle voices telling me it was going to be all right. I wasn't to worry. My flood of tears continued nonstop and no one expected me to explain why I was crying. I think they knew somehow and understood! Still, I felt so incredibly undone!

The group walked me the short distance to my own doorstep. Once there, Helen leaned close and whispered in my ear, "You should give your doctor a call in the morning." And that's exactly what I did. I suppose it turned out to be a kind of a melt-down. My doctor suggested some pills for what he called anxiety. I think they were valium. I certainly hadn't realized how very vulnerable I was.

After that, I remained on the executive board with my friends, which was now minus Lila, and I did not receive any further phone calls from her. I was told she'd been directed to professional counselling and that news put my mind at rest knowing she was receiving the help she needed. Most of all, I was able to resume my normal life again.

54. Life's Ups and Downs

Our lifecycles ebb and flow, forever moving us forward and teaching us by our experiences to grow and develop. I think it happens so subtly sometimes that we scarcely notice we're becoming more mature with the passing of time. Then again, sometimes we set goals for ourselves with the desire to improve in some areas. This was now the case with me. As a young mother, I wanted to try to develop a better sense of humour. I was tired of taking life so serious. I realized that taking thing seriously was the result of the unsettling circumstances of my early years. Could I learn to worry less and laugh more? I wanted to try! So I made a conscious decision to focus on being more relaxed and find the funny side of situations when possible.

So, without any warning, the very next thing that happened did loosen me up and even caused me to chuckle to myself. A man knocked at our door one morning and handed me a picture, asking if I'd like to purchase it. He was a photographer and the picture was of a little girl in a cowgirl's costume sitting in the saddle of a Shetland pony. When

I looked closer, I recognized the little cowgirl astride the pony as none other than our Chrissy! What a surprise! Seeing her there shocked me at first, but I paid the man the price he asked and the photograph became mine. In studying the photograph more closely, I couldn't help smiling.

Chrissy did look cute perched there in those child-sized chaps and cowgirl hat. However, my cautious nature told me I should ask some serious questions of our carefree little lass when she returned home from school that day. And from her I learned that this nice pony-man had set up his camera near her school the week before

Chrissy, the cowgirl.

and offered to take anyone's picture. He had a line-up of willing little customers in no time at all, including Chrissy. Why not! She wanted to join in the fun and take advantage of an opportunity to sit on a Shetland pony. Of course! It was all that simple, except she'd forgotten to tell me about it!

I did talk to her about being cautious around strangers, just to set my own heart at ease and she listened. Even so, all these many years later I still smile when I look at that photograph. I've had it made into a fridge magnet for both Chrissy and myself to remind us of one of life's precious childhood moments that was meant to put a grin on both our faces.

It's hard to explain, but times in general were quite different growing up in the 1950's and early 1960's. We all lived a much freer life in the uninhibited and stress-free world of those far away days. Young children were not accompanied everywhere by adults as they are today! Their play time was spent in the outdoors with their friends enjoying the fresh air. I must admit though, I often took a stroll down the lane to make sure of my children's whereabouts even then. I had to know they were safe and not following the more adventurous leader-types and putting themselves in danger.

I also chose to peek out our kitchen window when they were playing in our own back yard. We had a very tall Mountain Ash tree close to our back lane which they all loved to play beneath. Was the attraction all those red berries? Probably so! Still, I kept a watchful eye on them in case anyone tried to climb high into the sparse branches at the top of the tree where the limbs wouldn't support a climber. It was definitely too dangerous for young ones to be up there.

By and large, my fears for Leslie and Chrissy were for naught! If, perchance, I did spot a climber it was more than likely their cousin Debbie, who often spent time with our girls. She was a fearless little girl, probably due to the fact she was raised with an older brother, David, six years her senior, urging her on. The two of them did have numerous trips to the hospital's emergency room for stitches over the years. This was just a fact I couldn't help noticing. The four cousins did have lots of fun and many adventures together in their growing up years, all of which turned out safe enough. I was a mother who worried, sometimes unnecessarily.

Leslie with her pennant.

In June of 1964, Leslie graduated from grade six at the Chief Maquinna Elementary School. She had excelled in her exams and won the school's coveted Scholastic's Award. As her Mom and Dad, we felt very proud of her as she was exceptionally smart, but had also studied and worked hard throughout the year. Her name was attached to the pennant that her school gave to the outstanding student for the year.

It was at this time a terrible accident happened to Johnny Peters, who had been Leslie's best friend since they were just three years old. Leslie was not with Johnny that day, but was told about it later on. Apparently Johnny and another boy from school were in the Peter's backyard trimming some bushes with a pair of long-handled pruning shears, when the awful disaster happened. Somehow, and unintentionally, the sharp blade of the shears pierced Johnny's right eye. There was nothing that the team of doctors at the hospital could do to save Johnny's eye. A real catastrophe for a young boy of twelve! We all felt so sorry for Johnny and Leslie was terribly upset as the two of them had been very close since age three.

Unfortunately, Johnny and his future after that accident will always be a mystery to Leslie and all of us. You see, at about that same time, our very own family's future was given a shake-up in ways we could never have dreamed or expected.

55. *Our Move*

Jim and I loved Vancouver and seriously thought we would live out our entire lives there with our family. So it was upsetting to find ourselves in the midst of events that were beyond our control during 1964. We were literally forced to sell our home and move away from our beloved Vancouver. The Teamsters Union had organized the EMCO warehouse employees and they were unable to come to an agreement with the company. This meant EMCO was given no choice but to close down their Vancouver operation, causing many of their workers to be unemployed, and others were asked to accept transfers to offices in other provinces. Jim, in the capacity of salesman, and Doug McKay as purchasing agent, were both offered their same positions. But, it meant moving to Edmonton and working in the branch office of EMCO there. Jim and I decided, after talking it over, it would be wise for him to accept the offer and go to Edmonton. And for us, his family, it meant a very big disruptive move and relocation.

Leslie was almost twelve and Chrissy was eight years of age. They were both sad to be leaving friends they knew in Vancouver behind, but were willing to go. We just hadn't been prepared to be uprooted so suddenly from all that was familiar to us. Yet there was nothing we could do about the big turn of events. We tried to look forward to our move with enthusiasm even though it presented its own set of challenges, like all moves do.

By August of 1964, everything we owned was packed into the mover's truck and our family set forth on a road-trip heading to Edmonton. In the trunk we had our tent in case we needed to use it on the way. The first lap of our journey followed Highway One along the Fraser River in a northerly direction until we reached Kamloops, where we stayed briefly with the Walkers. Irene and Ted and their kids had relocated from

Vancouver to Kamloops and now Ted was working in his Dad's sawmill. Their son David was now in his teens and Debbie was twelve, the same age as Leslie. Our two girls enjoyed spending a brief couple of days with their cousins, despite the extreme summer heat that Kamloops is famous for.

Once we were on the road again, we followed Highway 97 through Falkland and drove through the Okanagan Valley. I vaguely recall being impressed with the beauty of Okanagan Lake and the picturesque mountain scenery as we crossed over the floating bridge as we left Kelowna. Little did we realize at that time Kelowna would play such a big part in our future.

Next, we travelled to Creston which brought back warm-hearted memories to both Jim and I of our teenaged courting years when we first met. From there we drove on to Alberta through Radium and stopped at a campsite north of Calgary. We assembled our four-man tent and spent the night much to the delight of our two girls, who loved sleeping the night in their sleeping bags. The last part of our trip was just a short drive north bringing us to Alberta's capitol, Edmonton, and our newly adopted city.

The excitement of arriving at our destination was shattered when we found out, though we were in Edmonton, none of our furniture was. Everything we owned was still in the mover's truck somewhere on the way! So at this point, we decided to drive to Lashburn for a visit with Hazel and family. It was a warm sunny August day as we headed out of town on Highway 16. We were glad it was still summer holiday time and Chrissy and Leslie were off from school and were looking forward to the visit as part of their holiday.

Suddenly we noticed some white stuff in the air and a few minutes later we found ourselves in the middle of a snowstorm! Was this summertime on the prairies, we wondered? Later we learned it was not unusual in Alberta to see snowflakes fall from the sky even in the summer months of the year. We did drive out of the short-lived snowstorm quickly and crossed into Saskatchewan that day. Hazel, as usual, had the welcome-mat out when we arrived at their place and amazingly it had only been a three hour road-trip from Edmonton! We rejoiced and gave thanks we were now living a lot closer to one another at last.

56. Edmonton

Arriving in Edmonton, we weren't sure of what to expect for winter weather. Then, 'old-man' winter stepped in and showed us what a prairie winter was truly like. We were about to be shocked. I recall waking up one Monday morning and looking out on a bitterly-cold, winter day and thinking, we live here now, so we have to adjust. I bundled the girls up in their newly acquired thick winter clothing to walk the few blocks to their schools. Once bundled up, off they trudged in the snow and frigid air.

Then to my surprise, they returned shortly, nearly half frozen to death. They told me neither of their schools was open. Why weren't they? The radio conveyed the news to us. A city-wide school closure was in effect due to the minus 95 degree wind-chill outside! With coming from Vancouver, we were not used to school closures due to weather. But we learned quickly enough, schools in Edmonton shut down whenever their winter temperatures dipped to their rock-bottom lows. And, that very first winter we lived there, we were introduced to some cold temperatures that broke all-time records.

We had bought a home in Edmonton at 8718-162nd Street in the Meadowlark area. It was a plain, ordinary three-bedroom bungalow on an ordinary street, but the area around us was a lovely one. And soon after our move in, we purchased a new Bell Windsor piano from Woodward's store and used our older-upright model from Vancouver as a trade-in. We wanted our two girls to continue their studies in music and began immediately to look for a piano teacher to tutor them in their Toronto Conservatory classical program. And it wasn't long before we found someone to fit the bill as a tutor.

Our girls attended two different schools in the public school system in Edmonton. Chris entered Elmwood Elementary and Leslie started at the new junior high school, called Hillcrest. This school was the latest, state of the art school, designed with a circular shaped floor plan and was windowless. It had one main hallway that went around the building in a circle with classrooms on both sides and a large gymnasium in the middle. You could quite literally 'walk around' at recess! Leslie was thrilled to be attending such an unusual and innovative school for her first year of junior high.

Being transferred by EMCO along with the MacKay family automatically drew our two families together from the very beginning. Doug and his wife Marian had an older teenaged son, Craig and a daughter Sandy, who was two years older than Leslie. They bought a house in the same vicinity, fairly close to us and Sandy was in Leslie's grade seven class at Hillcrest, as she had previously failed a couple of grades in school.

Once we settled into our new surroundings, Doug and Marian suggested that we plan to play the card game of bridge with them every Friday night. So this became a habit throughout the time we all lived in Edmonton. I have always loved cards, but I was a real beginner at the game of bridge. Being Doug's partner weekly did help me begin to get the hang of it as he was an astute player and always wanted us to be the winning team.

In conversations around the card table, the MacKay's repeatedly expressed their discontentment in having to leave their home at the coast and move to Edmonton. They were determined not to like anything about living in their new city. Jim and I missed Vancouver like they did, but we had decided to make the best of our new location by getting involved in the community. And so we did!

57. Brownies

As a family, we joined Edmonton's St. Timothy's Anglican Church and found we were just in time to enroll Leslie for the confirmation classes. We were happy about that. I also wanted to get involved in our new community, so in October, when it was announced there was a Mom's Tea at the Elmwood School and they needed volunteers, I offered my help. After all, our Chris was a pupil there. My invitation to be part of the volunteers was from the principal himself, Mr. Seale. I liked this school immediately! Then by serving at the tea, I gained new friends and one was Penny Linden's Mom. Penny was Chris's newest best friend at Elmwood, and her mother was the Brown Owl leader of the local Brownie pack. Eight year old Penny was a member of her Mom's pack and loved Brownies so much she convinced Chris to become one too.

The Brownie organization offered so many positives how could I not agree? I had read up on why the Brownie organization existed. And I was delighted to discover their mandate was to help young girls develop their own sense of identity, to make friends and acquire simple skills and cultivate their own special talents. And this was only a short list of the things the Brownie's offered. Older girls, twelve years and up, were also given a similar program, called Girl Guides.

Both Leslie and Chris were enthusiastic when I told them what I'd learned and they wanted to join up, receiving their appropriate uniforms as a Brownie and a Girl Guide. They went once a week to their pack meetings and made new like-minded friends and worked hard towards getting the many badges offered. I think they must recall happy memories from back then.

Then, to my total amazement, I became one of the Brownie leaders myself! One of the Brownie leaders moved away and I was asked to take her place. How could I say no when I was so 'sold' on the benefits of the movement? I became the Pack's Tawny Owl, teaching the young girls the moral values and principles I so admired and wanted for my own two daughters.

Meanwhile, life was moving forward with momentum in other areas of

In uniform all three.

our family. Jim had taken up the sport of curling with some of his friends at work and had adjusted nicely to his new sales territory in the city of Edmonton. Our social calendar was a busy one. The rage at that time was the cocktail party. And I soon learned they were nothing more than an evening party of endless drinking and smoking. I quickly became a master at 'nursing' one drink throughout an entire evening and I never needed alcohol to enjoy myself up to this point in my life. Why start now?

When it came to smoking I felt forced to 'join the crowd', otherwise the smoke-laden atmosphere was just too hard to bear. I kept my Menthol cigarettes in the freezer so they'd be fresh when I brought them out a few at a time for social gatherings or for our on-going Friday night bridge games. The MacKay's and Jim all smoked, as it was common to drink and smoke in the 1960's. We hadn't yet learned they were detrimental to our health. And if you recall, I discovered at an early age, smoking was widely modelled for us by the Hollywood movie stars and in the many magazines' full-coloured ads. No wonder most of us tried the 'habit' and many were innocently addicted.

That second Edmonton winter, I bravely took a Canadian Red Cross beginner's swimming class at nearby Jasper Place Sports Centre. I passed too, although that didn't mean I actually learned how to swim! The instructor was a young fellow who finally gave up on a few of us older 'fraidy-cats' and passed us anyway. It was my first attempt to learn to swim as an adult, but would not be my last!

Edmonton's winter ice and snow was also put to good use. The accumulated snow in our backyard was flooded with the garden hose and converted into a near-perfect skating rink with temperatures always below zero to keep it in its frozen state. We all acquired skates and although I was far from an accomplished skater, Leslie or sometimes Chris would patiently help me maneuver around our small rink. In the long run, our whole family benefited from the fresh air and exercise involved in skating. It was fun!

58. Our Family Expands Again

Once the ice and snow of the long prairie winters melted, most people looked forward to a holiday away. Jim and I knew in advance we'd be out of town on a particular weekend in the month of July and had arranged to leave our girls with a neighbourhood girl keeping a watchful eye. Leslie was now almost thirteen years of age and Chris nine, and both had looked forward to being home and mostly taking care of themselves for the first time. They also knew they could call the MacKay household nearby, in case of any emergency.

It was during our absence that an unexpected event happened! We had an unforeseen visitor arrive! Who? Well none other than David Walker, our nephew from Kamloops. He landed, unannounced, on our door step while we were away from home and the girls were alone. He had driven his Volkswagen from his hometown and brought all his belongings with him. He told Leslie and Chris he had come to live with us permanently and promptly moved into our unfinished basement bedroom.

When Jim and I arrived back home, we tried to talk him into returning to his Dad and Mother in Kamloops, but David's mind was made up. He had run away from home, he said, and was not going back. He was eighteen years old!

At thirty-five years of age, I wasn't ready to have a teenaged boy in the house, but what could I do? In the end, he became another member of the family. David started to look for a job and unbeknownst to us, went to EMCO and applied there. And surprisingly enough, they hired him! In his interview, he didn't tell them he was related to Jim and, of course his name being Walker, they were unaware he was Jim's nephew. However, the truth came out the first time David let his guard down and "Uncle Jim" came out of his mouth at work. EMCO had a policy about not hiring family members, but Jim as a salesman was out and about in his territory most days and David worked in the warehouse. So, the two of them never did actually work together.

Meanwhile, both our girls were settled into their busy routine of homework, piano practicing and lessons, as well as their involvement in Girl Guides and Brownies. Leslie was also attending confirmation classes at St Timothy's Church. And, by the springtime of the next year, the planned ceremony took place and Granny, Grandpa and Auntie How came from Vancouver to be part of the family celebration. The Confirmation Sunday turned out to be a beautiful, cloudless sunny day with all the remaining snow melting on the streets and lawns. Leslie wore a white-embossed cotton dress I'd fashioned for her on my reliable little Singer sewing machine and she beamed with happiness that day. She was twelve years old.

Leslie (on the right) at Confirmation.

At that time in my life, I was immersed in instructing the Girl Guides group and had also joined Penny Linden's Mom as a member of a weekly bridge club. One of our bridge players was the wife of a local radio talk show personality, which, of course, rated as a VIP to me. When the bridge game met at my house, which was once a month, I literally took the house apart and put it back together, cleaning every nook and cranny. Everything had to look perfect, including whatever extravagant looking dessert I could dream up and create in my own kitchen. It would never do to serve anything as mundane as store bought! Not on your life! The hoops I put myself through in those days and I wasn't even fond of playing bridge!

Then, something of prime importance to our future happened: EMCO's head office in Toronto asked Jim to take a Company Management course. He flew to Toronto for it and later on received a certificate showing his successful completion of the program. We were not told what it meant regarding Jim's future, but we hoped it was preparing him for an advancement of some kind. We'd find out, no doubt, and in the meantime life was running smoothly once more within our expanded family.

And it was not long before EMCO announced Jim's big promotion, which meant, as a family we would be moving to Calgary, where Jim would take over as manager. He would not only be managing the Calgary operation, but also the smaller Lethbridge branch, as well. It was a surprise to us and we were excited! The effective date was to be May of 1967. For us it meant buying a new home in Calgary and a change of schools for the girls, but we were all happy about the change.

Naturally, the MacKay family members were disappointed that we would be moving but EMCO offered Doug a promotion to assistant manager of the Edmonton branch. Nonetheless, it didn't work out for them and we heard later on that Doug had quit EMCO and they had moved back to Vancouver.

I felt our time in Edmonton had a very positive effect on our family life. Perhaps it was the long winters or the depth of the sparkling snow drifts, but we drew closer to one another as a family. We had been a happy family all along, but those three years knit us together in a way that seemed to bond us as a family.

59. Calgary

So it was in June of 1967 that we arrived in Calgary, but minus our daughter Leslie. That year was the Canadian Centennial year, which was celebrated across Canada and Leslie's junior high class had the privilege of traveling by train to Montreal to join in the festivities. They were well taken care of and billeted onsite at the Expo grounds. Upon her return she shared how much she enjoyed the many exhibits and meeting other people from across the country. They were taken on a day tour of Quebec City where they saw the old cobblestone streets and grand old buildings. It was such an exciting trip for her.

And meantime in Calgary, we had settled in and from the beginning we found Calgary to be a friendly, welcoming city. We felt right at home, especially when we moved into the wonderful home we had purchased in the south west part of Calgary at 2815 - 63rd Avenue. It was located in a beautiful area called Lakeview. The custom-built white-sided bungalow had many unique features I instantly appreciated. There were three bedrooms on the main, an eat-in kitchen with built-in wall oven and a finished family room with a wet bar. The downstairs was accessed by an open stairwell surrounded by railings with planters. I loved the house immediately.

It was also handy to Chris's elementary school, Jennie Elliott, and near a small shopping Centre at the end of the street. Leslie had to be bused to Lord Beaverbrook High School for her grade ten classes, as the new Central Memorial High School was being built. She would eventually complete her high school there. We also learned very quickly that we had an Anglican Church called St. Lawrence within walking distance and we started attending there as a family.

For the first time in my life, I felt inspired to decorate our new house and make it look even more beautiful. After all, Jim was now the manager of a business and we could easily afford the cost. Jim agreed. I took pleasure in having the living room painted a pale green, ordering the custom-made sheers for the windows and buying all new living room furniture. It was by far the nicest house we'd owned yet and we knew we were going to enjoy living there.

Yet, little did we understand that our family was going to experience tremendous changes, bigger than we'd ever faced and they would all happen during the ensuing six years we lived in our newly adopted city of Calgary.

60. Dad Arrives and Art Class

The first change came about early on when I received a phone call from Hazel in Lashburn. She asked me if Tony, our Dad could come and live with us in Calgary. Earlier in the year she had invited Dad to move from Idaho to Lashburn and to make his home permanently with her family. She now admitted to me that plan was not working out. The reason why? Eddie had developed a drinking problem and with their two young children in the house, it was becoming too much for Hazel to care for Dad as well. Of course, I said yes to her request and suggested they travel to Calgary for a visit at Christmastime and bring Dad with them.

Dad was seventy-five years old by this time and had very bad rheumatoid arthritis in the joints of his hands and feet. He was unable to manage stairs. Therefore, Chris's bedroom on the main floor became his and Jim built a new bedroom in the basement for Chris. She was just eleven years old and it was hard for her to give up her room, but she did it anyway. It made us so proud of her for doing it.

Grandpa and Chris soon became good pals and even shared a mutual love of playing the game of cribbage. She'd often come home from school on her lunch break to challenge him to a card game. I felt both of our girls benefited from an ongoing relationship with their Grandpa Posing. He loved to tell stories of his young days and how different the world had been back then. As for me, however, having three generations together under one roof was somewhat trying at times. But I did try my best to keep life as peaceful as I could.

I enjoyed my Dad's company too, as he was a great communicator. His mind was sharp and he was in good health except for the rheumatoid arthritis. He had a robust appetite and loved desserts of any kind. Pie was his bigtime favourite and he'd say, "If we're not having dessert just give me a spoonful of sugar to satisfy my sweet tooth."

I don't recall ever having to pass him the sugar bowl at the end of a meal. I always provided some form of dessert that pleased his 'sweet tooth.' Dad taught me how to make Posing Stew, the secret ingredient being the addition of a rutabaga, which changes the flavor dramatically. The two of us got along very well and Dad often shared with me the many stories of his younger life. I learned all about my Dad and Mother in their early married years, when they were in love and also about my three older siblings growing up. Mother had never shared many memories with us kids, especially good memories. Therefore, the stories my Dad told were all interesting and I could see he'd been a storyteller from birth, a gift I believe he passed along to me.

The way I coped with any stress at that time, was to explore the channels of interest I felt drawn to and had never acted upon. After all, our dreams are meant to be pursued, aren't they? I signed up to be a weekly volunteer at the Children's Hospital and continued to visit there throughout the six years we lived in Calgary. There were so many youngsters in those wards with devastating injuries. I recall one little girl of six, who was burned dreadfully when her nightgown caught on fire. How heart wrenching that was!

I took golf lessons during my first summer in Calgary, too. My efforts though, were never very successful. The golf course was teeming with mosquitos that year, which didn't help me concentrate on the game. Not when my bared flesh was constantly under attack by those pesky stingers! However, because of my interest in golfing I made three new friends who, like me, didn't take the game of golf all that seriously. The four of us enjoyed each other's company and looked on the game of golf as a form of exercise.

Next on my agenda of things to do, was to take art lessons. I had felt drawn to the world of art all my life and so I talked my three golfing pals into coming along with me. However, I never thought it would turn out a total disaster in the end, like it did. But then, that's a story in itself.

We signed up for the Beginner's Art Class course which was offered through the School Board night-school program. We arrived for the first class not knowing what to expect. When the instructor introduced himself at the front of the class, we did feel a little suspicious. He was young enough to be one of our sons and, of all things, wore a kaftan! In spite of this, the four of us settled in and set out our paint supplies and canvas as instructed.

About that time, an attractive lady entered the room and walked to the front. And there she disrobed! My friends and I were stunned! She didn't leave a stitch of clothing on! Our instructor didn't bat-an-eye, just calmly informed us we were to spend the next hour capturing the distinct colour of real skin. Believe me, none of us accomplished that task!

The following week, the four of us very hesitantly showed up again and things went from bad to worse. Standing at the front of the class was our model, a very handsome fellow even younger than our instructor. We were told we'd be working on getting the parts of the body in correct proportions that night. It was then that the handsome guy casually cast his clothes aside and stood facing us, stark naked! Good grief, I said to myself, the parts of this model, in my shrewd estimation, were certainly out of proportion! It was disturbing to say the least!

Just then, one of my friends sitting behind me whimpered in a feeble voice, "I want to go home, now!" And that's what the four of us did, never to return to the evening art class again.

61. Driving Lessons

It hadn't taken us long as a family to put roots down and begin to love Calgary, calling it home. The girls were doing great in their respective schools and taking piano lessons. My Dad had settled in with us and insisted he wanted to pay me room and board. It was at this point, that the next big change came about. My Dad, because of health problems, wasn't able to use the public bus system and so he asked if I would get a car and learn to drive. He would need to be driven to his numerous doctor appointments, he said, due to his rheumatoid arthritis. And he would provide me with the money to buy a car by paying me for his room and board in advance. The amount he estimated as a fair price for rent was thirty dollars a month. So that was settled between us. The whole idea of driving pleased me as I wanted to learn how and have my own car. So, I courageously set out to take driving lessons.

Having sat in the passenger seat all my life, I was unaware of road signs, speed zones and other driving rules. This didn't help in preparing me to climb behind the wheel of a car. I was definitely starting from scratch in my mid-thirties. And although I was no spring chicken, I still possessed a great determination to succeed in whatever I undertook. And it's a good thing too!

The Alberta AMA in those days did not take a person out by themselves to learn to drive. Rather, each instructor had two people attempting to learn in the car at the same time. This was unfortunate! You see, I was teamed with a much older lady, who from the start seemed a bit eccentric to me. We each took turns driving while the other one became a passenger in the backseat of the car.

I experienced multiple nightmares in that backseat, believe me! At times we sped through red lights, zipped well over the speed limit and went careening through playgrounds. The teacher was trying to give her instructions, but often ending up shouting precautions. Only the fact that he had a brake pedal on the floor on his side of the car saved my sanity. However, it was still a stressful way to learn to drive! But despite it all, I finally gained confidence and took the exam and passed. What a relief! I'm not sure if the bizarre lady got her license or not. I didn't ask. I just hoped I'd never meet her on the road.

Next I went looking for an older car and found one that wasn't too ancient and was in good running order. It turned out it was a push-button Plymouth Valiant which was a bit unusual. But, I soon became used to starting the car by pushing a button and another to change gears.

My Dad's first request for transportation was to drive him to the Hudson's Bay store in order to be fitted for a brown suit. When I asked him why he wanted a suit, his reply was short and to the point. He wanted the brown suit to be buried in! "I want to be ready," he firmly told me.

That became quite a standing joke in the family as time went by, for my Dad wore that brown suit to a great many celebrations, a wedding, a confirmation, a baptism, and other events in the upcoming years. Still, just having it hanging in the clothes-closet gave him peace of mind.

62. The Stampede

The Stampede-bug bit us very hard, you might say, that first summer in Calgary and we attended the wild-west show a number of times. One weekend, two family visitors arrived that were determined to enjoy all the stampede events that they could. Floyd, who was single again after Gigi and he had parted ways, was thrilled to fulfill his dream of coming to Calgary's world-class rodeo. Our other guest that same weekend was Auntie How who, being a lover of horses herself, also came to town. They made quite a pair, walking arm in arm as they toured around the Stampede Grounds with us. The four of us had a great time taking in all the sights.

Floyd suggested getting ring-side seats for the rodeo, so we did. Sitting there in the in-field seats, where we did that July day, would cost thousands of dollars today, so I`m told. And even back then, they were hard to come by as it was where all the contestants sat. However, Floyd stepped right up to the ticket booth and asked for the seats and they were sold to us. He always did look the part of a cowboy with his Stetson and boots and perhaps it paid off that day. We were surrounded by cowboys waiting to take part and we could almost reach out and touch the horses. It was all so exciting! Auntie How was 'tickled pink' to be sitting so close to the action! Floyd said we would experience all the sights and sounds sitting out there and indeed we did!

As the ferocious bucking bronco horses were let out of their chutes with a cowboy astride, the air was filled with the horse's fierce snorts and farts as he put his tremendous energy into every buck. "See I told you," Floyd said, "We won't miss a thing out here!"

We laughed, but it truly was exhilarating to be so totally involved in what was and still is called, 'The Greatest Show on Earth.' Naturally Floyd was comfortable in the rodeo setting, as he had loved and respected horses all his life, even taming a few wild ones in his younger days.

That boyish grin of excitement never left his face during the whole show. It was so great he'd finally experienced his dream.

As it turned out, we almost had more excitement than we'd bargained for that day. A young boy had left his parents who were sitting above us and climbed down to sit in the front row, which was right below us. During the bucking horse event, Floyd pointed out how very slick the in-field was from the hard rain the day before. And sure enough, almost at that very moment, a dangerous, alarming accident began to unfold before our eyes! A wild, bucking bronco, having bucked-off his rider, lost his balance in the slippery mud and flipped over on his side and came sliding with great speed towards the very row of bleachers where we sat.

Floyd, my quick thinking brother, reached down in front of us and in one mighty scoop of his hand, lifted that little boy up and out of danger, depositing him in the row up behind us. And then there was an enormous explosion of sound as the massive pile of horse-flesh came smashing into our wooden grandstand benches. It sounded like a thunderous locomotive had crashed through and the flimsy wooden benches at our feet, splintered into pieces, flying in every direction. It was just like a scene out of a Wild West movie!

Auntie How, Jim and I scrunched low and hung on to our seats when the horse landed with all four legs kicking, right where the boy had been sitting moments before. Floyd's quick rescue of that youngster may have saved his life or, at the very least, prevented some grave injures. Floyd took it all in his stride though and calmly said he'd learnt a few things about horses, having been around them most all of his life. And, what had he learned? "Horses can be mighty dangerous," he said. No truer words were ever spoken! We'd just witnessed that reality!

63. Life Goes On

Having reached the management level with the company gave Jim some perks! Yearly, EMCO held a Western Canada Manager's Convention either at the elegant Banff Springs Hotel or in the likewise posh, Jasper Park Lodge. I enjoyed attending those yearly conferences with Jim, where he could meet the other manager's and I could get to spend time with their wives. I soon discovered though, it was also a time of excessive drinking. Nonetheless, as I had learned from experience, I didn't have to enter in. I knew it was always my choice to drink or not.

The conferences were fun otherwise, and I liked preparing to go and finding new outfits to wear while there, as I'm sure the other manager's wives did. When it came to purchasing new clothes I could afford the best, but I tried to buy my fashions on sale. It was a part of the inherent thriftiness which I still possess today. For me it's a game, the more money I save, the more I win. I'm a very scrupulous shopper and if there is a bargain to be found, I'm not one to miss it.

Our roots as a family were planted deep in Calgary by 1968 and we felt like we'd lived there all our lives. We were involved in the Anglican Church of St. Lawrence and had friends among the people there. The priest was Peter McCalman, who was about my age and a friendly, down-to-earth man who wore his clergy collared shirt casually with his blue-jeans. He and his wife had a teenaged family, so we related well in that category, too.

One afternoon when I was downstairs in our house doing the laundry and my Dad was napping, I heard some music coming from the stereo in our front room. Both of the girls were at school so I came upstairs to investigate. I found our priest playing a vinyl-record he'd brought with him. It seems he'd arrived on his bike and got no answer to his knock, so he just came in. That's right, we didn't lock our doors back then!

Peter was a very unceremonious, relaxed kind of a guy. We liked him a lot! And our friendly Priest was also a bargain-hunter like me. At church one Sunday morning, he announced he had a box of the new non-traditional Bibles called *Good News for Modern Man*. And Peter said he would sell them to us at the rock-bottom price of two dollars each. Everyone clambered to buy one. We got two, so I could give one to my Dad. It was the first Bible any of us had ever owned.

My Dad started to read his Bible every day in his bedroom before he took his nap. An hour later he would emerge from his room and want to discuss what he'd read. I would patiently try to help him. Of course, the Bible was all a mystery to me, but I tried my best, using my common sense, which I thought I possessed in abundance. Talk about the blind leading the blind!

It was during the spring of 1968 that Chris took Confirmation classes given by Peter, our Priest. And when the big day of her Confirmation Ceremony arrived, it was a very special occasion, not only for Chris, but all of us. Granny and Grandpa Rolfe were happy to come from Vancouver for the event, as well as Auntie How, who after all was Chris's Godmother.

Chris by the church after her Confirmation.

For Chris's special day, I'd sewn a white dress for her to wear, of lovely lace-embossed cotton. She had selected the sewing-pattern herself and it made her look so grown-up in it. Always tall for her age, Chris stood-out among the candidates in the way she carried herself. Earlier that year, she'd attended a modelling-school course, which had given her a great measure of self-assurance. She was poised and had a certain confidence about herself that was very obvious to us all! We were very proud of our youngest daughter that day as she was confirmed in her faith. No two ways about it, she looked beautiful with a captivating smile on her face.

64. The Accident

Basically, we were enjoying our lives in Calgary when one of life's many difficulties happened. An accident came our way. It happened in the summer of 1968 when Leslie was fifteen and had just completed grade ten. She was a passenger in the front seat of a car that was involved in a horrific accident. The result was that her head went through the car's windshield. Back then, cars not only didn't have seatbelts, their windshields were made-up of only a single sheet of glass, unlike today's cars that have laminated safety glass. So when the impact to the car happened, the windshield did not shatter, but broke into large jagged pieces and Leslie was cut from one side of her face to the other, just below her eyebrows. Sounds terrible? Yes it was!

When Jim and I were called to the hospital that night, they told us she had a cut on her forehead. What an understatement! Fortunately for Leslie, a plastic surgeon was available in the Emergency Ward and he did a fantastic job of suturing her face with many, tiny little stitches. Sixty-eight of them! When Jim and I were finally let in to see her, the sight of her face hit me very hard. I felt dizzy and I thought I might pass out! I didn't, but still I couldn't help thinking that this trip to the hospital made up for all those childhood stitch-free years she'd enjoyed as my little girl.

The hospital released Leslie to us once the bleeding stopped. Her face had been numbed and she was fine other than the jagged scar running across her face. We took her home with a huge bandage wrapped around her head. I was worried sick, as any Mother would be, and I cried myself to sleep that night. My little girl was hurt and it wasn't something small that I could kiss and make better.

The next morning, very early, as I lay staring at the ceiling, an idea formed in my mind. After breakfast I drove to St Lawrence and found it unlocked as all churches were in those days. It felt strange to me, being in church without the people in the pews, but I walked to the front and knelt at the altar. There, I bargained with God. I told him if he would heal Leslie so she wasn't disfigured, I would permit him to do whatever he wanted to do in my life. I didn't know exactly what I was articulating, as I'd never prayed a prayer like that before. When I stood to my feet again, I felt somehow God had heard my prayer and would answer. So, immediately I felt better and not so worried anymore.

Did the prayer work? All I know is that afterwards an astonishing change started to happen in Leslie. Grade ten had been a difficult year for her with the move from Edmonton and she had begun 'partying' with the new friends she was making. Her grades at school had plummeted with her lack of attention to her work. She had always been an honour student before this and now, amazingly it seemed, she was once again restored to her former self.

Following the accident, Leslie really seemed to have a new outlook on life and appeared to grow up almost overnight. I recall one of her girlfriends from school came to visit and gasped at the sight of Leslie's wound, exclaiming, "If that happened to me, I'd kill myself."

Later, when her friend had gone, Leslie said to me, "I can't believe how immature some of my friends are." As if by some sort of miracle she was seeing through new eyes.

And to this day, I believe there was another person involved in the phenomenal turn-of-events Leslie experienced! That person was a guy by the name of Mike, who appeared out of the blue to visit her shortly after her accident. He was a former chum of her cousin, Debbie's, who she'd met on a visit to Kamloops. He was a big husky young guy, with a very noticeably kind and winning way about him. He spent hours talking in private with Leslie. And later, she told me how his 'being there' for her, had helped her so much. What had he said? It wasn't for me to know. But as quick as he'd come, he was gone, and we never saw him again. Mulling it over later, I came to the conclusion he surely must have been an angel sent by God!

65. Ceremonies and Friends

As chance would have it, Leslie met Stan Phelps the next spring after her accident. She was in her new high school now, called Central Memorial and was in her grade eleven year. She had met Stan through a girlfriend of hers and he lived on the north side of Calgary. At first, Jim and I didn't approve of Stan as a boyfriend as he was three years older than her, which seemed like a real big age difference. And he had already finished high school and was working, with plans of going to university. At the time they met, he had had a falling-out with his Dad and was living in his antiquated car.

This didn't sit well with me and, though I'm somewhat ashamed to admit it now, I didn't always make Stan feel unwelcome in the beginning of their relationship. I had always imagined Leslie would eventually find a boyfriend that was more like her own father. Doesn't every Mother? Even so, my actions did not deter Stan and I finally gave up. Love conquers all, so they say, and it proved to be true in their case. And incidentally, it wasn't long before things got resolved between Stan and his Dad, and Stan was restored back into the family home again.

With time scurrying by, as it seems to do so often, Leslie's high school days at Central Memorial were fast coming to an end and the year of 1970 appeared on our calendars. And then came the big day of Leslie's graduation from grade twelve. Graduation day filled our entire family with a rush of excitement.

Stan was now Leslie's steady boyfriend and a frequent visitor at our house. On this day, he arrived at our door, looking ever so nice as Leslie's escort, dressed in a nice suit with a white shirt and tie. And he brought a beautiful pink corsage for Leslie that looked perfect on the shoulder of her soft pink sheer graduation formal. As her parents, we had to admit they made a good looking couple and it was quite obvious they were in love.

Central Memorial had been newly built when Leslie and her peers started attending there for grade eleven, so Leslie's class was the first to graduate from the new school. This caused a major celebration, as these Grads were making a mark in history that day. Our first-born had reached a milestone in her life by completing twelve years of education and now wanted to study at university. It was an important day! Leslie's name along with her classmates will forever hang in Central Memorial's hallway, commemorating the school's very first graduating class.

The next step in Leslie's journey of education was to seek a scholarship. During her final year of high school, Leslie's marks had been at the top of the class and we discovered Rolex Canada offered a scholarship that was open to the families of Emco employees. Leslie's scholastic marks were forwarded to Rolex and she was declared the Scholarship winner! It paid for her tuition and books for her entire four year program at the University of Calgary. Jim and I were so very happy and proud of our daughter's accomplishments. And, I might add, she excelled from the start in her chosen field of Microbiology at the University of Calgary.

Are you wondering if Chris had turbulent teenaged years? Thinking back, it seemed she was a child of exemplary conduct most of the time, perhaps becoming wise in 'what not to do' after watching her older sister. It was a cinch raising her! With her happy disposition, she sailed through high school surrounded by a great many friends, because if you recall, Chris had been social even from a young age. Her Dad and I never had to worry about the friends she would choose, either. Chris, to our way of thinking, always made wise choices.

Chris's best friend and 'bosom buddy' in Calgary, was a girl by the name of Kirsti, who lived only one house away from us. From the start, they spent most of their time 'hanging out' at Kirsti's house and no wonder, her mom worked, which gave them the freedom of an empty house most of the time. I admit I really never got to know Kirsti's mother, Jo, very well, as she was not a stay-at-home mom like me. She held the position of a professor at the University of Calgary and she and her husband lived very busy lives. But I certainly did hear a lot about Jo in those years through Chris, who loved her dearly.

There was also another friend of Chris's named Robyn, who lived close by us in our Lakeview neighbourhood. I recall how the three of them, Chris, Kirsti and Robyn, formed a happy trio of friendship, spending much of their time together and having heaps of fun.

The year Chris celebrated her 16th birthday and got her driver's license was certainly an 'outstanding' year for her. That year held a surprise for her as well, one none of us had anticipated. Our dear Auntie How asked us if we would let Chris accompany her on a six week holiday to Europe. What an opportunity for Chris! Naturally, we said yes to Auntie How's plan. However, we did find it somewhat difficult to spare the amount of cash needed for her fare to fly over there. Yet, it was a chance of a lifetime for Chris and we wanted to make it possible for her to be able to go. The memories of a trip like that, would last for a lifetime.

Another good thing came out of Chris's vacation time away for six weeks. A year earlier, we'd had a concern about Chris developing an on-going friendship with Simon, a boy in her class at school, who lived right across the street from us. It was very well-known, he was a marijuana smoker, but we trusted Chris to say no to drugs even though her friends may not. What else could we do? Upon her return from Europe, Chris ended their relationship which made us, as her parents, very happy.

After that Chris was kept busy with a lot of other things. She had gone through Guides, just as her sister had and held a regular babysitting job right on our street three nights a week. And her music, not only piano, but now the flute, filled up her extra time. She excelled at playing the flute and was in the high school band, a marching band, as well as an orchestra that performed for stage productions. She loved music and performing.

Meantime, Jim was having some health problems. Even though he enjoyed his role of manager, it was stressful to the point where it caused bouts of indigestion and other stomach problems for him. There was a lot of tension involved in managing the large staff in both Calgary and the Lethbridge branch. Definitely it was taking a toll on him physically and his doctor suggested he quit smoking.

I saw in the Readers Digest magazine, an article about quitting the cigarette habit that was easy and unique. I gave it to Jim to read and as instructed, he set aside a date far ahead on the calendar, when his smoking would come to an end. Then, little by little he began getting used to what it would feel like not to smoke. It was a process of believing you could do it when that day in the future finally arrived.

I suppose it was mind-over-matter, but it worked! The appointed day arrived and Jim was ready and prepared to become a non-smoker. And at this point, it was important for him to tell everyone around him, he no longer smoked, but had quit. That was an important step and he did it! Once all his work-buddies and friends knew he'd quit they no longer offered any temptations his way.

In two weeks he had mastered the cravings and could honestly say he was free of the addiction. In support, I also joined him, but for me it was easy to quit, as I had always been just an occasional participant. You may recall how I used the freezer to store my cigarettes?

66. Travels and a Wedding

In 1970, Jim ordered the most luxurious car we'd ever had for his company car, a Mercury Marquis. I couldn't help running out to admire the shiny new vehicle in the driveway on that first day he drove it home. I called for my Dad to come and see but he said he could view it well enough from the large picture-window in our front room.

Later I asked my Dad if he liked the car and he said it was a good thing that it was a big one, it would protect Jim when he had an accident. I agreed that the car was big, but felt my Dad's point of view was somewhat negative. I assured him we weren't expecting Jim to be involved in an accident. However, Dad insisted an accident was overdue simply by the fact that Jim drove on the busy roads every day. I pooh-poohed those words and dismissed them, thinking my Dad was developing a pessimistic attitude in his old age.

However, what Dad predicted did come to pass within two weeks. The accident happened while Jim was stopped at a red light on his way home from work. When the light turned green and Jim pulled out, a car that was unable to stop ran the red light, swerved and smashed into Jim's Marquis. Not once, but twice! It hit the right front fender, caving it in, and bounced off and back again to hit the right rear fender. Jim wasn't hurt, but his car was badly damaged front and back. And yet, it was still in running order.

After spending time with the at-fault driver and the police, Jim decided to drive the car home, having arranged to get the repairs done the next day. When my Dad got up the next morning and saw the car out the window, he was not surprised at all. He just had one question, "Were there two cars that hit Jim?" he asked, "One in the front and one in the back?" From Dad's point of view it surely looked that way, with the two fenders both bashed in.

By the time another year rolled around, Jim and I began to ponder the thought of where we might want to settle in our retirement years. Jim was partial to Creston and a move back there, but I was not. I was thankful I'd met Jim there, but my memories of Creston weren't all positive ones. Besides, I was sure by now the people we'd known in Creston during our courtship days would have moved away, just as we had. It wouldn't be the same town.

I had hoped for a new location for both of us and for some reason, unbeknownst even to me, I suggested Kelowna. I really didn't know anything about Kelowna, as I barely remembered passing through the area on our way to Edmonton in 1964. However, my mind was set and after many more discussions Jim and I came to a mutual agreement to look for some land to buy in Kelowna.

So in the fall of 1971, we embarked on a journey to Kelowna with the thought in mind to buy some property, perhaps even an acre or two. It would be the place where we could eventually move to settle down. We found a real estate agent in Kelowna who showed us his listings. Not one of them fit our dream of a place, but we weren't ready to give up yet. In due course, we viewed some parcels of land in East Kelowna. The one we liked best was a nice view property on June Springs Road, but it had an unsightly junkyard in the neighbour's lot next door. With nothing else to consider buying, we decided to purchase the place, regardless of the junk. I couldn't actually feature us ever living there, yet it made a good investment for our money. Little did we know at the time that I needn't have worried? We were never meant to live on that land, but it did give us an important connection with Kelowna.

On our return to Calgary, there was great news awaiting us. Leslie and Stan had decided to get married and were excitingly making plans. There were a great deal of things to do for the big day and so we were all kept busy working toward getting it all done. We met Stan's parents, George and Alice and found them to be very nice people, who already knew and loved our Leslie. I was excited to be the 'Mother of the Bride' and I could already imagine their walk down the aisle in our beautiful church of St. Lawrence with our friend, Peter McCalman, officiating.

The day of the wedding arrived and Leslie was a beautiful bride in her traditional picturesque wedding dress. It was a conventional, long white dress with a finger-tip veil and Leslie carried a bouquet of yellow flowers in her arms. Her bridesmaids were her sister Chris and her cousin Debbie from Kamloops. It was their first time being bridesmaids and they looked very beautiful in their floor-length yellow dresses and big, floppy-brimmed yellow hats. Granny and Grandpa were among the wedding-guests, as was my Dad in his brown suit, which he had bought to die in, but now made him appear quite dapper under these joyful circumstances.

Chris, Leslie & Debbie.

I wanted to savour the happy moments of the wedding, but it was impossible to do so, as the ceremony was over in what seemed like the blink of an eye. And the next thing I knew, we were descending the stairs to the church hall below where the wedding supper was laid out for us. The St. Lawrence Auxiliary ladies had worked hard to decorate the dining hall and provide a wonderful meal for us. Our family members gathered together with the group of friends and professors from the University of Calgary and rejoiced over the happy occasion. Jim and I enjoyed getting to know Stan's parents, who now had become family. It felt strange to me, yet our first-born daughter was now a married lady with a brand new name of her own.

Once again, our lives in Calgary returned to normal after the wedding, though not for long! Quite unexpectedly, something truly disastrous happened! Don, one of our dear friends, died suddenly of a blood-clot to his heart. He was a salesman on Jim's staff who, only the

Dad (in his brown suit!), Marie, Granny and Grandpa Rolfe, and Jim.

week before, had gone into the hospital and had successful surgery on his back. We had visited him just the day before and he had laughed and joked with us.

Now on the phone I was being told he was dead. The impersonal voice asked me to inform Jim and the other employees. I was stunned! It couldn't be true. Don and his wife Monique had been special friends of ours ever since Don joined the staff several years back. He was a mere thirty-six years of age and he and Monique had five children with the youngest not much more than a baby. The whole idea of Don's death was just too horrible for me to accept.

I hung up the phone in utter disbelief. No one close to us had ever died before and Don's death hit me very hard. It was a Saturday morning and Jim and the other salesmen were out golfing. What was I to do? How could I reach them? I didn't have the will to act. I got into my car and drove to Leslie's place. Even then, I had difficulty verbalizing what had happened, but I finally blurted it all out. Together we decided to phone the golf course and have Jim paged. Death was frightening to me and my lack of experience in that area of life more than overwhelmed me.

I'll never forget Don's funeral held in the Roman Catholic Church where they were members. It was a difficult day and especially so for Monique. Yet there she was, such a brave and calm Mother, assisting each of her five children to approach their Dad's open coffin and view him as he lay there. She told me later it was the only way they would understand that their Daddy had gone to heaven and wouldn't be coming home from the hospital. It was truly one of the saddest scenes I've ever witnessed.

67. Surprises

We were more than ready after that to receive some happy news. And it was fast in coming! There was to be a Twenty-Fifth High School Reunion held in Creston for Jim and all of his school mates from the class of 1946. We were delighted the organizers hadn't forgotten Jim and had somehow been able to locate him where we now lived. We could hardly believe that twenty-five years had flown by so quickly since Jim had graduated! Of course, he said we'd come and we immediately made plans to take a holiday from his work to drive to Creston by car for the weekend of the celebration.

The Creston Valley never looked more beautiful than when we arrived for the Class Reunion. Everything about the town seemed the way we remembered it from so many years before. Of course there were a few new buildings, such as the motel where we stayed and a sprinkling of little shops on the main street. Basically though, the town where we'd met and fallen in love was much the same and felt familiar to us both.

Joining the other arrivals, we assembled at the dinner hour in the Wynndel Hall, just outside Creston. At first glance, many of Jim's former colleagues looked too old to be his age. Then again, as we got closer and talked with them, we recognized who they were and enjoyed getting reacquainted. I stuck to Jim like glue, as none of my former classmates were in the group there. I was three years behind Jim's class at school, so I wondered if any of Jim's fellow-graduates remembered me, I certainly remembered them.

Our group enjoyed a meal together and then each graduate was asked to share their life's journey since they graduated. Jim was the first to speak. He gave a great rundown of his work life and how he had moved from Vancouver to Edmonton and more recently to Calgary. Then he told about managing EMCO, a wholesale plumbing and heating company and as his story came to an end, a voice in the crowd called out, "What about Marie?"

Jim had mentioned only his work career and forgotten to tell about our marriage and being a father to our two daughters. I suppose he had felt nervous in front of his former school classmates. However, he recovered quickly and fitted in the details of our marriage and being a father to Leslie and Chris. When he finished, everyone gave him a good round of applause.

It was very interesting to hear all the different stories of where life had taken each of the graduates, but I was surprised that none had married their highschool sweetheart. Jim and I were the only exception.

Our reunion festivities continued over into the next day with a tour of our former highschool building. I enjoyed seeing the classrooms again and recalled my own happy days in those familiar rooms. Our time of reminiscing together had turned out well and we parted feeling a renewed and friendly closeness with each other.

Back in Calgary once more, we decided to deal with the ongoing challenge of Jim's position as manager. Although he enjoyed some aspects of his work, Jim felt under pressure and was regularly struggling with acute indigestion and tension. As well, the company's head office had recently announced all the branch managers were to be shuffled from one location to another. This meant Jim would be moved and Saskatchewan was the place being considered for his new location as manager.

After five years of hard work developing EMCO in Calgary into a more profitable and productive organization, Jim didn't feel he had the energy or desire to start over again somewhere else. Besides, Jim liked being a salesman and having only the responsibility for his own territory. With Jim's positive determination and my added support, we were certain it would all work out well for us. So, it happened as planned and Jim stepped back into his former position of salesman and found it was enjoyable and worked much better for him.

It was around this time that I decided to see if I could get a job, so using my long time experience of volunteering at the Children's Hospital as a reference, I found a position in a nearby Preschool Daycare. It was caring for the one and two year olds. The little ones, who were hardly more than babies, acted out their unhappiness at being dropped off and cried incessantly. It was heart wrenching for me! I spent my time picking the little ones up and cuddling them which seemed to help ease their flood of tears. I was kept extremely busy.

Sadly though, my job didn't work out well at all. I began catching one sniffling, coughing virus after another from those precious wee ones. It seemed I had no immunity at all to resist the ongoing colds and flu germs they inevitably brought with them to the daycare. And then, after a particularly bad flu that had put me in bed, I simply had to stop going, for the sake of my own health. I was sad about it, but I managed to carry on with my hospital volunteer work, which I dearly loved. Ironically, it seemed there at the hospital, I wasn't in such close contact with viruses and it was one day a week, not daily.

The next big event that appeared on the horizon of our lives was special to us all. Leslie was pregnant with a baby on the way, which would introduce both Jim and I to the wonderful world of being Grandparents! I hadn't thought I'd become a Granny until I was old and grey, yet here I was, about to be a first time Granny in my forty-first year! It was ever so exciting and I eagerly looked forward to the baby's arrival.

At that time, Leslie and Stan were living in a basement suite quite close to us. Leslie and I spent time together almost every day, visiting and shopping together. Chris was in grade eleven and was away at school five days a week, so I had time on my hands. And I found it was a lot of fun getting ready for the coming of the baby, scheduled for mid-August.

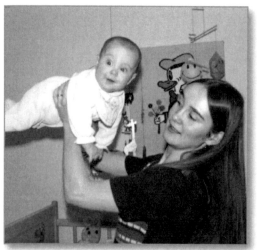

I found most everything concerning babies had changed so much since my pregnancies twenty years before. So, it was fun to join Leslie in discovering the brand new things now on the market. Spending so much of our time together drew us very close as mother and daughter, and without a doubt we both enjoyed the time we shared.

Baby Trish and Leslie.

Leslie's health was excellent and her months of pregnancy flew by rapidly until on the thirteenth day of August 1972, little Tristian made her entrance into this world. She was such a beauty from the very beginning, with her wide open eyes, dark hair and joyful disposition. Leslie made frequent visits to our house with our tiny granddaughter and my Dad became very taken with little Tristian. He would watch her for hours on end, as she smiled and flexed her arms and legs in her little cradle-seat that was placed on the kitchen table. Very often my Dad would make the same comment, saying, "I've never seen a happier baby in my eighty years on earth." I was so glad my Dad had lived to see and enjoy his darling great-granddaughter.

68. Fitzroy

Changes were constantly coming our way in those years and this time, it was in the form of an amazing person, one we would long remember. Fitzroy Richards arrived in Calgary as the new Anglican Priest of St. Lawrence Parish, replacing Peter McCallum. Before Fitzroy arrived in person, he sent a letter of introduction to our congregation which shook us all up. Why was that? Because he had a very different idea about what our parish would look like under his charge.

He announced there would no longer be two church services like we were used to. No! From now on there would be only one gathering which would be a Communion service every Sunday. It broke all of our traditions! And if any of us were displeased about this change, he said, we could look for another church, which he suggested was probably right down the street. We couldn't believe our ears when his letter was read out loud to us on a Sunday morning. We were all in shock!

Can you imagine how upset we felt upon hearing all this? Our neighbourhood church was not used to change. We were offended by his brashness and, after all, wasn't he a total stranger to us? Then again, we couldn't help admiring his self-assured boldness and we secretly looked forward to meeting this outspoken man of the cloth. Were we disappointed? No, we weren't at all!

On his first Sunday in the pulpit, Fitzroy greeted us with a broad smile and told us his life's story about being raised in a Christian family in Trinidad. He also shared that God had given him a great love for us here in his new parish already. He knew he'd been called to serve us at St. Lawrence by God. In spite of our former thoughts of his pluckiness, those humble and appealing words endeared him to us all.

Fitzroy was surprisingly small in stature for a man, but he made up for it with his larger than life personality and colour, in more ways than skin tone. His vestments were made of extravagant hues of red and other bright colours which he wore with immense pride and dignity. He would even outshine the Bishop when he came in his purple robes!

Fitzroy admitted in his first sermon that he was an avid preacher and the truth of that we would very soon discover. He was well acquainted with the scriptures of the Bible and patiently began to teach us from them. Because he was a charismatic-type speaker, we listened, but most of what Fitzroy said was well over our heads spiritually. Even so, we looked forward to his messages every week, as he was not afraid to speak on any subject or theme. He shared his opinion freely in his bold and passionate way.

One Sunday, Fitzroy looked out over the congregation and asked a question. "Where on earth are the men in this Parish?" It was a rhetorical question, for sure! Our church was typical of most Anglican churches of that day, basically attended by females. Then, he called several of the youngsters by name, as he was good at remembering everyone's first name, and gave them all instructions. They were to go home that day and lovingly encourage their Dad to come to church by giving them this message. "Tell them the sermon today was about being born-again," he said, "and being born-again will help them become better fathers."

Fitzroy not only cared for us in church, but he was also thinking of our loved-ones at home. Often he talked about the Trinidadian fathers in his native land, who apparently were spiritual leaders that brought their wives and families to the church. He used his beloved homeland of Trinidad as an example to us, yet he managed to make us still feel loved and cared for too. It was easy to relate to Fitzroy's enormous heart of love for us all.

Leslie had started to attend St. Lawrence Church and was bringing our little granddaughter, Tristian, too. Having a great love for her child had refocused Leslie and I suppose my tales about our new priest had captured her interest in church once more. "It felt like coming home," she told me after her first Sunday. Rightfully so, as she had been raised from a young age in the Anglican Church and the prayer-book service was still familiar to her.

Leslie arranged with Fitzroy to do the baptism for Tristian when she was about eight months old and the Rolfe family joined us from Vancouver. Tristian was Granny and Grandpa's very first great-grandchild and she was precious to them. Chris, as well as my Dad Tony, in his now 'famous' brown suit, were also present for the baptism. It was indeed a time to happily rejoice together. Little Tristian looked beautiful in the white baptismal gown that her own mom had worn twenty years earlier.

69. The Bible Study

Fitzroy's presence certainly made a difference in the normal life of our Parish. For instance, he shared with us he'd like to start a weekly, home-based, Bible group and astonishingly, it quickly came to pass. I'd never been involved in anything similar to a Bible Study class before, but I volunteered our home as one of the host-homes without giving it much thought.

I immediately began worrying about what I'd done, as I knew absolutely nothing about Bible Study groups. Would I be embarrassed by my lack of knowledge, I question myself? I wanted desperately to do things right, so I found our copy of the Good News Bible and placed it prominently on our coffee table. For some reason that made me feel much better!

When the door-bell rang on the appointed night, Jim and I graciously welcomed the small group inside. Beyond that point, we didn't have a clue what was going to happen. However, Fitzroy arrived and put us all at ease by telling us how he had prayed for a Bible Study group like this to lead. Then he launched into how very much he loved God's Word, all the while hugging his Bible to his chest. I'd never heard anyone speak or act like that before, but then I remembered his fondness for the Bible from the sermons he'd preached. I started to relax!

And as the weeks went by, all of us in the group started to grow in a new understanding of what he was teaching from his beloved scriptures. Our meetings became enjoyable and we began sharing out loud, our own individual points of view. This helped us to get to know each other better and soon we were all the best of friends.

In the meantime, I was living a busy life as a grandmother every day, either at Leslie's house or having her over to ours. I was receiving so much pleasure in seeing every little change in Tristian as she progressed month after month. Babies bring such joy! And Leslie and I were becoming so very close, able to relate much easier now that she was married and a mother, and far beyond her rebellious teenage years. Then, even before Tristian had taken her first steps, a big turn of events in our lives began to play out. It made me unexpectedly happy and upset at the same time.

What was this news? Jim received a job offer that was too good to refuse, but there was definitely a downside to it. The job Jim was offered was a manager's position with a well-known company called Westburne. This prominent company was one Jim knew well because they had been a competitor of his. They knew all about Jim and his history as both a salesman and manager with EMCO. And this new job would have us residing in Kelowna, B.C. Yes, the very place where we already owned a piece of land. Amazing!

Jim's work would see him travel throughout the Okanagan, developing new business for Westburne, all the while being based in Kelowna. He would be working out of an office in our own home at first and then later, a Branch Office and Warehouse would be built and Jim would become the manager over a staff he could hire himself.

It certainly was a great job opportunity for Jim as he still had a lot of energy and desire to work at forty-five years of age. Better still, the job sounded like there would be much less pressure on him than he had with EMCO. He knew of Westburne's reputation as a good employer. So together, the two of us decided in favour of the new appointment and began thinking about our move to Kelowna.

But the downside was it would mean we would have to move away from Calgary which had been our home for the past six years. Leaving Leslie and our wee grandchild behind was a very hard thing for me to do. I tried not to show it, but it felt like my heart was being broken into pieces. Perhaps, only a first-time grandmother could understand the feelings I was having, leaving such a big part of the family behind. And even though I knew Jim and I were making the right decision in going, I still felt inwardly sad.

I tried to not think about the distance this move was putting between me and my daughter and grandbaby. Wasn't it a whole day's drive? I thought about how I was going to miss them. It made me want to cry. I'd feel silly explaining my tears to anyone, wouldn't I? Hadn't something wonderful happened to us? We'd been given this great opportunity of a fresh start in Kelowna and I'd have to learn to handle my feelings of loss. I really hoped I could!

Thankfully, Chris didn't have any problem with leaving Calgary, even though she had just graduated from grade eleven and would be entering her final year in a new high school in Kelowna. She actually seemed very excited about the new adventure that was ahead of her in a new school and a new city. I was most pleased about that.

70. Kelowna

The move to Kelowna went according to plan in the summer of 1973 and we were happy with the house we found. It was on the west side of Okanagan Lake in the district called Lakeview Heights, halfway between Kelowna and Westbank. The new home was a rambling two-storied, eight year old house with two bedrooms on the main floor and another in the basement. It sat perched on a hill overlooking the gardens of Byland's Nursery, where they grew a multitude of trees and other greenery. And the house certainly met all our needs as there was space in the downstairs area for Jim to set up a business office. Everything appeared to be working out for us in a great way.

The first thing on our mind in our new location was to settle in and then find a church, as we'd grown accustomed to attending church every Sunday while we lived in Calgary. We drove to the town of Westbank and discovered a small, white-sided church with a sign identifying it as St. Georges Anglican Church. We found some very welcoming people there and the service offered an informal contemporary style which was similar to the one we'd attended in Calgary. The friendliness of the parishioners, sparse as they were, made us feel at home and we decided to put our church roots down there.

If I recall accurately, it was just a couple of Sundays later when we returned home after church with the parish offering money in a bag. St. Georges was in need of a new Treasurer and Jim had been asked to accept the position, which he did. We couldn't help smiling over Jim's new financial position and chalked it up to him having such an honest face.

Meanwhile at home, our Chris spent the remaining weeks of summer at the beach or around the house, quite happy despite having no friends her age to hang-out with. She would also be going into her grade twelve class without knowing anyone in her school. It made me think back to my own days in Creston as a newcomer in High School. It definitely had an adventuresome quality about it and I hoped it would turn out that way for our Chris.

Then, when September arrived and school started, Chris settled nicely into George Pringle High. She had been given a choice to either take her final year at Kelowna High School or the one in Westbank. They both required travelling by bus as we lived half way between them. Yet, without hesitation, Chris chose to attend George Pringle in Westbank. She wasn't even aware her choice greatly affected her life from that point on, just like all major decisions in our life do! She was happy with her choice and after a brief time of adjustment, settled nicely into her new school. As for myself, I still grieved inside over our family being separated. What was wrong with me?

Within weeks, as fate would have it, Chris met up with a certain someone, by the name of Dan Ashman, a classmate in her grade twelve class. They caught the same school bus and Dan had conveniently sent his friend Ed up to sit beside Chris that first day and find out who she was and all about her. Dan lived in the Lakeview Heights area, quite near us and before very long the two of them were going steady. We learned that Dan's father had passed away, but had been a roofer by trade and had actually put the tile roof on our house, with Dan helping him. Both Jim and I were very pleased Chris had found someone as nice as Dan and it was a serious romance from the start.

As time passed by and we settled into Kelowna and its lifestyle, we acquired a love for our new location and felt at home there. We grew more involved at St. George's Church and before long got to know the whole congregation by their first names.

Chris was very popular by now at her school and enjoyed a wide circle of friends that always kept her on the go. She had settled in very well to her new life. We were happy to acquire an organ for her to play, as we had left our piano in Calgary for Leslie.

And Leslie and I were in touch a lot, not by expensive long-distance phone calls, but by letter. We both also made cassette-tapes and mailed them back and forth as we loved hearing little Tristian's jabbering sounds as she was attempting to talk. It made her seem close. But in spite of everything good in our lives, in my heart there was still an ache. Who could heal it?

During the winter we reveled in the milder weather in Kelowna and when the springtime of 1973 arrived, we were surprised when our family members grew once more. It was Jim's sister, Irene and her husband Ted who unexpectedly decided to move from Kamloops over to Kelowna. They said they wanted to live closer to us and they bought a duplex in the Rutland area. Ted and Irene were empty-nesters at this point and were feeling a sense of freedom. We saw them fairly often, although they liked to camp on the weekends in their trailer and go sailing on the Shuswap in their houseboat. They kept it moored in a little place called Canoe, on the Shuswap Lake, when not in use.

Before long, Irene got a part-time job at Sears and Ted got his 'ticket' to become a plumber. One interest Irene got involved in about that time was numerology. She studied the many books of the psychic Edward Casey, as well as other books pertaining to tarot-cards and horoscope readings. These strange things were something I had never dabbled in and I had no interest at all in. And although none of us were aware at the time, a terrible family tragedy was looming on the horizon for Ted and Irene. If only we could see ahead and prevent catastrophes from happening, but we can't do that, can we?

Jim's work as a salesman was a good fit for him and he was doing well, free of the pressures of selling in the big city. I tried to find fulfillment getting involved in activities to occupy myself. There were a great many courses offered in our new locale and before long I found one in Floral Design. It was fun and I enjoyed making the fresh flower bouquets as well as corsages, but when the sessions ended I was ready for something else. And my search took me next to pottery making, as clay had always fascinated me. I enjoyed the classes and made new friends, but again, I was back where I started at the end. I had a need to be filled and who could fill it?

In December of 1973, even though we were enjoying a stretch of mild temperatures here in Kelowna the three of us journeyed to Calgary to celebrate Christmas with Leslie and her family. Our family enjoyed togetherness once again for the holiday week. That truly meant a lot to me! While we were there, we accompanied Leslie and sixteen-month old Tristian to the Christmas services at our former church of St. Lawrence. It was good to see our old friends again.

During a discussion in the coffee time afterwards, one of our close friends, Jill, mentioned a book written by Dennis Bennett, that many of them at their church had been reading. "Do you think the book is a real life story?" Leslie asked.

Obviously Leslie had read the book and had questions. A reply was promptly given by Walter, Jill's husband. "The book is true, alright, as my sister even speaks in tongues since she read it."

We knew Walter to be a no-nonsense type of guy. And though I didn't entirely grasp what they were talking about, later on Leslie offered to lend me her copy of the book in question, saying, "We can discuss it after you've read it." Little did I realize at the time, this particular book would play a life-changing role in my life?

71. The Book

Once we were home in Kelowna again, I tossed the book from Leslie into one of my dresser drawers. I had good intensions about reading books, but I didn't always follow through and actually read them. And sure enough, the book lay forgotten in the drawer unread while the rest of the winter months drifted by. And, like the old saying goes, 'out of sight, out of mind'.

Finally, the month of April arrived and springtime started to creep into our Okanagan valley once again. Jim was scheduled to attend a Westburne Conference in Vancouver for six days that month and I was uneasy about him being gone for that length of time for those feelings of broken-heartedness were still bothering me. The time of Jim's departure on a Sunday arrived and we kissed goodbye and he drove away over the hill. I knew I was going to miss him during the week ahead and end up counting the days until his return.

Early the next morning, Chris caught her bus to school and I started feeling edgy again, with nothing to do. Then I recalled the book in my dresser-drawer and thought this would be a good time to start it. I opened the drawer and dug it out. I recall it was April the eleventh, 1974.

The book was titled *Nine O'clock in the Morning*, which didn't tell me very much about the book. I was about to find out it was one title I would remember the rest of my life. It wasn't an overly thick book either, which suited me fine. I was feeling an obligation towards Leslie to read it, so I settled into a comfortable living room chair and began to read.

From the very beginning, I had to admit it wasn't like any other book I'd read before. It had been written four years previously by an Episcopal (Anglican) Priest in California by the name of Dennis Bennett.[2] He told how his life had been altered beyond his imagination by a deep spiritual experience he'd undergone. He also claimed his book was not fiction, but a true story! I was curious and fascinated at once with the book's storyline. I couldn't help recalling how I'd felt when listening to Fitzroy preach in Calgary and thinking there had to be more to faith than I had encountered. Could this be it? The Reverent Bennett said it was a true story! And I felt open to believing him. After all, wasn't he an ordained priest in the very denomination I had willingly joined as an adult? My interest in reading this unusual book was beginning to grow by the minute!

The book went on to tell about how the charismatic renewal movement had swept through every church denomination worldwide back in the 1960's, ten years previous to my time of reading the book. And, this charismatic renewal was still dynamically active in the church today. Not that I had ever heard the words 'charismatic renewal.' The term was completely foreign to me! Nevertheless, Dennis Bennett went on to tell the compelling story of how he had become acquainted first-hand with the experience connected with the renewal.

He told of a young couple at a neighbouring church who had both received this experience and their lives had been dramatically changed. The name of this experience, they told him, was Baptism of the Holy Spirit and it was an infilling of the Holy Spirit accompanied by speaking-in-tongues. Dennis was intrigued!

He continued on in his book to say that at first he naturally resisted everything the couple was saying. After all, he was the Rector of a

---

2 *Nine O'Clock in the Morning*, Dennis J. Bennett, Logos International, 1970. Plainfield, New Jersey.

church with 2,500 members in Van Nuys, California and he had never heard of this charismatic renewal before, let alone a so-called Baptism of the Holy Spirit. Dennis had many questions which led him to study the Bible references found in the Book of Acts that told of this experience and how the people had received it.

At that point in the story, I remembered back to Calgary and how my friend at the coffee time had said his sister spoke in tongues after reading this very same book. Could this mean it was a real experience? I was very interested in all of this, so I decided to study the passages that convinced Dennis Bennett. First I'd have to find our copy of the Good New Bible, the bargain book I'd got for just two dollars. The lost was soon found and I began reading the scripture references for myself.

In Dennis's story, he studied those Bible passages for three months and learned that the experience was indeed a biblical fact. Dennis, unlike me, possessed a degree in theology which helped him understand all the deep bible truths behind the experience. But just the same, I wanted to be convinced that what I read was factual and not some made up story. I had never been a fan of fiction, and it was history books or biographies that had always been my choice of reading material.

As I continued to read Dennis's book, I realized he viewed the experience as a valuable encounter offered to all believers, not just the people within the pages of scripture. As he relates in the book, it had taken Dennis a long time to do his Bible study, but finally he ready to take his 'leap-of-faith,' as he called it. He asked God for the fullness of the Baptism of the Holy Spirit. It was a daring move on Dennis' part, but one I was now considering to take myself.

As I could see, the references were clear. The Apostle's, along with other people in the Biblical record, received the Baptism of the Holy Spirit and then prayed for other people to receive the same experience by speaking-in-tongues. The four Gospels as well as the Book of Acts in the Bible told of these accounts. It was meant to be a natural second step after one had become a born-again believer. How had Dennis missed seeing this before? Well he saw it now! And so did I!

Dennis shared in his book how the Lord Jesus Christ filled him to overflowing with the Holy Spirit in a supernatural way. He said the event was one of great joy and the indisputable reality of God's presence with him. And Dennis also began speaking fluently in a foreign language he had never learned. He assumed this new language had to be words of praise, for they flowed from his mouth easily and without effort on his part. Dennis accepted it all as a gift from his Heavenly Father and began to teach about the experience in his large California church. This caused him all kinds of trouble with the hierarchy, but that's another story and his story to tell.

Bible references that I've incorporated into my faith (mostly from the NIV version):

The four Gospels proclaim Jesus as the Baptizer in the Holy
Spirit. Matthew 3:11, Mark 1:7 & 8, Luke 3:16, and John 1:33.
Acts 1:1-5, the promise of the Holy Spirit /
Acts 1:8, the promise of power
Acts 2:1-15, the day of Pentecost / Acts 8:4-25,
baptized believers receive the Spirit
Acts 9:17-19 and Acts 10: 44-48 and Acts 13:9 and Acts 19:1-7
1 Cor. 14:15, all are to speak in tongues / 1 Cor. 14:18,
Paul spoke in tongues
Mark 16:17, Jesus said believers would speak in new tongues.

72. The Second Book

Coming to the end of Dennis Bennett's book, *Nine O'clock in the Morning,* I knew without a doubt I wanted the experience that the Reverend Dennis Bennett had received. However, I was at a loss as to how to go about it without some further help. In desperation, I flipped to the very back of the book, past the chapter references and tucked away under the Publisher's Note, I found my answer. Dennis and his wife Rita had co-authored an additional book called, *The Holy Spirit and You,* described as a study-guide on the Baptism of the Holy Spirit. This was just what I needed in the adventurous quest that lay ahead of me.

I sat in my chair meditating on what I had learned by reading *Nine O'clock in the Morning* and studying the Bible passages. Together they had revealed a clear path to becoming a born-again believer in the three-fold nature of Father, Son and Holy Spirit. The facts were all there once I believed the Bible to be true. It was as plain as day! John's Gospel in Chapter 3 verse 16 said plainly that, "God sent His Son into the world and whosoever believes in Him will not perish, but have eternal life."

This verse was like the Gospel in a nutshell, and I so wanted to be one of those 'whosoever's' that wouldn't perish, but have eternal life.

In all my years as a churchgoer, I'd missed the reason Jesus came to earth and died on a cross over 2,000 years ago. By His death, which is a historical fact, Jesus took away the separation of sin between me and God. He reconciled me back into a loving relationship with my Heavenly Father. I wasn't a bad person in God's eyes, only a person separated from His holiness as everyone is when they are born on this earth. This truth became clear, but it required me to believe it by exercising my faith.

Jesus Christ was a bridge between me and God that I could cross over by believing Him, that is Jesus, to be my Lord and Savior. This is basically the good news of the Bible and it makes this fact so clear even a young child could grasp and accept its truth and become a believer. Wow, what an eye-opener! Learning all this encouraged me to take the next step of faith and receive the Baptism of the Holy Spirit. So, with no delay, the very next morning, which was April the 12th 1974, I drove into Kelowna and purchased the Bennett's second book at the Gospel Den Bookstore in the Capri Centre.

At home once again, I settled into my cozy living room chair to read *The Holy Spirit and You*.[3] This second book was laid out as an instruction manual that started with an explanation of what it means to become a Christian.

Firstly, I was to ask God's pardon for living my life for myself and not for Him which was all part of the separation between me and Him.

Second, I was to ask for forgiveness of all my sins and have them cleared away, so I could live every day freely forgiven. This part is called repentance.

And lastly, I was to ask to be converted or born-again! This meant to invite the Lord Jesus Christ into my heart and life and make Him my Savior and Lord.

My mind was made-up! I'd never been so sure of anything before in my life, so without any hesitation, I began with number one and prayed through each step. And God, my Heavenly Father, not only heard my words, but saw my heart and granted me the gift of eternal life. I was born-again that very day by the Spirit of God.

---

3 *The Holy Spirit and You: A study-guide to the Spirit-Filled life*, Dennis J. Bennett, Logos International, 1971. Plainfield, New Jersey.

The book then led me to pray and ask for the second step, the Baptism of the Holy Spirit. This meant the Lord would touch my inner spirit with His Spirit and I would begin a new dimension of my spiritual life. It would make it possible for me to be led by the spirit, the inner part of me that is eternal and lives forever. This spiritual part of me would one day ascend to heaven and live in eternity. How amazing! And that wasn't all! I would also be given the gift of communicating with God's Holy Spirit in a very special language of the Spirit. The Bible called it speaking in tongues.

I prayed for the Lord to touch me a second time and then I waited, literally holding my breath for God to do something. Only the silence of the room surrounded me! Suddenly a twitch in my leg got my attention. Was that a sign? How silly! Right then and there, I realized my imagination was working overtime and I laughed at myself and decided to just keep on waiting.

I had followed closely the book's instructions on how to receive the Baptism of the Holy Spirit, so what more could I do? Then, a thought came into my mind that maybe kneeling before God, like I did at the altar in church might help. So I retired to the bedroom and knelt beside my bed. I was determined to press through for this experience no matter what!

"I'm not getting up until I receive from you in some way, Lord", I heard myself saying. Woe, was that impertinence on my part? Could I offend God and cause Him to turn away? No! I was sure He could look into my heart and see I wanted this infilling of the Spirit more than I'd ever desired anything before. I loved God now and the anticipation of what I was asking for only gave me a greater desire for His holy presence.

73. The Encounter

Silence continued to surround me in my bedroom as I knelt beside my bed, waiting expectantly for the Lord to appear. I felt every fiber of my being ready and alert to meet this mysterious God of the universe that somehow I now believed existed. A thought came to my mind. If I praised Him with words of love perhaps whatever was delaying my encounter with Him might be resolved. Taking a deep breath, I began to express my yearning and desire to know Him better. My love for Him poured out of my mouth and suddenly, quick as the blink-of-an-eye, everything abruptly changed!

My senses became aware of someone in the room with me! Incredible as it may sound, I knew I was not alone anymore and I wasn't frightened either. A pleasant feeling seemed to wash over me, as if a good friend had come by. My eyes focused on the bright light coming through the window and in one split second it happened! I beheld Christ standing in front of me with His hands stretched out toward me, in a gesture of inviting me to draw closer.

The Spirit within me leapt forward, as surely as if I had done so physically and I felt a magnificent connection with Him. I desperately wanted to voice my love to Him and I opened my mouth to do so. And, to my utter surprise, the words that came tumbling out were not recognizable to my ears. I heard myself speaking words that were unknown to me and certainly not English, the only language I knew. It wasn't gobbledygook either, but a clear and highly inflected, expressive language.

As I listened to myself speaking, I sensed those unintelligible sounds were not my words, but those of the Holy Spirit. I was worshiping the Lord in words I didn't understand, but I felt God did. There was a physical sensation happening as well, for my mouth and lips were tingling as I expressed myself in my new language. This reassured me that what was happening was both physical and spiritual. Inwardly, I felt my heart was expanding in size to accommodate all the love being poured into it by the Lord. It was a supernatural feeling I'd never felt before! And I knew and understood for the first time in my life, Jesus loved me, He really loved me. How much? Enough to die for me!

It is hard to explain, but in that very short moment of time, I was made aware of another dimension to my life, something I'd never been conscious of before. It was my spiritual side. And the insecure person I once saw myself as, had been transformed into a new person of the Spirit, filled with confidence and love. I felt light-hearted knowing I was now a child of God. It was a thrilling and mindboggling experience for me at the same time.

And meantime, I was still praising God in this unknown language only He could understand and I didn't want to stop, ever! Yet, I knew I could stop anytime I wanted to and return to speaking normal words of English again. The choice was mine! I'd been given a language of the Spirit and also with it came the freedom to use it or not. I closed my eyes and slowly let my words of praise to the Lord come to an end. The sense of spiritual joy in my heart did not diminish and I knew it wouldn't. I had encountered the Lord of the Universe and I was a changed person! The gift I had received was a new heart of love and a special language so I could communicate with my Heavenly Father. And I knew, from the Bible, if I used my language it would build me up in my innermost being. What a remarkable gift!

74. Sharing

Suddenly, I had a strong desire to share what I had experienced with someone, but whom? Then I remembered Leslie and how it all started with her giving me the first Bennett book to read. I got up from my knees, eager to call her on the phone. As I said previously, I rarely phoned Leslie and especially not in the middle of the day when the phone rates were sky high, but today was an exception! I had gone through a life-changing event and I wanted to share it with her.

She finally said, "Hello" in answer to the ringing of her phone and quickly explained to me that I'd caught her at a bad time. It seemed that her outdoors clothesline, laden with baby clothes, had minutes earlier crashed to the ground and she was in the process of retrieving them from the muck-and-mire of the dirt in her backyard garden.

Nevertheless, it would take more than a mere clothesline catastrophe to dampen my spirits. I told her the details of my morning and at once she entered into the joy of what I had gone through. She became excited, and wanted to know if this experience was for anyone who wanted to receive it. I was able to reassure her that it was. Hadn't it happened to an ordinary person like me? Leslie's wet clothes were forgotten as she began plying me with more and more questions.

I answered, as best as I could, being careful to explain that I had had a great desire for the gift and I believed somehow that that played a big part in my receiving it. I sensed now that Leslie wanted this wonderful gift for herself and that pleased me so much. By the end of the call, she had firmly decided she was going to seek the spiritual baptism for herself. And of course, that is really her story to tell, but suffice it to say, she had a unique experience of her own which followed a few weeks later.

Meanwhile at home, Jim was due back from his convention in Vancouver on Saturday. Would I share my 'mountain-top' experience with him? I had to, as life would never be the same for me again and I wanted him to know that. Finally Saturday arrived and I waited in expectation until I heard his car pull into our driveway. I literally ran down stairs to welcome him home. I threw open the door and confessed outright, "You've got a brand new wife!"

Jim had no idea what I meant by that announcement, of course! Later, I would explain how something wonderful had happened to me. I was totally honest about the fact I had received God's amazing gift of salvation and I wanted him to know I was a changed person. Thankfully, I had a husband who loved me and was happy for me even though he didn't fully understand.

The following day, and for many days to come, I had ample opportunity to explain my experience further and to show Jim by my changed life that I was a born-again believer. For indeed, my life was greatly altered and I would be forever changed in the way I lived my life. I was now aware that Christ was alive in my heart and living out His life through me.

Jim, in the course of time, had his own encounter with the Lord and because we are all unique individuals in God's eyes, Jim's experience was totally different than mine. And to say I spent a great deal of time praying for him is an understatement. I prayed unceasingly! It was a tremendous blessing for us both to find togetherness in our new life in Christ our Lord.

Not very long after all this happened to us, we made plans with Leslie to come to Calgary for a visit. Leslie told me about a group of people meeting at the University of Calgary for charismatic meetings each Saturday and did I want to go? My answer was a firm "yes" and I began praying for the Lord to open the door of possibility, so indeed it would happen.

The time soon arrived for the three of us to travel the eight hours to Calgary for our family visit. The change in little Trish was tremendous and it was great to hear her now bubbling with words of her own. Leslie was also excited to tell us that she was two months pregnant with her second child. It was such wonderful news! We loved the role of being grandparents and little Trish was now at the age to want a little sister or brother.

The Saturday morning of the charismatic meeting at the University arrived and along with it, a spring blizzard with blowing snow that quickly covered everything with its white fluffiness. That wasn't very unusual for Calgary weather, but it was very disappointing to Leslie and me. You see, our plans were all made and Jim was going to look after little Trish so we could go. But once the snow began to fall, Jim wouldn't hear of us driving across the city on the snow covered streets.

Naturally, I was devastated, but as a new believer I now had the option of reacting in a Christian way. And that was to pray! Did God take away the snowstorm when I asked? Incredible as it may seem, that's exactly what happened! No sooner had I prayed than the skies began to clear and the snow began to melt and by the time we left for the University, the sun was out. I remember the only evidence of the storm, was a steamy vapour rising from the wet roads we traveled on to the meeting.

Without a shadow of a doubt, I believe God turned that storm away because He is good and wants to answer our prayers. Leslie and I were quick to give Him our grateful thanks, also. Does God always grant the answers to prayer so easily? Certainly not! But I believe our Heavenly Father sometimes does want to show His favour towards us in the same way our earthly fathers do. As the old saying goes, "God works in mysterious ways, His wonders to perform."

Both Leslie and I were buoyed up with happiness that day as we joined the group of other worshippers in that meeting. They had gone through a similar experience to the one we had and we felt a kind of kinship with them and felt God's love flowing between us. We experienced a peace that passes understanding as we realized we were all members of the great and awesome family of God.

75. Women's Aglow

The day following our meeting in Calgary, Leslie took me shopping for some books at a Christian bookstore she had discovered. The proprietor of the store was a friendly person who confided that he, too, had experienced the Baptism of the Holy Spirit. When I asked him if he knew any likeminded Christians in Kelowna, he said he did and promised to pass my name on to someone. I wrote out my name and phone number on a piece of paper and left it with him.

When we returned to Kelowna I did not forget the man's promise and made it a priority to pray and ask the Lord to guide that piece of paper into the hands of a certain lady and have her contact me. I believe God heard my prayers and had a plan to fulfill in His own timing. My part was to pray. And I did, while waiting for what was going to happen next?

Well, close to a week later, while I was kneeling in my place of prayer beside my bed, the phone rang and a lady's voice on the other end of the line said she had received my number from a bookstore in Calgary. My heart leapt! It was so exciting to have the answer to my prayers came so quickly. The lady introduced herself as Julie and asked if I could meet her the following week at a lady's meeting in the ballroom of the Capri Hotel. Of course, I said I would.

The gathering turned out to be the second in a new series called, Women's Aglow Fellowship, especially designed to minister to Christian women of all denominations. And Julie, as it turned out, was the Founder and President of these monthly charismatic meetings and I learned this when she introduced herself at the front, while opening up the meeting. God is so full of surprises! There were several hundred women gathered together on that day to grow in their faith. The name they had adopted, Women's Aglow, was from the King James Bible, in the Book of Romans, chapter 12 and verse 11, where it says, "Be aglow with the Spirit of God."

My experience in that first meeting was very enlightening, as I'd thought up to now I was alone in my understanding of the new life in the Spirit.

I recognized anew there was a Charismatic Renewal going on in people's lives and in churches, not only locally in Kelowna, but in our country of Canada and around the world. It was a continuation of the renewal Dennis Bennett had introduced in the early 1960's. I was excited to be part of such a movement, especially as I could not deny God had directed me to the Bennett books and now drawn me to this fellowship meeting. So, straightaway, I joined the organization and planned to attend their Christian meetings every month. I distinctly heard them make a promise to teach from the Bible, as well as to help us live out our new life in God's Spirit with boldness. I was in need of both and so also, were a lot of other ladies there, it seemed.

Throughout the year of 1974, so very much had happened spiritually, and yet there were changes on the home front as well. Chris finished her Grade Twelve year and graduated, as did Dan. Jim and I were so proud of them both. Dan had become her one and only boyfriend ever since they met the year before. There was a big celebration and dance for the graduates and I remember how great they both looked as they got all dressed up for it. Chris wore a lovely turquoise evening gown adorned with a white orchid corsage, Dan's gift to her. He wore a suit and sported one of the biggest bowties I'd ever seen. They made a striking couple and it was very easy to tell they were in love.

Meanwhile at that time, trouble brewed in Saskatchewan. Hazel was phoning me more often concerning her family situation, which had decidedly gone from bad to worse. Eddie was drinking heavily and his health was going downhill. Hazel thought his problems started when he was refused a pilot's license to fly, due to his diabetic condition. This was very devastating for Eddie as he had served in the Canadian Air force during the war and felt that gave him a right to fly. Eddie's brother Ivor owned and flew his own plane regularly, having an air-strip at the Reckwell farm now. The situation was a major setback to Eddie and caused him to turn to drink even more in his frustration and depression. And Hazel, along with Marie and Jack, were finding it hard to cope with the growing problem.

How could I help? When praying I felt led to invite Hazel and her children to Kelowna for a much needed break away from the difficult circumstances. She agreed to come while her two children were still on summer vacation from school. The three of them arrived soon after in

Kamloops by CN railway. We drove there and picked them up and Chris and her cousin Marie were thrilled to have some time together. And we all took pleasure in the lovely days of summer in Kelowna.

As Hazel's visit started to come to an end, I sensed the Lord was encouraging me to share my faith experience with her. Up to that point, I hadn't mentioned my spiritual awakening, but now I began to wonder what would happen if I did. God's inner voice was speaking so persistently about it, I was losing sleep. I loved my sister very much and I did believe God was her answer.

The last day of Hazel's holiday arrived, and I was trying to have a nap, from of my lack of sleep the night before. However, sleep wouldn't come and I knew why. I got up and joined Hazel at the kitchen table where she was playing a game of solitaire, a game she loved. Our young ones were busy outside in the backyard, so it was a perfect opportunity. I opened up to her in detail, divulging all that had happened to me concerning being born-again and experiencing the life of the Holy Spirit. I ended by telling her, just how very much God loved her and wanted to give her a completely new life as well. Hazel had sat listening to my story in silence and then she said, "I'm happy for you, Marie, because you've always been a good person and deserve it all, but God doesn't love me."

Appalled by her statement, I reassured her God's love was for everyone and had nothing to do with being good or deserving it. However, Hazel's mind was made up and I could tell she wasn't hearing what I said anymore. She wasn't going to change her mind. She could be stubborn!

In desperation before she left, I found a book written by Pat Boone who was one of her favorite singers at that time. I gave it to her. I'd read the book and it was about how Pat and his wife had become Christians and the difficulty he had in accepting the Biblical fact that God loved him. In the telling of his story, Pat shared how he conquered his doubts and experienced a really unique encounter with the Lord. I thought perhaps Hazel would listen to someone she admired, like Pat. Time came once again for us to part and we all hugged with some sadness.

Once Hazel got home, she wrote to say she had enjoyed reading the book, but as far as I could tell, the message of God's love for her was not received. I felt so very disappointed and helpless and I knew I couldn't do anything more, only God could. It would take a miracle to transform Hazel's thinking. And this is when God once more stepped into the situation.

76. Erica

Following Hazel's visit, I kept on praying for my sister and then a couple of weeks later, when I was driving to the monthly Women's Aglow meeting, an odd feeling came over me. I felt like something significant was going to happen that day. What could it be? I could only speculate that it would be something good, for God is good. The thought of Hazel never entered my mind.

When I arrived at the meeting I was early, so I stopped by the book table to have a quick look. As I stood there, a lady came up beside me and picked up Dennis Bennett's book, *The Holy Spirit and You*. I couldn't help but notice! After glancing through the book in her hands, the lady turned to me and asked inquiringly, "Have you read this book?"

What a question? Dennis Bennett's book was surely the ONE book on the table that God knew I'd read from cover to cover. I answered the lady's question by telling her how God had used that very book to reveal his plan of salvation to me. She smiled at me, paid for the book and then asked if I was alone, and would I sit with her in the meeting? I agreed. I had no other plans! Did God? We walked together into the Capri Ballroom and found seats side by side at one of the tables. This left only one vacant chair at the table, the one beside me on my right.

As usual, about two hundred women were in attendance, busily seating themselves at the linen covered tables. It was already getting crowded in the spacious room. Yet, no one sat in the seat on my right. I chatted with my newfound friend and learned our special speaker that day was one of the National Board Speaker's from the United States. It was a treat having her on our agenda that day. Then what happened next seemed to be quite normal, or was it? A lady approached our table and asked me if the chair alongside me was taken. When I said it wasn't, she promptly sat down beside me, just as the meeting got underway.

Our guest speaker for the day began her teaching on the subject of 'How *to Hear God's Voice Speaking to us in Everyday Life*.' And to start off, she said she would relay an example from her personal life. God had spoken to her that very morning concerning the dress she'd chosen to wear that day. What a strange way to begin a talk, I thought to myself! And then, at this point the lady on my right who had just joined us, leaned over to me and whispered, "Not only does God care about what you wear, He also cares about where you sit."

I was surprised with her remark, but she went on to say, "I was sitting across the room and the Lord told me I was not sitting in the seat I was supposed to sit in." Then she added, "I was directed to this chair beside you."

Immediately my spiritual senses perked up! Who was this lady, anyway? Why had she been sent to sit beside me? My mind entertained a hundred thoughts and possibilities as the guest speaker continued her speech up front. The message on hearing God's voice in our lives was ever so interesting and all of us there listened intently, right through to her closing remarks.

Then, I turned to engage the newly arrived lady beside me in conversation. I quickly found out her name was Erica and she was visiting from out-of-town. She said she had even borrowed the dress she was wearing from her sister Linda in order to attend the meeting today. Was it just a coincidence that of all the people in Kelowna, I knew her sister Linda when she told me her last name?

I had recently joined a neighbourhood Bible Study in Lakeview Heights and her sister, Linda was also a member of the group. Erica promptly told me she didn't often come to these meetings as she lived in Lloydminster on the border of Alberta and Saskatchewan. Now it all added up! Lloydminster was only a twenty minute drive from where my sister Hazel lived in Lashburn.

Had God orchestrated this situation? I believed so! And I shared Hazel's situation with Erica, who was not a stranger any longer, but now a friend and sister in Christ. Erica listened while I spoke and then told me she felt God wanted to use her in bringing some encouragement to Hazel. And, perhaps even help her turn her life over to God. I was thrilled to hear her say that! It seemed natural then, to go forward together and ask the Aglow ladies to pray about all this.

The first day Erica went to see Hazel, she wrote me a letter afterwards about what happened. She said the welcome mat was definitely not out. However, Erica and I were in agreement, that she was not to give up, but to go another time. It seemed the Lord was not in a hurry to make any changes. And what could Erica and I do, but wait and pray for God's timing.

Eventually the day came, when Hazel reached the end of her rope, so to speak and in a state of desperation called the phone number Erica had given her, by then. The two of them eventually become close friends and in due course, Erica took my sister to a Women's Aglow meeting in Lloydminster. There, Hazel went forward and surrendered her life to the Lord. Was that the end of Hazel's problems? Certainly not! But from then on, Hazel had an inner strength and the Lord`s help to guide her and reassure her she was greatly loved and never alone.

And, just a short time later, Hazel was greatly blessed when her daughter Marie attended a Crusade meeting and accepted Christ as her Saviour and Lord. It was another family miracle from the hand of our loving God. And would there be more? Of course, as our God is a miracle working God and the events to follow about Ted`s life just verify that fact once more.

77. Ted

And now, the months were shifting by in the year of 1974 and though much had happened to me spiritually, Irene and Ted were unaware of any of it. I had tried to talk to them about God, with no success. I had even tried to turn Irene's interest away from her numerology to the Bible, but she said she'd read it and it didn't appeal to her.

In June for our 25th anniversary, Irene and Ted invited us to their place for a backyard BBQ. Some members of our family, as well as some of theirs, were visiting, so we all joined together and had a good time. We were greatly surprised with their gift of a silver tea service.

Then the year 1975 appeared on the calendars, and as summer turned into fall, Ted and some of his buddies began making plans to drive north to Canoe and remove his houseboat from the waters of Shuswap Lake. Ted asked Jim to join them, but Jim was busy setting up his new green-house. It had arrived boxed up in sheets of glass walls needing to be assembled. So, Ted and his friends went ahead to retrieve the houseboat without Jim. Little did anyone know their journey was destined to be a very disastrous one, at least for Ted?

The trip up there went as planned and Ted and his buddies removed the houseboat from Shuswap Lake. Then they anchored it securely on top of the boat trailer, high up in the air behind the truck they were driving. A party atmosphere had prevailed and continued now as they set out for home. Ted, and one of his pals, had chosen to ride inside the houseboat atop the trailer, as there wasn't room for more than three in the truck's cab.

The disastrous accident took place as they were heading homeward. Ted and his friend up in the houseboat realized the truck had pulled off the highway and stopped and for whatever reason, Ted opened the door of the houseboat and stepped out. He fell from the great height of the elevated houseboat and injured his head on the way down and as he landed on the pavement below. It was a real significant fall.

Surprisingly though, Ted did not pass out, and only received a cut above his eye, which was bleeding. His friends patched him up and insisted he ride the remainder of the way back in the front seat of the truck. The driver later admitted Ted had acted peculiar during the drive home, grabbing at the steering-wheel at times. Even so, when they reached Ted's house in Rutland, Ted was let out at the door and his friends drove away.

Unfortunately, Irene was not at home, having flown over to visit their son David, now living in Calgary. Upon entering the empty house, it seemed Ted had tried to go down the stairs leading to the basement and fallen, collapsing unconscious at the bottom. He lay there on the cement floor until the next day, when a curious neighbour noticed the side door of the house was open and went in to investigate.

Regrettably, Kelowna's only neurosurgeon was out of town that weekend and so Ted, still in an unconscious state, was taken by ambulance to the Kamloops Hospital for surgery on his brain. Irene had been notified and flew directly from Calgary to Kamloops, while Ted underwent a lengthy surgery. Ted came through the operation, but did not regain consciousness. The doctors, at this point, were very pessimistic about Ted's recovery.

Irene contacted us by phone. She was very upset telling us about Ted's awful accident and we immediately drove to Kamloops to be with her. I was a Christian of eighteen months at that time, and my Bible went everywhere with me. So as we drove, I had it open on my lap and was reading the list of Beatitudes in the fifth chapter of Matthew's Gospel. The very first Beatitude seemed to stand out to me and I read it out loud to Jim as he drove. "Blessed are those who know they are spiritually poor for the Kingdom of heaven belongs to them." Would this verse be helpful to Irene? We didn't know, but I wrote the reference down anyway and asked Jim to remind me to give it to Irene. Then we prayed for both Irene and Ted.

When we arrived in Kamloops, we found Irene in very bad shape, physically and emotionally. She was visibly shaking from head to foot and crying incessantly. We tried our best to comfort her and give her hope about Ted, but nothing we said helped to calm her down. She was in a terrible state. We were glad she was staying with her daughter Debbie and her husband and would not be by herself.

We joined them in going to visit Ted, even though each time we found him in the same unconscious condition and not improving. We still prayed for him each time. Soon it was time for us to leave and return to Kelowna, as Jim had his job to attend to. We said our goodbyes to Irene and were heading for our car, when I recalled the Beatitude scripture. Jim took the Bible reference back and gave it to her, asking her to read it for some encouragement.

78. Irene

And the following, is how God works in circumstances to bring forth His goodness. Irene told us she couldn't sleep after we left. She got up and found a Bible in the middle of the night and those words of Jesus in the first Beatitude spoke to her deeply. She was overwhelmed with the realization that she was indeed one of the "poor in spirit" and needed a relationship with God. The next morning, a long-time friend of Irene's came by to see her and, in an effort to help, took her to a Bible study she belonged to. The teaching on that particular day was, of all things, on the Beatitudes in the Gospel of Matthew.

But this was no accident! I believe it was God, for sure. Irene shared with the group how she wasn't able to cope with the tragedy of her husband's accident and the group prayed for her. Then they explained the way of salvation to Irene and encouraged her to relinquish her life to the Lord so He could help her. And she did just that! Ted's condition didn't change, but Irene's did. She was born-again into the family of God.

When the surgeon in Kamloops transferred Ted to the Kelowna General Hospital, he was still in a coma with the same grave prognosis, but Irene was now dealing much better with the situation. And as well, she was feeling renewed in her newfound relationship with Jesus. She understood the Lord was with her and her trust and faith was now, not in what she could do, but what God could do. This helped her believe Ted would eventually get better. Once in Kelowna, Irene wasn't up to returning to the duplex she and Ted shared, so she moved into our extra bedroom, saying it would be temporary, but it did extend to four months.

During those months, I often accompanied Irene to the Kelowna hospital to look in on Ted and pray with him. It was difficult to see him, day after day, in that comatose condition, exhibiting no signs of regaining a life of any kind. His appearance was dreadful as a large portion of his skull bone had been removed during his brain surgery and there was a huge hole that sunk deep in the side of his head, covered only by skin. Sometimes his unseeing eyes opened and one eye stared at the ceiling and the other looked straight ahead. I recall Chris coming to visit Ted at this time and saying it was just too difficult to see her Uncle like that, so she couldn't come back.

We began to wonder if Ted's situation would ever change, but unbeknownst to us, God had a plan which was slowly being working out. Looking back, it seems a type of spiritual housecleaning was in order first for Irene. Remember her involvement in the things of the occult, numerology, tarot cards and horoscope readings? I didn't know much about such devilish stuff, but God's own Spirit convinced Irene of her former misplaced passion. It was through the pages of the Bennett books I lent her, that her eyes were opened and she returned to their duplex and destroyed everything there of an occult nature. She was obedient to what she felt God was leading her to do and after that, Irene experienced yet another change. She was filled with God's Holy Spirit.

79. Healing

We had travelled to Vancouver to pay Granny a visit because of her deteriorating health, and when Jim and I arrived back home again, we found Irene very excited about her new spiritual in-filling and as well, she had great news to tell us about Ted. He was beginning to recover! We wondered, could it really be happening at last?

I joined Irene the next day when she went to see Ted and indeed, it was true. Ted was sitting up in bed, his familiar crooked smile on his face and looking a great deal better than he had up until now. So from then on, Irene and I began making routine visits to Ted's bedside and praying over him to be healed and to someday talk again. Time passed by slowly until one day, after our prayer, Ted began to whisper. At first his voice was almost inaudible, but as it gained intensity we heard him asking for a pencil. Irene quickly found him one and fitted it between his fingers and gave him some paper to write on.

With confidence, Ted began to write at a rapid rate of speed across the paper. Irene and I stared at each other in disbelief! What was he writing? When he stopped, we realized he hadn't been writing words at all but a series of symbols and weird shaped markings in a straight line across the paper. We couldn't make heads or tails of it. We were disappointed when we couldn't decipher his message and decided to call it a day and go home. The next day when Irene finished her four hour shift at Sears, she went to the hospital again to see Ted. She arrived early before visiting hours were in effect and took a seat in the hospital lobby, the customary place she waited.

Sitting there, Irene noticed a King James Version of the Bible on the table beside her which was placed there by the Gideon Society. She opened it up at the beginning and on one of the first pages, there was a scripture written in English as well as several other languages. One of them was Aramaic, the language Jesus spoke when he walked this earth.

The Bible scripture was from the Book of John, the 3rd chapter, verse 16, where Jesus says, "God so loved the world that He gave His one and only Son, that whoever believes in Him shall not perish, but have eternal life." The Aramaic letters she saw written there looked familiar. They seemed similar to the markings Ted had written on the paper that she'd given him the day before. Could it be that Ted had written in an ancient dialect? Only God knows!

And it was shortly after that, when Ted miraculously started to speak in a clearer voice. He told Irene and I, or anyone who would listen, how the Lord had come and sat on his bed and talked to him when he was in the coma. We had to admit this new 'raised-up' Ted not only knew about the Lord, but seemed to have a close connection with Him. There was no way of discovering whether what Ted claimed was true or not, but as the old saying goes, 'the proof is in the pudding.'

And indeed, from that time on, Ted talked freely about his friend Jesus and made every effort to introduce Him to as many other people as he could. I also might add, when Chris came to see Ted again after he could talk, Ted remarked on the long time it had been since her last visit. Somehow, he knew Chris had visited him when he was in that coma! Whatever else was revealed to him in that state, God alone knows?

Ted was released from the hospital when he was capable of looking after himself, yet physically, he never fully recovered from the ordeal of the devastating brain surgery. That's not to say he didn't enjoy a happy life. Irene continued working part-time at Sears and Ted had the company of their little dog, a dachshund, with him at home. Going out walking for exercise, Ted had all kinds of adventures to share when Irene returned after work. If perchance Ted crossed paths with the Jehovah Witnesses in the neighbourhood, he would boldly tell them about Jesus, his Lord and Saviour, so who is to say that wasn't his ministry.

Around this time, our Church of St. Georges held a walkathon to raise money for the expansion of our church building. And it wasn't an easy feat to accomplish the walkathon either. The route extended along the Westside Road out to Camp Owaissi, approximately a fifteen kilometers distance. And who should register to do this walk but Ted! He was sincere about getting sponsors, but by the looks of him, none of us thought he'd be able to do it. Understand that Ted wasn't well-coordinated after his accident and tended to weave when he walked and was even sometimes mistakenly called a 'drunk.' Ted, of course, would pointblank deny this remark and loudly proclaim, "I don't drink and I don't smoke and I go to church on Sundays." And all of those things were true.

A new wheelchair-ramp was built onto the front of St. George's Church to accommodate Ted and two of his friends who came from Cottonwoods Care Center every Sunday morning in Ted's latter days. And as always, retaining his good sense of humour, Ted referred to the three of them as the 'three Musketeers.' When it came time to give the new wheelchair ramp a name, Ted was quick to reply, "Call it the Sinner's Ramp!" He was a believer who understood he was a forgiven sinner. Yes, Ted was well-known and loved by the whole congregation.

Chris holding Tania.

80. Family Changes and The Sermon

In the fall of 1974, Chris entered Okanagan College to work towards a diploma in Bookkeeping and Dan departed for Vancouver to begin his studies at UBC for a Metallurgical Engineering Degree. In that same year, three days after Christmas, our second little granddaughter Tania was born in Calgary. And I was privileged to travel there and care for Trish who was now two years old, while Leslie was in the hospital for a week.

And, when our Tania was just a few weeks old, Fitzroy suggested doing a service of Thanksgiving for Childbirth out of the prayer book, for Leslie and her new born baby. None of us had ever witnessed this service before, but it turned out to be very beautiful. In the ceremony Leslie knelt at the altar rail holding Tania in her arms, as Fitzroy covered them with his floor-length cape and pronounced multiple blessings over them. Then, our dramatic Priest led us in his rich, melodious voice in the old, familiar hymn *Amazing Grace*. We all joined in.

It was a few months later, on Good Friday of 1975, little Tania was baptized and her Auntie Chris was thrilled to be Godmother. Again, the service was awe-inspiring as Fitzroy dramatically lifted our tiny grand-daughter high in the air towards the large Cross behind the altar and offered her up to God.

Back at home in Kelowna, I was experiencing my own everyday mir-acles. For instance, I'd never dreamed I'd ever be speaking from a church pulpit on a Sunday morning, but that is what God's plan for my life al-lowed me to do in that year of 1975. Our priest at St George's church, Ray Bray, phoned me one morning and asked if he could come and have lunch with me, as he had something to ask me. And so he came, and after our lunch of a soup and sandwich I grew a bit nervous, wanting Ray to get on with the task he had come to do.

It was then he told me he'd been keeping an eye on me ever since he understood something of a spiritual nature happened to me. I was shocked to hear that, but he went on to say that he thought it was now time for me to share my testimony of that experience with the congrega-tion. He asked if together we could plan a Sunday for me to do that. Now it was my turn to ask a question. "Don't you want me to share with you what I'm going to say?"

Ray promptly answered, "No, I trust that what you say will be the truth." Wow, such faith he had in me!

We agreed on the Sunday I would speak in place of Ray's sermon and our lunchtime was over and Ray was away to another appointment. I was thrilled to have this new opportunity to share, of course. But, must it be to the entire church congregation? Ray had responded to that ques-tion as well during our talk together. In his practical no-nonsense way, he said, "If they have difficulty with what you say, it is not your problem, it is theirs!"

The Sunday morning of my sermon arrived, and I was ready with prepared notes to keep me on track. The church service unfolded at its usual pace until the sermon time arrived. At that point Ray introduced me, by coming down where I was sitting with Jim in the front pew and escorting me up the few stairs into the pulpit.

Looking out over the church people gathered, I was amazed at how many people were crowded into the pews. I hadn't known what to expect, but it was full to overflowing! The previous week Ray had an-nounced to the parishioners I would be sharing my spiritual experience on the following Sunday morning. The thought did occur to me at the time, they might all stay home and sleep in. Yet, that didn't appear to be what happened.

I didn't exactly feel comfortable in the pulpit, but I felt this opportunity had been given to me by God, so I plunged right into my talk. I explained how I had searched for years to find an inner peace and fulfillment, but always ended up feeling empty and without purpose. I was aware there must be more to faith than I had experienced. I told how I'd tried to fill the emptiness inside me with new knowledge and fresh skills learned, but couldn't find satisfaction there either.

Next, I shared about moving and leaving part of my family behind, which left me with the experience of being inwardly heartbroken. Finally I got to the part about discovering the Reverend Dennis Bennett's books and how they brought a new reality of God and His Holy Spirit into my life. Did I discern some raised eyebrows at this point? I didn't care. I held absolutely nothing back, describing my encounter with the Lord in detail and daring to hope it would help those whose faith had not yet come alive.

I explained in plain words the anointing I received from Jesus and the Baptism of the Holy Spirit. And about the blessing of speaking in a language I hadn't learned, but which I felt glorified God. I could see every upturned face from my position in the pulpit and they seemed to be intently following my story. My twenty minutes were almost up, so I ended my story on time, wanting to be obedient to what Ray had asked of me.

Afterwards, only one lady asked to borrow the Bennett books, whereas the others only shook Jim's hand and congratulated him on having such a fine wife. What did they mean? For being brave enough to speak about what God had done in my life? Perhaps! I tried not to feel disappointed and concentrated on what Ray had so wisely told me. What they did with my testimony was up to them, it wasn't my problem.

81. Huntley Street

In those early years of faith, I became a big fan of *100 Huntley Street*, which was, and still is, a Christian television program, shown daily right across Canada. I even volunteered to pray and council with anyone of an Anglican background that phoned into the Kelowna station. I wanted to be used by God and I met some interesting people that way. I desperately wanted to continue to grow spiritually and *100 Huntley Street* and Women's Aglow had many knowledgeable speakers that imparted their experience and wisdom to us.

I also got involved in my church and became a teacher of a Sunday school class. They were busy years, but I saw my involvement as doing God's work and looked to Him to give me strength to do it. And I must say He did.

I do so well remember a special event that happened in 1976 when David Mainse, the founder and host/director of *100 Huntley Street* came to Kelowna with his television show. Irene had been asked to be a guest and to share about how God had worked the miracle of Ted's conversion while in a coma. I had gone to the studio early that morning with Irene, and was sitting in the first row of the audience near the cameras. I had a ringside seat when the cameras began to roll for the live interview with Irene. It was very exciting!

Then, unexpectedly something happened that drew me into the scene in front of me. David Mainse had asked Irene to share about what happened to her husband Ted, and she did. Then he inquired, if she was praying for a miracle for her husband during that time? Irene answered by saying, "My sister-in-law and I prayed together all the time."

At that response, David asked Irene if her sister-in-law was in the audience. Irene nodded yes! Then, turning his face towards us in the audience, David called out, "Come over here, sister-in-law!" I didn't want to go in front of the cameras, but I was trapped and I had no way out, so I got to my feet and just a few steps took me into range of the cameras.

I sensed David was going to ask me a question and suddenly I felt camera-shy and started to draw back. But just then, David reached out and took hold of my hand. It was a perfectly normal thing for him to do, but the instant his hand clasped mine, I felt a powerful current of fiery electricity shoot from his hand into mine. Then that liquid fire washed up and down my entire body, paralyzing me from head to foot and rendering me speechless.

I heard David asking me what my name was, but I was unable to respond. I just stood there frozen to the spot. I tried to open my mouth, but all I could do was stammer helplessly. The fire inside me caused my mouth to go dry and I felt weak, not only in my knees, but all over. David asked my name again, but I was a prisoner with no voice and couldn't answer him. Smiling at me then, he said the first thing that came to his mind, "It's alright," he said, "Thank you for praying anyway," and he let go of my hand. What a relief!

I immediately felt normal again and I stumbled back to my seat. I knew it wasn't electricity that I'd felt, but it was God's Holy Spirit coursing through David's body and connecting with the Holy Spirit in me. It was my one and only experience of that type and it left me with the definite impression that David Mainse was indeed a Man of God, no doubt about it. The only other explanation I can offer, is when Jesus says in scripture that He has risen from the dead and is alive, living by His Holy Spirit in us, He was not kidding!

82. Forgiveness

As time passed by, I was steadily growing spiritually little by little, on my pathway of faith. I studied the Bible daily because I loved God's Word and I formed a Prayer Group at St. George's church. I also followed the *100 Huntley Street* Christian program on television and attended the monthly Aglow meetings, where the speakers were gifted with wisdom on many subjects of Biblical truths.

I particularly recall the teaching on inner-healing at one particular Aglow meeting and about the importance of forgiveness. It helped me to gain new insight and forgive a lot of people.

First on my list to forgive was my mother, for her inability to show me love and to care for me as a mother should; next was my Dad for being an absent father when I was a child growing up; and also my brother Bud, for being dishonest and undependable. And, under the speaker's wise council, I also came to the place of forgiveness for anyone else I could think of.

Then, quite suddenly, the name of Curtis loomed big in my mind. No, I told myself, not him! Certainly I couldn't be expected to forgive him! It was asking far too much! Curtis had taken advantage of my innocence as a child in so many ways, not to mention the horrible night of his attempted rape in the cabin. I considered that a despicable act, utterly unforgiveable.

However, the Aglow speaker, leading us through our inner-healing prayer, said that by not forgiving I was wounding myself and not my perpetrator. It was much like I was swallowing poison and hoping the other person would die. She emphasized further, to forgive would unload the weapon I was pointing at my offender and flush out the hatred in my own heart. At that point, she instructed us to close our eyes and let our minds go back to our own particular trauma scene, and ask the Lord to give us some new perspective on what happened there.

I visualized Jesus in the scene with me and he had His arms around me. I felt safe there as He told me how much He loved me and how I didn't deserve any of this happening to me. It wasn't my fault it took place. And, he wanted to remove any shame or blame I'd put on myself over it. Incredibly, Jesus was doing it now, as well as giving me freedom from the grip anger had on me. He told me this other person had chosen to cause this to happen, but now I could choose God's way to respond. And that was by forgiving him! And I only needed to be willing to do it!

And in that very moment I became willing! Inconceivable as it seems, I did want to be rid of all that bitterness and hatred I had stored up in my heart. By God's grace, I was enabled to forgive Curtis. After so many years of carrying around this animosity towards my brother-in-law, I was at last able to lay it down and to grant him forgiveness and be set free. For me it was a life giving moment.

83. Cursillo

The year 1976 was a significant year for Jim and me. It was then that the Anglican Bishop of our diocese invited both of us to become involved in a new church movement by the name of Cursillo. This weekend event originated in Spain and the word in Spanish is simply explained as a short-course in Christianity. For us, it meant Jim would go to Seattle to experience a men's Cursillo weekend and I would follow a month later, attending one for ladies. Why the Bishop chose Jim and me to do this, we didn't know, but perhaps he saw us as potential leaders for the movement he wanted to develop in our very own Diocese of Kootenay.

My initial Cursillo weekend as a candidate in Seattle was both a bitter and a sweet event for me. Looking back now, I realize I went into the weekend with a huge 'chip' on my shoulder. The 'chip' consisted of knowing I was already a Christian and doubting that the Leaders of the Cursillo could teach me anything exciting enough to compare with my own conversion experience. What a bad attitude! Even the opening night started out wrong for me, as the evening was designed for us, as candidates, to undergo a time of self-evaluation.

I felt I already knew myself, or at least I thought I did! I couldn't relate to the talk about the Prodigal Son and so I didn't gain much from the exercise. Instead I kept wondering why I'd even signed up for such a weekend. It was said that the weekend was an encounter with Christ, but it wasn't until Saturday that I finally shed my bad mindset and my spiritual sense came alive and I entered into the weekend experience.

As candidates, on Saturday we were invited to what was called the *Marriage Supper of the Lamb.* As we were led there by our team leaders, we entered a room which was ablaze with candles, revealing many tables set-up in the shape of a giant cross. When I took my place, I saw that the linen covered tables were laden with hundreds of candles and banks of fresh flowers, which had an intoxicating effect with their perfume. It was beautiful beyond compare! And I sensed at last, that it was a heaven-like atmosphere of holiness I was in.

We all sat waiting, as if momentarily the Lord Jesus Himself would be assuming the empty seat reserved for Him at the head of the cross of tables. At that moment I grasped the awesome realization of how important my faith in Christ was to me and I opened up my heart. The amazing love of Christ began to wash over me in wave after wave and I knew Christ was my hope of Glory, just as the Bible stated.

Music filled the air and for the first time since I'd arrived, I really joined in, singing the familiar hymns and inspirational songs with enthusiasm. A generous piece of bread was placed before everyone there and we were asked to share it with our sisters in Christ around us. My heart was overwhelmed with the love I could feel coming from those around me, as I shared my bread with them. I felt my tears on my face, but I let myself enjoy the enormous love of knowing I was part of a big Christian family. It was indeed a holy moment!

The remainder of the Cursillo weekend was a series of phenomenal happenings, one following after another until in the end, I knew without doubt, it had been one of my most remarkable spiritual encounters ever. I came away from my Cursillo weekend as a dedicated member of that movement, just as Jim did. And following that, we both worked as team leaders on many such weekends, both in Seattle and in our diocese, as well as Calgary. We wanted other people to have that same phenomenal Christian experience we'd had.

In due course, I would serve in the position of Rectora and Jim as Rector. That is, we took the leadership role of a Cursillo weekend, which was comprised of up to sixty people making up the team, as well as the many candidates. To this day, we are great enthusiasts of this special Christian movement.

84. Wedding Bells

It was in August of the year 1976 that the wedding of Chris and Dan took place in Westbank, on a bright sunny Saturday, the 21st day of August. It brought together our family members from Saskatchewan, Calgary and Vancouver, including Granny Rolfe who was now confined to a wheelchair.

St. George's Church was where the ceremony was held and I did my best to enhance its beauty by placing two huge bunches of our own homegrown gladiolas, in tall vases on either side of the altar. The Reverend Jim McCullam from St. Michael's church in Kelowna had been asked to officiate, as St. Georges was in the process of acquiring a new Priest.

Chris literally was glowing with happiness on her special day and no wonder! She was marrying the tall, handsome man of her dreams and we already loved Dan and thought of him as a son. I recall a very vivid memory at the very beginning of their wedding service, when Dan and his best man, Ed Skutshek, walked up the aisle to the front of the church. This was a signal the wedding ceremony was about to begin and Ted, seated in the front pew, turned and called out loudly, "Welcome to the family, Dan."

A chuckle rippled through the wedding crowd in response to Ted's spontaneous greeting. We all loved Ted and were quite familiar with his impromptu behavior. Ted`s nature was to be a friendly individual and that part had never changed.

Then, it was all silent again and we all sat waiting for the moment when the bride would appear and proceed down the aisle on the arm of her Dad, denoting the wedding had now truly begun. Chris looked so lovely in her elegant high-necked wedding-gown of white silk and carrying a bouquet of her favorite flowers, white daisies. Her cousin, Marie, and her best friend, Kirsti, were her two attendants. They were in long sheer-flowered dresses and carried white daisy bouquets, as well. Trish,

Chris & Dan`s Wedding.

the little flower girl looked adorable in her long turquoise blue dress, carrying a basket of flowers.

The order of service went forward exactly as planned, with the vows spoken by Chris and Dan to each other and everything running smoothly through to the very end. During the signing of the register, the Beatle's song, *Here, There and Everywhere* played in the background and then the proclamation of Dan and Chris as husband and wife and their kiss ended the ceremony. Their smiles said it all as they walked back up the aisle and photos were taken outside the church as well as on the back lawn of our Skyline Road home.

The wedding reception with dinner and dance was held at the Royal Ann Hotel in downtown Kelowna with all the family and friends mixing together and enjoying each other's company. And as usually happens, after dinner many speeches were given, followed by a piece of wedding cake distributed to each guest personally by the bride and groom. I had baked the traditional three-layered wedding cake from my own fruitcake recipe and a bakery had beautifully decorated it. A dance finished out the evening with many musical favorites of both current times and of days long past. Jim had happily supplied a few tunes from his collection of old jazz records. It was a day of perfection in every way.

The atmosphere was joyful as the Ashman clan and Rolfe clan became one big family that day. It seemed to me like God had worked it all out flawlessly, bringing us to Kelowna just at the right time so that Chris and Dan could meet and fall in love and now get married. And I sensed, even then, it was going to be a marriage of longevity, lasting a lifetime.

Dan, at that point in time, was a student in his second year at U.B.C. working towards his degree in Metallurgical Engineering and Chris would now be joining him to live and work in Vancouver. Luckily she was able to transfer with her job at Scotiabank and she easily moved into a new life in the big city. Chris going away would cause Jim and I to become 'empty-nesters' and we certainly were going to miss having her around the house.

85. My Final Visit with My Mother

Later that same year of 1976, my mother, in a very ill condition, was transported to St. Paul's hospital by ambulance from that hotel where she still lived. I was called by the hospital staff to come once they discovered she had a daughter in Kelowna. Of course, I went immediately! They told me she only had a matter of days to live, which truly shocked me. She had always reassured me on the phone that she was fine, but now I saw the weak and frail condition she was really in.

Despite this, she maintained her need for privacy. When I asked where Bud was she said she was sure he was fine. In other words, she didn't know where Bud was. He had moved away leaving Mother alone and didn't tell me. He made me so mad. How could he desert his own mother when she was so weak and sick? Then again, should I expect him to be different now? He'd never had any scruples or sense of doing right before. It seemed nothing ever changed with my brother.

I stayed with Chris and Dan in their Kitsilano apartment and used the bus to get back and forth to the hospital to visit Mother. On one particular morning, I was praying for Mother before leaving to catch the bus and I felt God asking me a question. Would I be willing to share with my mother the great love that He had for her? I drew courage from the fact that she had been raised by a Godly mother and attended church at one time. Still I wanted to be sure this was not out of my own imagination. I prayed and said yes to God, but then made a request of Him. Would He confirm to me, in some way, that I was hearing His voice correctly? Just how He would do that, I left up to Him.

I walked to the bus and boarded it, carrying my purse and my Bible just as I usually did. I took a seat by the window about half-way down the aisle. At the next stop a young lady got on the bus and bypassed several other empty seats to sit in the one right next to me. I sat there holding my breath and remembering my prayer for a sign from God.

The young lady's first words to me were, "I'm a Bible believer myself."

I knew God had sent her and I quickly explained to her what my circumstances were. I asked if she would pray for my mother to be open to God's love that day and she immediately did. She said she felt God had engineered the circumstances of bringing us together.

At the hospital bus stop, we said goodbye and I got off. We hadn't even bothered to exchange names with each other, as somehow we knew we were like two ships passing in the night and wouldn't see each another again. Sounds dramatic, but that was what happened.

In the hospital, I hurried down the hall and found Mother where the nurses had propped her up in a chair. She was very weak, but smiling. Without hesitation I reached out and placed my hand on her shoulder and asked, "Mother, do you believe in God and His love for you?"

Her answer was quick. "Yes," she said, "at this point I have to believe."

My heart leapt for joy and I prayed with her, trusting her into God's mighty hands. The next day I noticed Mother appeared much more peaceful and at rest. Even the other lady who shared Mother's hospital room mentioned the change in her, which was obvious. Having peace in her heart made such a difference.

On the way out of the hospital I was told that the doctor who was assigned to my mother wanted to speak to me. I knew my mother had no doctor of her own and as far as I knew she'd never been to a doctor's office in her entire life. The drugstore was where my mother went for her medical advice.

This hospital doctor was waiting to see me in his office and he had a very stern look on his face. I was unprepared for what occurred during the next few minutes.

To my surprise, the doctor lashed out at me in angry words. "Why haven't you looked after your own mother?" he said first of all. And then next, he asked, "Did you not know the conditions that she was living under in that skid-row hotel?"

I did not answer.

Then his final statement, "That hotel had lice and there was evidence of it when the ambulance brought your mother here." His anger had caused his face to redden, but after a pause he drew a deep breath and I saw his rage beginning to fade away as he gained control of his emotions.

I stood there silent, completely understanding his fury as I had felt it many times myself and in even greater measure. And as for his finger-pointing at me, I already felt tremendously guilty, so his words were not able to penetrate very deep. Some questions of my own whirled in my head! Should I ask him if he was aware that some people absolutely chose the hell they wanted to live in? Didn't he know some people were determined to live only the way they wanted to, regardless of anyone else? And thirdly, wasn't it true, we can't force change on someone else, we can only change ourselves.

Arguments in my own defense tried to rise up, but were stuck in my throat as I stood there speechless. It was obvious it had helped this doctor to express his anger and I couldn't help but sympathize with his feelings of fury and helplessness. Hot tears swelled up behind my eyes, but I swallowed them back. This was not a time to cry! I reached out and took the black garbage bag he held out to me, explaining it contained the few items belonging to my mother. I turned and walked out of his office feeling inwardly down-trodden, but still it wasn't a time to cry. That would come later, alone on my pillow.

My mother died shortly after that and I did have tears, lots of them. Partly for the tragic heart-breaking way she had lived her life, but also for the great joy of knowing God redeems and makes all things new and that includes people. She was with Jesus now in a place of perfect peace where there is no more death or mourning or crying or pain. It tells us this in the final book of the Bible, Revelations chapter 21 verse 4. And with all my faith, I believe it to be so.

86. More Final Moments

After that time in Vancouver, death seemed to come knocking at our door more often, taking away people we loved. Just a year later, Hazel's husband Eddie died of cirrhosis of the liver, at the young age of fifty-three. Was it that God hadn't heard our prayers for him? No! God did miraculously heal Eddie once, but when he refused to turn away from alcohol, that healing was lost and the cirrhosis returned with a vengeance. Jim and I joined Hazel for Eddie's funeral in Lashburn and it was during the service that Hazel, in the midst of her feelings of loss and grief, experienced a supernatural touch from God. He reassured her of His everlasting love and that Eddie was in His eternal hands.

Our dear Granny Rolfe's departure from this earth occurred next, in 1979 and it was a great loss to all the family. Nonetheless, once Granny ended up in a Vancouver care facility, struggling with dementia and suffering additional strokes, we couldn't be sad. She knew where she was going and had peacefully prepared herself much earlier for the end of her life. She believed the Lord was with her always, often asking us to play her the hymns she enjoyed, calling them her 'Jesus music.' We lost her at the age of seventy-seven, but her legacy of love lives on in our hearts and lives. Yes indeed, all of us who were privileged to be part of her family.

And the next year, 1980 brought about the death of Tony, my Dad and with it a story I must tell. Dad no longer lived with us in Kelowna, having returned to his beloved Idaho about the time of our move from Calgary in 1973. My brother Floyd had made his home in Boise Idaho and so Dad relocated in that area.

Many times my brother Harold and his wife Glenys from Denver would meet Jim and I and Hazel in Idaho to visit with our Dad. We had some really wonderful times, but that was all before my life-changing spiritual experience and my mother's deathbed prayer in St. Paul's hospital. After those events happened, I wanted to go back and share it all with Dad while it was new and fresh. I prayed and asked the Lord to arrange an appropriate time to visit him.

It was not very long afterwards that we felt we should make the trip to Idaho and visit my Dad. He lived in a retirement care home in Nampa Idaho, on the outskirts of Boise and his health had deteriorated to being wheel-chair bound. But, despite his frailty, he cheerfully welcomed Jim and I, thanking us for travelling the great distance to see him. I had prayed to talk privately with my Dad and so when the opportunity arose, I got right to the heart of the matter with him.

I explained to him that the God of the Bible was real and I knew this to be a fact. The expression on Dad's face as he listened showed he was following what I said closely and wanted to hear more. And he had questions, too, as I explained about the details of my experience and so I answered them as honestly as I could. At the end of our time together, Dad asked me to pray for him, asking God to do for him what He had done for me. I happily obliged.

A week after our return to Kelowna, I received a letter from my Dad who enthusiastically stated he was now a member of God's family. Such wonderful news! Dad's letter told me that when Jim and I left Nampa he couldn't wait to know the God of the Bible, so he voiced his own simple prayer, asking the Lord to come into his heart and "become real to me just like You did for Marie." And wondrously, God faithfully answered him, granting my Dad the desire of his heart.

The letter went on to say that now Dad was busy telling everyone around him in his care home about the amazing gift of eternal life he had received. He said he was simply asking them if they wanted to meet his Lord and Saviour. I rejoiced with Dad in his new awareness and desire to evangelize. How amazing God is!

87. Life on a Farm & More Grandchildren

As our busy lives of ministry moved forward, Jim and I did have our share of family concerns, especially when Leslie and Stan's marriage broke up and they separated. We certainly tried to be there for Leslie in the difficult time of her becoming a single mom. But then, soon after the divorce came through there appeared someone by the name of Ralph in Leslie's life.

They married in 1980 and moved a short distance east of Calgary a year later, to a small acreage near Langdon. It was a great change for Leslie and her young girls. Leslie enjoyed the country lifestyle right away and had an abundance of energy for the work required. There was a cow and goats to milk, as well as pigs to feed and a flock of chickens to gather eggs from. Turkeys and chickens were raised over the summer, along with a large garden which provided fresh vegetables for their family. A horse was later purchased for the girls to ride. Residing on a hobby-farm was indeed a great adventure, though lots of work too!

Meanwhile back in B.C, Chris and Dan had now left Vancouver and moved to Trail, in the West Kootenay area. Dan had graduated from U.B.C. and accepted a position as an engineer at the Cominco smelter and there was a job for Chris in the purchasing department as well. They both loved the fact that Trail was a small, friendly town after living in the ever expanding city of Vancouver. We were also happy to have them just four hours away, making it possible to see them often.

It was astounding how quickly those next years in the 1980's went by. The year of 1981 was a significant year! It was with great excitement, Chris and Dan announced they were pregnant and on December 10th of that same year, little Timothy James, our first grandson, was born. He was given the middle name of James, after his Grandpa Jim, which was very pleasing to us. Little Timmy was a high-spirited and healthy little boy, who won all our hearts with his big eyes and mischievous smile.

Chris and Timmy.

Just a year later, in October of 1982 in Langdon, Colin Christopher was born to Leslie and Ralph, giving Trish and Tania a little brother and us a second grandson. Colin was a real joy. He was a contented baby, as his sisters had been before him. Trish and Tania welcomed their new brother with enthusiasm, proudly wearing their matching yellow T-shirts given them by the hospital which spelled out "New babies are fun, we have one."

It wasn't long before there was good news from Chris and Dan once again. Another baby was on the way and on the 31st day of March, 1984, our third grandson, Bradley Daniel, was born. He was such a happy, laid-back baby with nothing but smiles for everyone around him. His birth gave us a total of five grandchildren to love and enjoy. Truly, each one is a unique gift from God.

Leslie and Colin.

Chris and Bradley.

88. My Baptism

A prayer I had persistently prayed over the span of eight years was answered. Our Bishop consented to my request to be baptized in Okanagan Lake. I had desired water baptism since my conversion in 1974 as my only baptism had been in the Mormon Temple. Now, in 1982, the Bishop was not only giving his approval of my baptism by immersion, but was saying he would baptize me himself! What a wondrous answer to my prayer!

A lake baptism was unheard of in the realm of Anglicanism and would actually be a first, and last, in our Diocese of Kootenay, so far as I am aware. Again I was reminded afresh how dependable God is when we ask and leave the details up to Him. I had not wanted the Anglican tradition of sprinkling water over my head for the reason that my Temple baptism had been by immersion and I wanted as much for my Christian baptism. After all, baptism symbolized 'an outward and visible sign of an inward invisible grace.' And I was willing to wait on God's timing for this experience.

The scene of my baptism was much the same as the one in Mark's gospel where it describes the baptism of Jesus in the Jordan River. The water of Okanagan Lake on that twelfth day of September, 1982, was cool after storm clouds had cleared away, revealing patches of blue in the sky. The Bishop led the way into the water of the lake and I followed, with our priest from St. Georges, John, after me.

We were all in white robes and we slowly made our way out through the water until it was well past the level of my waist. We were directly off the shore of the Anglican Church camp and witnessing my baptism was a cluster of my friends on the sandy beach. They were singing praise songs to God, accompanied by their guitars and their voices rang out over the water to me. I felt so full of joy over the way it was all unfolding, moment by moment.

My baptism in lake Okanagan.

My friends were my witnesses, as the Bishop plunged me underneath the water of the lake, just once, in the name of the Father, Son and Holy Spirit, signifying that my baptism by immersion was now over and accomplished. And, at that exact moment, the sun burst forth from behind a stray cloud and gloriously lit up the scene with brilliant light. It seemed to me as if God was smiling down on me and was well pleased with my baptism.

Later in the afternoon, having changed into an appropriate white dress, I joined my crowd of well-wishers in the camp's outdoor chapel. There I was confirmed by the Bishop into the traditional Anglican Church. Such a magnificent day I was experiencing. And I found I was feeling like a true Bride of Christ, which the Word of God tells us we are all called to be. Love surrounded me in the person of my devoted husband, Jim, a sincere group of friends and the Holy Spirit of God, so tangible I felt I had sprouted wings and could fly.

89. A.F.P. and Church Travel

It was only a matter of weeks following my baptism and confirmation that the Bishop called me into his office and asked me a very personal question. "Are you a praying person, Marie?" When I answered in the positive he explained that he wanted to appoint me as the Diocesan Representative of the Anglican Fellowship of Prayer (AFP). It was an international church movement that he wanted to establish in our Diocese of Kootenay. The diocese itself was huge, including the Okanagan, the East and West Kootenay areas, south to the U.S. border, west to Princeton, and east to Alberta – an area covering some 83,000 square miles.

As the A.F.P. leader, I was to form a team and travel throughout the extensive diocese doing workshops on prayer at any Anglican Church that invited me to come. Wow! What an opportunity! I was very happy to be asked, but not totally surprised to be singled out for such a position. You see, during those eight long years of waiting to be baptized, I'd prayed for God to give me a new ministry following my baptism. In the Gospels of the Bible, I'd clearly seen how Jesus set about doing His ministry after His baptism, so that was my desire also. So now, there was no way I could refuse the Bishop's request. It was an answered prayer. I gave him my yes!

As the leader of this new prayer movement, I formed a team and included a priest, as the Bishop had also asked me to do. My team consisted of Jim and our good friends, Rena and Martin and a newly appointed priest by the name of Paul. Then I began advertising the availability of the workshops to the many parishes of the diocese.

I'd met Paul at a Diocesan Synod Conference in Penticton when he was the incumbent at the East Kootenay Church at Fernie B.C. I found him to be a very friendly person. He shared with me at that time, how he was not happy serving at the Anglican Church there and asked me for a prayer request. Would I pray for him and his wife and family to be appointed to a church in Kelowna? He explained they were from India originally and that was why they didn't like the long, cold winters in their present town.

During the weeks that followed, I did remember Paul's request and prayed, but even so, I was surprised when the Bishop appointed Paul to the Parish of St. Aiden's in Rutland, a suburb of Kelowna. From then on, it was like I was a 'saint' in Paul's eyes. Someone that could get all my prayers answered! So, naturally he was overjoyed to be part of my A.F.P. team when I asked him to join us. I was actually happy to choose Paul because of his vibrant faith, which I had spotted in our first meeting at Synod.

And Paul didn't let me down either! He was a master at always giving inspiring talks at our workshop seminars and both he and his wife Anna became close friends of Jim and I. In fact, they treated us like spiritual Godparents. Later on when Paul's son of six years of age became seriously ill, Paul called me to pray. And when his son Emmanuel recovered right away, Paul gave all the credit to my prayers. In fact, Paul told his son I had saved his life! That was downright embarrassing!

So with excitement, our team started reaching out to other Anglican parishes with our teaching workshops. Our traveling to reach the other churches was a lot of fun, as the five of us were packed into one car, with Jim as our responsible driver. There was laughter all the way. We took turns speaking at the prayer workshops and it was challenging at times, but enjoyable. We had the freedom to witness the message of the Gospel from our own personal lives and we all did so. I felt spiritually confident in carrying out this mandate, as the Lord had prepared me well with so many experiences in other Christian ministries. I enjoyed every opportunity God provided and an Old Testament scripture from Jeremiah 29:11 personally encouraged me many times. "For I know the plans I have for you, declares the Lord, plans to prosper you and not harm you; plans to give you hope and a future."

Our lives back then, were fulfilling and overflowed with busyness as Jim and I celebrated many other good things. We went to the very first Anglican Renewal West Conference held in Saskatoon with Hazel and Irene, as well as hundreds of other Anglicans from the four western provinces. How we enjoyed it when the audience began singing-in-tongues beautifully. Another thing on my agenda was attended my first AFP International Conference in Denver, Colorado. That was a miracle in itself, as I'd never travelled alone anywhere before. But, in the unfolding of events, I learned I was never alone, which basically I knew beforehand. Jim and I also went to the Montreal AFP Conference with our dear friends Rena and Martin and afterwards, spent a holiday sightseeing in Ottawa and the Niagara Falls area. Such a long list, where did we get the energy for it all?

90. Ordination

There was still so much ahead in life to celebrate. And a great and wonderful event was ready to take place on April the 25th in the year 1986. Jim was ordained as a Deacon in the Anglican Church by the Bishop of Kootenay. He had been studying under a mentor for three years and completed a three year theological course by extension from the University of Tennessee. The ordination took place at the Anglican Cathedral in Nelson, B.C. and our two daughters and many other members of our family, as well as friends, joined us there to celebrate this momentous occasion. Jim was so happy to be ordained into a life of serving the church and we were very proud of this pivotal moment in his life.

Leslie, Jim, me and Chris.

Jim's ordination fulfilled his mother's aspirations for him when he was a young boy. She had hoped he would become a banker or an ordained clergy and Jim fulfilled both callings, although she didn't live to see his latter accomplishment. Jim came to be the Deacon in our own parish and he enjoyed serving the people of St. Georges alongside our priest and dear friend, John and his wife Evelyn. The pair of them, James and John were nicknamed 'The Sons of Thunder,' an expression used in the Gospels referring to our Lord's two apostles with the same names. Our own two apostles shared the joy of serving together and seeing it transformed by God's mighty love.

As my busy life extended now into my sixties, I was still capable of fulfilling all I had taken on to do in my very active life. In fact, I managed to find the energy to join yet one more group, along with Jim, when we were asked to be members. This group of about twelve people was meeting together over their concern about how the Anglican Church of

Our family, back row: Chris, Tania, Trish.
Middle row: Leslie, Irene, Hazel.
Bottom row: Jim, Dan and me.

Canada was drifting away from its roots. God brought a leader into our prayer group who was a Greek New Testament christian, mature in his faith. Like any group that spends time together in prayer, we experienced the joy of God's presence and were committed to putting all of our concerns into His hands.

At this point in time, while we waited for answers to our prayers, Jim and I turned our focus more fully towards doing our AFP prayer workshops. We were pleased that about ten parishes in the Diocese invited our team to come and present our weekend workshop at their church, and we were happy to go. Our team worked well together and we felt our relationship with the Lord Jesus Christ was refreshed each time we were called upon to present the workshop.

91. Our 40ᵗʰ Anniversary and Trip of a Lifetime

Our celebration of forty years of marriage came up in June 1989 and Chris and Dan offered to host the family reunion at their home in Trail, in the Kootenay's. It turned out to be a great weekend of laughter and catching up with family members. Many of whom had travelled from the three western provinces and in addition, from the United States. My brother Floyd came from Boise as well as Harold and Glenys, who had the greatest distances to travel, coming from Colorado. It all turned

Jim and I.

Our family at our 40th Anniversary.

out to be an extra special time for the entire family who rarely got to gather altogether.

During our reunion, we had great fun playing games and the one we all played, no matter our age, was bocci ball. We reveled in endless games of this Italian game, tossing the ball on the well-clipped lawns and getting much needed exercise. And as a highlight of the weekend, all of us were given a personal 'walk through' tour of the Cominco smelter by Dan himself. He had been employed there at this point, for eleven years and incidentally, would continue to work for Cominco, eventually rising to a top-level management position and retiring at the young age of fifty-seven. A successful, long career to be applauded!

In the following year of 1990, Jim and I accomplished a long-time dream of ours to see Canada from coast to coast. We set out on a three month long car trip across our wonderful country, taking Hazel part of the way with us. First, we drove to Trail for a visit with Chris, Dan and their two boys. Tim was now nine and Brad, seven. We then drove on to Calgary and had a visit with Leslie, her daughter's Trish, eighteen and Tania, sixteen and Colin, who was now eight. Leslie and Ralph were still living on their hobby farm near Langdon.

Then began our trip east across the flat prairies without any further stopovers. The three of us did enjoy a tour of a Mennonite settlement south of Winnipeg and then travelled on to see the famous Dionne quintuplet's home in Steinbeck. As planned, we stopped overnight with friends in North Bay, Ontario.

We drove through Quebec where we saw a church altar made of real gold in one of the small towns. I remember we ate lunch in a restaurant where the waitress apologized to us about her English not being very good. Finally, we covered the distance left to reach the city of Halifax. This was where we would leave Hazel, as her daughter Marie and husband David lived there with their three young children, Tara, Steven and Cheryl. We had a great time seeing Halifax and even whisked the three youngsters away for a day's outing to visit Citadel Hill, the historic fort perched high on a hill overlooking the city. We had fun! From there, Jim and I continued on, by ourselves, leaving Hazel to enjoy a blessed time of six weeks with her precious family.

Jim and I drove through the Maritime Provinces and most everything we saw were highlights we will remember always. For instance, we visited Nova Scotia, where we took great delight in their Scottish music and talented clog-dancers. We saw the Bay of Fundy and witnessed a mind-boggling tidal bore for the first time in our lives.

After that, we journeyed to Prince Edward Island across the water by ferry as there was no bridge then, and enjoyed the unique red soil of the island, visiting the 'imaginary' house of the fictional character, Anne of Green Gables. We also saw the author, Lucy Maude Montgomery's, birthplace. We enjoyed driving all over Prince Edward Island and exploring Charlottetown, their amazing capitol city.

Newfoundland was our next stop and we reached it by a short ferry boat ride and instantly, it became our favorite province, mostly due to its picturesque scenery and the exceptionally friendly people we met there. In the capital city of St. John's, the owner of the B & B where we stayed was called 'The Mrs.' and she was one of those friendly people. She had an accent like the familiar Lancashire vernacular that Jim's parents had spoken in England. A most likable lady! We told her we planned to visit Clyde Wells, their premier, who was popular right across Canada at that time.

Our Mrs. was so thrilled for us and then told me I mustn't ever wash my hands after shaking hands with their premier. I laughed, but I think she actually meant it! The dear woman was a resident of St. John's, the

Jim and I meeting the Premier.

capital city and yet had never met the premier in person. She seemed to idolize him.

We drove to his office in the St. John's downtown and were given an appointment the following day when he would meet with us. It was the time of the Meech Lake Accord and Clyde Wells was admired, far and wide, for making his public stand against the Accord. Jim and I had a card of encouragement signed by our friends at St. George's Church and we were happy to have an opportunity to present it to him.

When we arrived at our appointed time to meet this famous politician, he came in and graciously shook us by the hand. We were impressed as he chatted with us informally and freely, offering his best wishes to our friends back in Westbank who had sent him their support. He said he knew B.C. well and certainly thought it was a beautiful province. I was utterly thrilled to meet and talk with him as he turned out to be a captivating and humble man.

All too quickly the time arrived to return to the 'mainland', as the people of Newfoundland called the rest of Canada. We learned it would be a three hour voyage on a huge ferry and that we would actually be losing sight of land in the Atlantic Ocean on our return passage. There was no short sailings like the one we'd come over on. This extended crossing made me very uneasy, but what was I to do about it? To calm my nerves, I prayed, asking the Lord to calm the waters even as the engines of the ferry were starting up in readiness to depart.

And, low and behold, the entire trip back was enjoyable with wonderfully flat and level water to sail on all the way. 'Smooth as glass,' was how the more experienced sailing people described it. Even so, I was seriously relieved when the sailing part was over, especially when we were told that only a week before, our very same ferry had experienced high thrashing winds causing all aboard to be violently seasick before reaching port. All I could say was hooray for prayer and expressed my thank-fulness to the One who is known to have walked on water. My prayers and the prayers of others I'm sure had saved us from a similar disaster.

We drove back through Nova Scotia again and returned to Halifax to pick up Hazel, bringing her delightful visit with family to an end. With her once more in the backseat of our car we crossed the border into the United States and headed west. Our travels led us through many experiences, such as some of the outstanding ones I remember and want to share with you.

We became what they called in that area, 'leaf-peepers,' meaning people reveling in the awe-inspiring sight of the autumn coloured leaves in the New England states; we got the chance to get acquainted with my ninety year old Uncle Nick, my Dad's brother, and several cousins for the first time in Kankakee, Illinois; we saw Iowa's extensive corn fields that were just as the song says, 'As high as an elephant's eye'; we encountered an overnight snowstorm at Mount Rushmore that made all the Presidents carved on the mountainside appear to be crying as the melting snow ran down their stone faces like tears. These are only a few of the highlights of our trip of a lifetime, crossing our splendid country of Canada and returning through the northern states of America, the beautiful.

When we reached Vancouver, our trip coast-to-coast was complete and we joined with twelve other members of our family in celebrating Grandpa Rolfe's ninety-fourth birthday. We were reminded again of the importance of family gatherings and the opportunity to create memories to help us all remember the past.

And on an added note, I brought back a bottle of water from the Atlantic Ocean and mixed it with an equal amount of water from the Pacific Ocean taken from English Bay. I then combined the waters of the two oceans in one bottle. Out of there I fashioned five small bottles of the two oceans mixed together and gave a bottle to each of our five grandchildren. It was an idea I had that I wanted to fulfill. And I did! Perhaps it was a rather odd thing to do, but the idea of producing something unusual, that had not been done before really appealed to me.

92. Ever-Changing Life

It wasn't much later, in the fall of 1990 that my brother Bud surfaced once again in our lives. I received a call from St. Paul's Hospital informing me that Bud was there in their critical-care unit and seriously ill. Jim and I returned to Vancouver immediately and discovered they had been keeping Bud alive by machine for two weeks following a major operation on his bowel. The bowel, which was filled with cancer, had burst.

Of course, he looked like death itself but he confided bravely, the doctors had given him just two years to live as the cancer had spread to his other organs. It was a devastating diagnosis, yet Bud seemed to be able to handle it and even jokingly said, "One good thing out of it, I've quit my cigarette habit." And then, with a half grin he added, "I haven't had a smoke for two weeks." The 'witty' Bud I knew so well was rising up again, with humour intact. That alone was something to find joy in!

Looking at him so sick in bed, I was reminded of the sixteen years I'd prayed for his salvation, ever since I'd become a Christian. But, not once had I been given any sign that my prayers had been heard. Still, by faith I knew all things were possible with God, so I decided to continue to wait and pray even though there was now, an expiry date stamped on the near future for Bud. Jim and I felt to reach out to him with our love and support in the meantime.

After we had returned home, we received a three-page letter from Bud and in it he explained that Jim and I, as well as hospital staff, had caused him to take a good look at his life and he knew he needed to make some changes. And they just might turn out for the better despite his terminal diagnosis. I couldn't help reading between the lines of that letter and recognize God at work.

As 1990 drew to a close, the prayer group we met with about our church concerns decided we could not agree with the current direction of the Anglican Church of Canada. In December, about thirty of us withdrew permanently from the church. I personally had to resign as the Diocesan representative of the Anglican Fellowship of Prayer. In the final analysis, all of us in the group worked through our disappointments and found peace. By faith we believed God would lead us in our search for a new home church.

93. A New Beginning Again

The idea that we would become evangelical Christians never entered my mind at that time of leaving the Anglican tradition, but that was the type of church where we ended up. Our friends, Martin and Rena, had left St. Georges Church before us and they invited us to join them at a newly-formed church called New Life, in downtown Kelowna. Their teenaged grandson was attending the youth group at this fledgling church and that is why they were there.

We made our first appearance in New Life Church on Sunday the 13th of January, 1991. From the moment of our arrival, I felt comfortable in this new place of worship, partly due to my involvement in Women's Aglow and other worship gatherings. There was no denying this was a charismatic church and I wasn't sure if it would suit Jim. But I was wrong! Jim's heart was touched with the joyful worship of the people and the abundance of young families there. He also had his 'buddy' Martin beside him. We settled smoothly into our new church along with most of the others from our former group. And we felt very blessed to be there as church was now a joy and not a duty at all.

Ironically, at that very point in time, the New Life Church was going through its own leadership difficulties. And as the weeks went by, the members of our group were amazed to see how their problems were handled. The undone, apologetic pastor confessed his wrong-doing on a Sunday morning before us all. Not only did he admit his guilt remorsefully, but he let it be known he was stepping away from his role as pastor and undergoing appropriate counselling. The answer to a church problem, we newcomers were not accustomed to witnessing.

Then, just weeks after our arrival, Wes, the Lead Pastor of the church at that time, took Jim and I out to lunch on a Sunday and asked if we'd like to join their Leadership Team. He said he envisioned Jim as sort of a wanderer, roaming around loving on people and the two of us as getting involved in the pastoral-prayer ministry of the church. It sounded good to us and so after that we set about doing what we were already experienced in doing, that is praying and loving people. And so, in our journey of following the Lord Jesus, we'd found our way to a restored place of blessing and ministry in a church of His choosing. Praise His name.

The size of the church we were in was forever growing rapidly, and before long we were divided into small groups called mini-churches. They met in small groups in people's homes during the week for worship, prayer and teaching, just like on Sundays. Jim and I were asked to begin visiting the different mini-churches to reach out and welcome the many newcomers. We felt privileged to do this as the groups were unique and exciting to attend and forever adding to their numbers. Jim and I began relating to everyone on a first-name basis.

94. Family Ups and Downs

In our family, we were experiencing some additional changes in the later months of 1991, as well. My sister Hazel, who had been a widow now for fourteen years, moved to Kelowna and rented a suite across the street from our Skyline Road home. I was so happy to have her close by again and she joined us in going to our new church. However, I soon realized Hazel`s move to Kelowna might not be as permanent as I had thought.

Hazel had met Art, who was a former friend of hers far back in her Vancouver days of the 1940's. Much to her own surprise, he had started to phone her nightly while she was still in Saskatchewan, even though he lived in Chilliwack, B.C. It had quickly become a long distant courtship and so by now, he was pleading for her to agree to marry him.

Hazel, however, had some grave reservations about being in another marriage where a drinking problem might develop. She suspected Art might be covering up a weakness for drink and asked us to pray for God's guidance in helping her to decide her future. I certainly understood Hazel's concern, even though Art was insisting he had no such problem. We prayed constantly but answers didn't come and so eventually the two of them were married in Chilliwack. Jim and I were members of their wedding party and there to give them our support. In the months following, we would often visit Hazel and Art as we drove back and forth through Chilliwack on our way to visit Auntie How and Jim's Dad, Thomas in Vancouver.

We had serious concerns regarding Jim's Dad, whose health was declining, necessitating a move from the family home into the Fairhaven Care Facility. When we visited, we always took him out for a drive and for lunch, which was always to MacDonald's for a hamburger with fries and a coffee. He was so easy to please! Thomas also liked buying 649-tickets, in hopes of winning their jackpot, which he never did. He remained his chipper-self throughout the final years of his life, but made it very clear he was ready to go 'home,' as he put it, whenever he was called.

While in Vancouver, we would also stop around to see Bud. He was going through the different stages of cancer treatment that the health-care program had set up for him. He claimed he was pain free, although he was confined, full-time now, to a wheelchair. Despite it all, I felt Bud had a liberated spirit, never losing his sense of humour or his natural flamboyancy. He would spin like crazy in his wheelchair and insist his life was just fine, regardless of the colostomy bag he wore and the ton of medication he took.

Yet, with the passage of time, Bud was forced to enter a hospice. But even in the face of that, he was positive. He bragged to us about how classy his new facility was, with all its modern 'state of the art' equipment to take care of him. He also liked the freedom he had to come and go in his wheelchair from the clinic whenever he wanted. Nonetheless, Bud's days were numbered and he knew it. Even so, he never let down his guard or was open to talk with us about the unescapable end of his life that we all knew was fast approaching.

95. Church Elders

Meantime at home, our New Life Church was growing incredibly fast with more and more people attending until eventually the mini-churches were asked to take turns staying at home or even attending another church on Sunday. This was to make seating space in our building, as we were that over-crowded!

And by now, Jim and I had been asked to serve as Elders on the church board. This was decided by a congregational poll and we were voted in unanimously, or so a ballot counter told us. And it was also around this time that the leadership at New Life decided to re-ordain Jim. And so it happened! After that, Jim was very busy preforming wedding after wedding and together we began doing pre-marriage counselling with the couples wanting to get married. Indeed, life was exciting!

As Elders, many of our leadership discussions centered on our need for a bigger church building and we started looking for land that we could build on. An acreage property in the Glenmore area looked favorable and we bought it with plans to hold it until the money for a new facility could be raised. Several years slipped by before the pressing need of a bigger building was addressed again. By now, our need for more space had sky-rocketed as there were lots of people standing at every service. And the plans for building a church in the Glenmore area had changed too. The prophetic people of New Life were sensing that God was revealing a different plan for our future.

At the prayer meetings, which Jim and I attended regularly, the intercessors were focusing their prayers on a large, free-standing building near the mall called Mainstreet Market as our possible future church home. It was an exhilarating time for the church, as being led by the Lord was the desire of all our hearts. We believed and wanted to be led, but then again, we knew we didn't have enough money for a down payment on that expensive building on the busy highway.

In spite of all these things, the Lord kept persistently speaking to us on that same theme through the intercessors. Then finally, in a meeting, God made it unquestionably clear by telling us to take the chicken down and to put up a cross. The Mainstreet building at that time had a chicken weathervane on its highest peak.

From that point on, the transition moved quickly. Our Church's parcel of land in Glenmore was put up for sale and we discovered it had miraculously tripled in price, paving the way for the huge Market building to become our church. Still, there was one more stumbling block to overcome. The zoning bylaw did not allow a church to be located on that expensive piece of land and so there was a great more prayers offered concerning that. It was then that we decided to just go ahead and take possession of the building. And that's what we did!

Our first Sunday in, we held a tremendous service of celebration of thanksgiving to God for His guidance and provision. Next, all the pastors paired up and went to City Hall, beseeching permission to have the bylaw changed. I remember Jim was paired up with Pastor Wes.

The final outcome was that the Lord very graciously granted all our requests and the city changed the zoning so that a church was allowed to be there. Miracle of miracles! We were not only in the new building, but we could stay and the first thing on the agenda was to take the weathervane down from the roof and put up a cross.

New Life Church.

Me and Jim.

96. Family Events of Death

Through the countless meetings and prayer times at New Life, Jim and I did our best to keep our focus on family as well. A series of unexpected events were beginning to unfold with our family members in that fall of 1991. The first one concerned my brother Bud. At the time, we were not aware he had reached his final days on earth, but it was so.

He was still at the Hospice House and had gone out in his wheel-chair to drink beer with some friends. At least that was what we were told. Just exactly what happened to Bud during his time out is unknown, perhaps a stroke or maybe the cancer rearing its ugly head? Neverthe-less, Bud was taken unconscious by ambulance to St. Paul's hospital. We were called to come immediately and we did, keeping him in prayer all the way to Vancouver.

Arriving at St. Paul's, the nurse in charge said my brother was dying and had lost his ability to speak, but could still hear if I spoke to him. At his bedside, I gave God thanks that I had arrived in time. Then, I simply gathered him in my arms and began telling him how much I loved him. And as well, I heard myself telling him that he'd always been my favorite brother. I had prayed for him so much over the sixteen years since I'd become a praying person, my love for Bud had no bounds.

Without hesitation, I told him, "Not only do I love you, but God loves you too." And, through my tears I added. "He loves you so much Bud, he sent Jesus to die for you so you can be forgiven of your sins and made in right standing with God." Then I whispered in his ear, "All you have to do is believe in Jesus and surrender yourself to Him. And even if you can't speak it out in words, you can say it inside your heart. Will you?" I asked.

At that point, I pulled myself back in order to look into Bud's face and I saw two giant tears welling-up in his eyes and beginning to run down his face. I knew he was saying yes inwardly! I felt the Lord was giving me a sign with Bud's tears, so I'd know he had surrendered his life to Him. Peace flooded my heart for I knew it meant I'd see Bud again in God's kingdom and some verses flooded my mind.

No eye has seen, No ear has heard, No mind has conceived. What God has prepared for those who love Him. (1 Corinthians 2: 9)

I left the hospital feeling so glad Bud had taken that spiritual step, albeit silently. He died later that evening and I was happy, not sad. I knew Bud no longer lived in that disease-ridden body, but his spirit had been released to heaven, so he could claim his new body.

Later, I scattered Bud's ashes in the shape of a cross on the sand beneath the nine o'clock gun in Stanley Park. It seemed an appropriate place, as Bud had often remarked on the faithfulness of that gun to function without fail. Perhaps he dreamed of adopting such a dependable attitude in his own life.

After our brief service on the sand, Jim and I visited Bud's skid-row apartment and spoke to a man in a wheelchair who said he knew my brother. He said he missed Bud, as in the past the two of them had wheeled down the street for a meal at the Gospel Mission. It blessed my heart to hear something positive from my brother's life and we asked the man to remember Bud when the gun was fired each night. He promised he would. I think Bud would have highly approved of this tribute to him.

After that emotional experience of Bud's death we drove back home to Kelowna. But, we hardly had time to relax before the next event five days later. We were called back to Vancouver as the health of Jim's Dad was going downhill and his many years on this earth had taken their toll. He was in good-spirits, but more than ready to 'go home' as he put it once again. The end was near and Dad knew it. His time of letting go of life was serene and peaceful. Later we gathered for Dad's funeral with Auntie How and Irene and as many of the other family members that could come. The head of our Canadian Rolfe family, Thomas, had proudly reached his 95th year and was laid to rest beside Alice Ann, his beloved wife of nearly sixty years.

97. Hawaiian Trip and More Changes

Previous to her marriage to Art, my sister Hazel had bought a condo-apartment in Westbank. Now she wanted to sell it as she had made her home in Chilliwack. Without any knowledge of how to do it, I promised my sister I'd sell her condo for her. And I did! With much prayer and the Lord guiding me, I ran just one ad in the local paper and 'low and behold' the condo was sold. Hazel insisted she wanted to reimburse me by paying the way for Jim and I to accompany her and Art on a vacation to Hawaii, which was planned for the following spring of 1992.

When the time for our excursion to Hawaii arrived, I was excited as I'd always wanted to experience the weather on a tropical isle such as Maui. And I was not the least bit disappointed! The lovely balmy climate of that Hawaiian island in March lived up to all my expectations.

During our ten wonderful days there, Jim drove us around in a rented car to see the many unusual places of interest. He and I even climbed up Mount Haleakala to observe an incredible early morning sunrise and to view the volcanic landscape high above the island. Hazel and Art weren't as ambitious and had no curiosity to see the landscape and sights around us. Hazel and I donned our bathing suits and really enjoyed the swimming pool at our hotel, not to swim mind you, for neither of us could, but just to cool off. The climate was just great, not too hot yet comfortable.

It was a vacation I'll always remember! The gorgeous sunsets and the warm ocean water as it splashed over our feet on the never-ending beaches, so empty of people. And the breezes! They cooled us in the daytime and nourished us at night with the sensation of being gently caressed by the tropical air. And I would be remiss if I forgot the flowers! I still have vivid memories of those giant multi-coloured native flowers blooming in towering hedges, everywhere. Truly a land of paradise, yes indeed!

Back home in July of that same year, 1992, we faced a major change in our lives that we knew was coming. After much thought and prayer we were moving once more and listed our home on Skyline Road for sale. We had decided to down-size from our two-story house to a newly built, no-basement house in downtown Westbank. No basement! Our past being revisited.

Oddly enough, I was feeling at the time that we should be moving across the floating bridge into Kelowna. As Jim had a long drive to work over that bridge to his office at the Church every day. But as yet, Jim wasn't ready to leave the small town atmosphere of the Westside behind, or his backyard green-thumb gardening. Moving to Kelowna and a condo would have to wait.

Leaving our Skyline Road home behind was hard, at least for me, as it held so many cherished memories tucked away in all its familiar rooms. For instance, I'd become a new Christian in that house and had experienced my unforgettable encounter with the Lord. We had reaped much family joy in living out those nineteen years in that home.

And during those years we had enjoyed watching our two daughters, Leslie and Chris, develop into the wonderful caring parents they were. They often brought our grandchildren for visits, Trish, Tania and Colin from Calgary and Tim and Brad from Trail. We'd had many happy and blessed times as family at our Skyline home, which provided vast areas of space for our 'little ones' to run and explore in their growing up years. Being grandparents was such a pleasure to us and having a spacious home had created the atmosphere for wonderful memories.

However, we did move in early January of 1993, to our new house on Majoros Road, close to the heart of the town of Westbank. At once we discovered a brand new home necessitates a lot of energy and attention, especially when the house is surrounded by a yard full of dirt.

As soon as springtime arrived, we were busy with plans for the outside grounds. We decided to plant a long hedge that would run the length of our lot from front to back. We purchased miniature cedar plants, a few inches in height and planted them in a long row on our property line. It changed the look of our place to have a hedge.

Next, there was the need for lawns, both the front and back yard needed to be sodded and it was during this particular time that something amazing happened concerning Jim.

I was at the back of our house painting the lathe wall of our patio with rubber gloves on, when Jim walked by me and asked if I would keep his wedding ring for him. He was about to begin laying the huge rolls of grassy sod down and thought he'd best remove his ring. The sod had been delivered that day and a couple of his friends were there to help this major job be achieved.

I didn't have a pocket to keep Jim's ring in when he handed it to me, so I pulled off one of my plastic gloves and pushed the ring onto one of my own fingers. It was much too big for me, but when I pulled my glove back on again, the ring was held in place. A safe enough spot to keep his ring, wouldn't you think? Nevertheless, later on when I was finished painting, I absentmindedly wrenched the glove off and must have launched the ring up in the air to fall wherever it may. But at that moment I was totally unaware of the fact that I was even the ring keeper for Jim at all.

After the sod was completely in place around the house, Jim found me in the kitchen and questioned, "How did my wedding ring get out in our yard?"

This was a surprise to me as I had forgotten all about his wedding ring! Then he explained. While he was working in the backyard near the patio he noticed a lump in a piece of the sod he had just fitted into place. Out of curiosity he lifted up a corner of the sod to see what was causing the big lump underneath it. And there lay his wedding ring in the dirt!

A ring couldn't possibly make a lump in that thick grassy sod, could it? Of course not! And yet, if the ring had stayed where it was buried, under the thick sod of the lawn, we'd never have found it. So, God somehow used an 'imaginary' lump in order to return Jim's ring to him. Talk about a mind-boggling Father in heaven watching over us! All our thanks were directed up to Him.

98. Family and Church Happenings

As we grew older, Jim and I reveled in the many opportunities to gather the family, or part of it, together. In May of 1993 we hosted our first family get-together at our home on Majoros Road to observe Jim's 65th birthday. Not all the family could come, but for those who did, it turned out to be a great time of celebrating and reminiscing. As a group, we banded together to play Bocci Ball as we now had the green lawns surrounding our house to play the game on. It was oodles of fun throwing those round balls forward, not with great accuracy at first, but gaining more expertise as we went along. During our hours together we decided it was far better to come together for a joyful occasion, such as a birthday, than allow a funeral to unite us.

Us at Jim's 65th.

As a family, we had already experienced a sad funeral in the month of January that year, with Ted passing away. Despite that horrific accident that had changed his life, Ted did enjoy the remaining years of his life, in his own unassuming way. He also remained a strong, faithful Christian to the end. My visits with him at Cottonwoods were always wonderful times of fun and sharing, due to his on-going sense of humour. He was well-loved by many and his funeral service was overflowing with the great many people his life had touched.

Left: Me and Auntie How.

Below: Our family group in Kamloops.

In 1995 we were invited to a family reunion gathering, hosted by Debbie and Fred in their lovely ranch home in Kamloops. Many of us were able to come and the focus of our time together, centered around the fine-looking horses that were available on their ranch to ride. Most of us were city-dwellers who rarely ever got to see a horse up close, let alone climb in the saddle and ride them. Not all of us did ride however, but the family's younger members excitedly took turns on horseback and for some, it may have been for the first time.

My brother Floyd, who had travelled to the reunion from the United States, along with Harold and Glenys, was right in his heyday. He stepped forward to help saddle up the horses so they could be ridden. Floyd was a real cowboy, as you likely recall me saying before, and oh, the many stories he could tell. He entertained us at length with his tales about working as a guide in the Idaho wilderness area. He guided men into those wilds for big-game hunting of moose and elk and as well, was a fishing guide. He took groups of men out for the thrill of a lifetime, on his fishing trips along the Salmon River and white-water rafting for the most daring of heart.

And, as a family, the focus of that reunion was also on the celebration of the 65th birthday of Auntie How and me, as we were both born in the year 1930. We received many gifts, but realized the best gift of all was just being together. We had a great lot of fun during our weekend and it still lives on in our memories to this day.

In the decade of the 1990's, Jim and I were kept busy in our role of elders at New Life Church. I had also become the Women's Ministry Leader at New Life and was overseeing the many different events held for the women, such as teaching sessions, breakfasts and annual retreats. I also led a church prayer group each week. There were many weddings taking place at New Life in those years too, which kept both Jim and I busy doing pre-marriage preparation as well.

At our church, we were holding a great many conferences and I remember the gigantic Dedication Celebration which we hosted so well. Our entire church was teeming with people at that time, filling the main-floor and the balcony and their cars overflowing the parking lot, too. It was the largest crowd we'd ever accommodated in our building up to that time and it was truly a joyful jubilee of honouring God for His goodness to us. We had grown into such a gigantic church, filled with wonderful families that were forever expanding as a congregation and welcoming newcomers all the time.

But, amid all our busy involvement at church we still spent time with our loved ones at every opportunity, especially with our grandchildren. Our interest in baseball blossomed in those years of the 1990's, when Tim, our oldest grandson, joined the Trail Little League Baseball team. Jim and I tried to support him by attending games whenever we could. And over the years, as he grew older, Tim advanced to the Little League All-Stars under Trail's baseball legend, Andy Bilesky. He was a gifted coach and became an outstanding legend in and around Trail.

Andy was both feared and loved as a coach. He had the ability to draw out the best in his young players and under his expertise, they not only learned about the game but they developed a love for baseball, like he had! At least our two grandsons did! Andy had a severely strict and tough coaching style and I can still hear him now shouting, "Get in the game!"

Under the tutelage of Andy, Tim developed into an astute pitcher and all the while, younger brother Brad, because of his extra height and ability, was finding his own place in the league as a first baseman. And in the long run, it was Brad who would seek a career as a left-handed pitcher of stellar quality.

As it sometimes happens, Tim's teen years arrived and although he was now on the Babe Ruth Prep team, his love of music and the guitar in particular, overcame his interest in baseball. I think he was more or less saying goodbye to baseball when he pitched an outstanding game at the Districts in his last year of ball. And even though Tim continued to enjoy sports, his focus switched over to the game of curling, a winter sport he grew to love and excelled at, reaching the Provincial level. He made us all so very proud of him throughout his sports career.

In the meantime, Andy recognized Brad's potential as a left-handed pitcher and gave him the opportunity to become a regular pitcher for the team. Brad loved baseball and was one of Andy's keenest players. As for us, even though we were now in our sixties, we kept right on enjoying the countless games that took place, in and around B.C. Yet now, we were following the games Brad pitched and they were exhilarating to us too, with another grandson on the mound.

It became evident, as time went by, that Brad was a very dedicated left-handed pitcher and his career was definitely on the upswing! Later on when he graduated from High School, Brad won a baseball scholarship to U.B.C. and also was selected as one of 15 students in B.C. to receive the Premier's Excellence Award for his outstanding service to

Tim.

the community, school and distinction in academics. As well, in the following years, Brad was selected to pitch on Team Canada at the World University Games in Chinese Taipei. As a pitcher, Brad was truly focused on making it to the Major Leagues.

Brad.

99. Calgary Changes

During those same years we were also closely involved with Leslie and her family in Calgary. Even though it was a distance to drive, we tried to visit several times a year as we sensed life on the farm was not going smoothly. When they had first moved to the farm Trish, being the oldest in the family, tried to adapt to the country-style way of life and the rural school, but as she grew older into her teens she had difficulty adjusting. And, there was an ongoing struggle in her relationship with her step-dad which only grew worse. She was happy to move to the city as soon as she was old enough.

Leslie was bravely attempting to 'calm the waters' around her, but finding it more challenging all the time. And then, because of a lack of money to support her husband's change of career that required years at the university, Leslie took on a full time job in Calgary at a Christian Book Company. These were exceedingly hard and complex years for everyone involved, especially Leslie as a mother.

Tania in the meantime, loved riding horses and had a horse of her own at the farm. She entered high school as a very conscientious student and got involved in many extracurricular activities, as well as sports. She remained on the farm until after her graduation and then went into the city to live with a focus on attending the University of Calgary.

Colin, eight years younger than Tania, didn't know any other lifestyle than country living and he loved the farm life. As a young boy he was imaginative and always full of original ideas about how to accomplish things that he wanted to do. He had many projects on the go! And even in his early grades at school, felt it was waste of time as he had so much to get done at home. I recall his hiding place in the barn hayloft back then and how he converted it into a hideaway, complete with a rope from the ceiling to swing on. And, Colin also enjoyed going to the Anglican Church and helping Allan, the Strathmore priest. Being not very tall at that age, Colin had no choice but to stand on a chair in order to serve at the altar with Allan.

Although Trish and Tania became very busy pursuing their careers and education in the big city, we always saw them and caught up on their pursuits whenever we visited Calgary. They were both loving granddaughters to Jim and I and when we visited the farm at Christmas they'd come out to complete the family circle along with Colin. We also appreciated the way they supported their mom, when a final break-up came and Leslie went through a separation and divorce.

As a result, Leslie and Colin also moved into the city and were fortunate to settle into a friendly neighborhood. Colin was able to attend the Alternative High School which allowed him to then pursue his chosen field of Computer studies in depth.

Tania, Trish and Colin.

100. A Conference in Norway

On May, the 15th of 1997, Jim and I realized a dream come true. We traveled to Bergen, Norway and stopped off afterwards in England, for a week's holiday in the city of London. We accompanied Roger, one of our New Life Pastors, to Norway so we could assist him in conducting a weeklong Church Conference. Pastor Roger was scheduled to do five days of consecutive teaching during the Conference in Bergen and we were there to pray with the people who asked for prayer at the end of each session.

On arrival I felt weary in body and mind and completely sapped of energy, as I hadn't been able to sleep on the long flight overseas. And, to top it off, our two suitcases had gone astray and didn't arrive with us. However, we were welcomed in the Bergen Airport by our billet family, who bore cheerful smiles and gave both of us hugs. I hid my fatigue under my own smile of greeting and I was indeed happy to finally get there.

The family billeting us was made up of Pastor Henry, his wife Ann-Marie, and two sons and two daughters. I promptly learned that according to Norwegian custom, the females were all given hyphenated names, so my name Marie, seemed to stand strangely alone. They were such a loving family and Henry was the Worship Pastor at the host church of the Conference.

At mealtime, we were given a huge traditional Norwegian meal and then whisked away to a nearby church to see a drama called *The Bride of Christ*. The drama was presented by a Messianic Jewish man named Barry who we enjoyed meeting and chatting with back stage after the performance. It was late when we returned home with our hosts, but nonetheless we were served a 'midnight' supper, the traditional fourth meal of the day.

I was completely worn out by this time but yet had difficulty falling asleep in the strange bed and unfamiliar surroundings. I was concerned also about our suitcases going astray, which didn't help to settle my mind down either. So, when we awoke Saturday morning, what were we to do but put back on the same clothes we'd worn for the previous twenty-four hours of traveling! Good grief, I thought! Where was God in all of this? As well, the day stretched ahead like an eternity before I could try to sleep again.

At the breakfast table we were told this was a special Saturday called Confederation Day in Norway. It was unique to their country and consisted of the local people wearing their national costumes and forming a long parade to walk the streets of the city. Their costumes represented where they were born and each one had their own design and vibrant colours. In Canada we do not have a holiday to compare to this one. I was impressed with these people and their love of their country and I enjoyed every minute. Jim and I had always been very patriotic Canadians ourselves and felt akin to them.

Later that same night, our Church Conference began, bringing all the churches of the Bergen area together in one huge building. The evening began with an hour long worship time and as I struggled to my feet, waves of weariness flooded over me from my lack of sleep over the two previous nights. The people around me were lifting their voices and hands joyfully in song, as the words appeared in Norwegian on the giant overhead screen. Knowing only English, I was unable to sing along, even though the melodies sounded familiar. But then, an interpreter appeared at my elbow and began speaking each line of the lyrics in English, into my listening ear. And, I found the lyrics were so full of spiritual truth and wonder.

Then, something strange began to unfold as those lyrics seemed to take on a life of their own. They prompted my heart to immediately open up and receive the joyful message of all the praise to God. It was an amazing feeling as my spirit began to expand, filling me with energy, beyond what I'd experienced before. And as well, my heart was strangely refreshed, so that by the closing time, when the crowd surged forward for prayer, I felt renewed with energy. Jim and I prayed with as many individuals as possible, then were driven back again to Pastor Henry's home, joining the family in the midnight supper. At a very late hour, we retired to bed.

I awoke the next morning at the first break of day and lay there watching the rays of sun trickle through the bedroom curtains. It was not yet six o'clock and I questioned why I was awake so early! It felt like I'd been shaken by someone and yet as my eyes searched the unfamiliar room and saw no one. Then, I recalled it was Pentecost Sunday, one of my all-time favorite days on the church calendar. I relaxed back onto my pillow to think about Pentecost and how this special Sunday was celebrated in churches worldwide as the time when the Holy Spirit was given to the followers of Christ in the first century. I had observed and loved Pentecost ever since I had received my spiritual in-filling twenty-three years ago.

I lay pondering this for several minutes and then incredibly, my entire body began to shake. I turned my head to look at Jim sleeping soundly beside me and my mind questioned how this was possible? And then, I heard a deep voice speak to me inwardly. "Do you not think I can shake you and not wake up your husband?" the voice asked.

I was surprised at the mention of Jim, asleep beside me and amazed that a voice was speaking to me at all. Was it God's voice? I chose to believe it was. And I had questions. Why was I shaking? And how was it possible for Jim to sleep when the bed was noisily rocking to and fro as my body vibrated?

God's voice spoke again asking me another question. "Do you remember how you felt last night?" And before I could answer, the reply was provided. "You were completely drained of your own abilities, before I filled you." And, He added, "I can only use you when you are empty of self." I now felt wordless, as I sensed there was power behind those spoken words.

Then I was given an explanation of the shaking, even as I was still being shaken. It symbolized in the physical what God was doing spiritually in the Church at this time. And the shaking would continue, I was told, until all that could be shaken off was gone to make room for more of His glory. I presumed God was referring to Himself. Then, two messages were given to me, one for Pastor Roger and a second one for Barry, the Messianic Jew I had met only briefly.

By now the sun was bathing the room in its bright light and my shaking was noticeably subsiding. I got up and wrote out the messages I had been given so I wouldn't forget what was said. How much time had passed, I wasn't sure, but I explained it all to Jim when he woke up. He found it hard to believe he'd slept through all that had taken place.

At breakfast, I decided to share my experience with our host, Pastor Henry, feeling he possibly would understand. And he did! With a smile he told me other people had experienced similar wonders in that same bedroom. How very extraordinary, I thought to myself.

Now, we had reached the second day of the Conference and upon arrival I found Barry and delivered my message to him, which he gladly received. Pastor Roger also listened while I relayed the words that were meant for him. Then, with a smile he said, "Be ready to be called up, so you can share what happened with the people in the Conference."

My heart momentarily stopped beating! That was not what I wanted to occur at all, but before I could protest, Pastor Roger was gone. Believe it when I say, I was under a certain amount of pressure for the rest of the day. But Roger did not call me up in either session, or even the next day. Now I was feeling relieved, thinking he'd forgotten all about it.

It was now Tuesday evening of that conference week, and about mid-way through the giving of his evening lecture, Roger's eyes roamed over the audience and found where I sitting. Then he spoke directly to me, "Come up here, Marie, and share what transpired between you and the Lord the other morning."

I felt everyone's eyes on me! What could I do? I had to do what Roger asked? I felt some comfort in seeing Pastor Henry standing there beside Roger, ready to interpret my English words into Norwegian, just as he had been doing for Roger in every session.

I climbed the stairs to the platform and just as I reached the microphone I felt my right hand start to tremble, then start to shake. Oh no, I thought as I looked into all the many upturned faces staring at me. I tucked my hand out of sight behind my back. I was ready now! Pastor Henry to the right of me spoke first, cautioning me to speak slowly so he could interpret each word and Roger, on my left, nodded for me to begin.

I took a deep breath and began slowly explaining what had happened to me, as clearly as I could. It was when I reached the point where God spoke to me that Roger interrupted with a question. "How did you know it was God's voice speaking to you, Marie?"

To myself I thought, Roger why are you making this harder for me? But, the answer to his question slid easily from my lips. "I just knew that I knew that I knew," I replied. Then, I continued to share my experience, feeling satisfied I'd answered Roger's question accurately. My nervousness had entirely vanished by this time and a sense of confidence overcame me. I felt calm and I knew the presence of God was with me. When my story ended, Roger turned to me, saying, "I'll pray for you now Marie."

I saw him lift his hand up, but at that precise moment I was overcome with a tremendous power and fell over backwards to the floor. In the act of falling, I experienced nothing but weightlessness, like I was a feather wafting gently downwards and coming to a rest on something both soft and stable at the same time. Then my entire body began to shake, starting with my feet and moving up my body to my head. Shaking in public would normally alarm me, as I am not one to embarrass myself in front of others. However, my shaking at this particular moment, seemed to be part of what God was doing, not what I was doing.

Next, the most amazing phenomenon of all happened when I had an out-of-body experience. This had never happened to me before. I had an incredible sensation of being lifted high up, over the stage and rows of people in the audience, to the highest part of the ceiling. And from that new perspective, I could look down and watch what was happening below. I saw Roger and I heard him as he continued to teach with Henry translating his words into English. I saw myself lying prostrate on the platform floor and my body was shaking from head to foot. It didn't make sense to me, but nonetheless, I was able to see it as plain as day.

Did the scene below upset me? No, it did not. You might say, I was in a state of peaceful tranquility in that high place covered over with what I can only describe as a heavenly blanket. Perhaps it was a GLORY blanket, as God's glory appeared to be radiating all around me and He alone was in control of what was happening. I personally had no sense of the passing of time as I rested up there, but all at once I realized Roger was ending his talk, by announcing the prayer time and I had no choice but to resume my place below. And so I did!

In a very natural way, I found myself getting up from the floor of the stage with the assistance of Jim's extended hand held out to me. Logically, I couldn't explain what had taken place during that interval of time, for only God held the answers. With the call for prayer having been given, I was ready for the opportunity to pray with those who were coming forward for prayer.

And then I was especially blessed, when a young girl in a wheelchair came directly to me, being pushed by her care-giver. She could not walk, but had brought with her a pair of new shoes, as a sign of her faith to be healed and to walk. With all the faith I could muster, I prayed and asked God to give her the ability to rise up and walk in faith. Next, I got her up on her feet with the help of her care-giver and though it seems incredible, she started moving forward with only the two of us balancing her underneath her elbows. Indeed, she did walk!

My heart burst with joy at that moment and I danced around her praising God and giving Him thanks. I couldn't help it! Complete happiness radiated from the girl in her newfound victorious achievement. I will never forget it! And then as the evening ended, a group of the older women in the Conference seemed to come from out of nowhere and began to form a circle around about me. I was puzzled and I wondered what they wanted. In their accented words of English, they told me I had been an inspiration to them. They could relate with me as a mature women, like themselves, who wasn't afraid to allow the Spirit of God work within me powerfully. I was sixty seven years old at the time! Their words pleased and blessed me and I felt God's love between us and we all continued to rejoice together. A perfect ending!

The next morning, we said our goodbyes and gave hugs to all our Norwegian family of friends and gracious hosts. We caught a flight to England for a week's stopover in London before coming home. It was thrilling to fulfill a long-awaited dream of seeing that great city and visiting all its historic places, some we'd only read about or seen on television. We had a superb time using the sightseeing bus as our means of transportation to get around the immense city, so as to view the Queen's palace, and all the other impressive places on our tourist's list. It was truly a memory-making few days!

We had also set aside time to visit our long-time friend Doug, who was living there and studying. He was married to Anna now and they were parents to their first two children. We had kept in touch with Doug, who was working towards his Masters in Greek Theology at the famed Queens University. This ultimately would result in his achieving a Chair at McGill University in Quebec, where he and Anna still live today with their expanded family of six children. We enjoyed our time with them and I was able to share about my amazing spiritual experience in Bergen. I think it was hard for Doug with his pragmatic mind to accept it all, but I assured him it was not a whim of my imagination, but a true happening in the supernatural realm. For it was.

101. The Lake-House: Our Little Piece of Heaven

On May 29th, 1997 we arrived back in Kelowna from Norway and our London trip and settled once again into the familiar environment of our home and New Life Church. After such a wonderful time away, Jim and I were hardly prepared for a turn of events that brought some health challenges into our lives? First, Jim had to undergo a hernia operation which was difficult for him to recover from. Then, I developed a growth that required surgery and my doctor said it could be cancerous. Not the words I wanted to hear! We surely had much to pray about!

This was the time Leslie was going through the difficult separation and divorce from Ralph and we wanted to give her as much support as possible. When I found out I had a month to wait for my scheduled operation with a gynecologist, I was glad to have time to act and pray about all these things. As well, I was kept busy sharing my testimony about my experience in Norway, as God provided.

It surely was the hand of God that gave me eight opportunities to tell my experience to groups of different sizes in that period of that one month. The first two occasions to speak, were at the Women's Aglow Meetings in Kelowna and in Oliver, as well. Each time and in every group, regardless of size, it was a blessing to me. And through it all, I had peace of mind about my impending surgery and our faithful God kept me believing only for the best. In the end I had my surgery and was given the verdict of no cancer. Both Jim and I rejoiced and gave thanks to the Lord for healing me through the skill of my doctor. God often works that way.

At the end of August, that same year, Jim and I made our very first trip to the lake property at Procter, B.C. After years of camping, Chris and Dan had decided to buy some waterfront property on the West Arm of Kootenay Lake, only the year before. The land had a very small, rustic

Us at the lake-house.

cabin on the high ground overlooking the lake and this is where we stayed.

What a restful place for a vacation it turned out to be! We enjoyed the fantastic view and watching all the activities of the boats on the lake. With the lakefront so close outside the door, we were fascinated by the arrival and departure of the Kootenay Lake Ferries at the wharf across the water. The two ferries run like clockwork every day and you can set your watch by them. Being lakeside was such a treat for us. We enjoyed everything about it, especially the sounds of the water activities and the squawking of the gulls and the honking of the geese passing by overhead. But most of all, we delighted in the deep quiet, so devoid of sound. What an exquisite location for rest and reflection, apart from the busyness of the world.

Throughout the years, this lake-house has become the family's favorite vacation spot and the tiny cottage has morphed during that time into a three bedroom A-Frame home with a loft, all designed by Dan himself. It's truly a wonderful lake-house now for many of us to enjoy.

Numerous times since that first time, Jim and I have vacationed there amid the intense wonder and beauty of that location. On that wide open deck of the lake-house there is a spectacular view of the water and mountains on all sides and it speaks to us of God's wonderful creation given for us to enjoy. We go there to be hemmed-in by its peaceful tranquility.

When we returned home from that serene setting at the lake-house, I was faced with another substantial challenge. When having my eyes examined on a routine visit, my optometrist discovered there was a fluid buildup at the back of both of my eyes. It could eventually cause glaucoma and even blindness. My doctor recommended laser treatment by a Corneal Specialist. I went immediately, and the specialist drilled a hole through each of my eye pupils with a laser beam. And, I was astonished to learn that in spite of the fact that other parts of the body heal up and close, these holes in my pupils will never heal shut. I believe this is another phenomenon in God's design of the body we inhabit. Those holes will remain open allowing any accumulating fluid to escape from my eyes is a sure indication of a Heavenly Father who cares. And I am grateful also for the modern technology that can do this.

Looking back to the year 1998, I recall a very happy occasion that took place in May of that year. Remember our nephew David, who left his home in Kamloops and came to live with our family in Edmonton? Well, this same David, eventually moved to Calgary and then Vancouver and to make a long story short, reappeared, wanting Uncle Jim to preside over his marriage to Janette, the 'girl of his dreams'. The two of them had it all planned for May 16th and so that was the way Jim and I spent his 70th birthday. Everything progressed beautifully with family members in attendance, but even so, Jim and I were surprised when we entered the reception hall after the ceremony and discovered it was decorated in a birthday theme in honor of Jim's big day.

102. Celebration

How does it feel to reach the milestone of 50 years married? Well, on Saturday the 27th day of June in the year 1999, Jim and I found out, and it was amazing! To honour our many years of marriage, we held a family reunion weekend with all of our loved ones and friends invited to join us in celebrating the big occasion. Quite a crowd to fit into our backyard all right, but we managed to do it.

Our hours together were spent chatting, recollecting past times we've shared, eating a lot and, of course, playing bocce ball on the lawns surrounding our Majoros home. Sandwiched between the games and all the chitchatting, we viewed old photograph albums, laughing at the style of clothes we used to wear, the different haircuts men sported and the funny hair-do's we ladies thought were so stylish. Basically though, we imparted our love to one another and enjoyed sharing our loving bond of being part of one big extended family.

The Rolfe Clan.

The next day, which was Sunday, our family came with us to the service at New Life Church. This pleased Jim and I so very much. We made such an impressive entourage as our family members filed in and took up a whole section of seats in the congregation. Pastor Ralph invited Jim and I up front on the platform and our fellow churchgoers greeted us with a great deal of applause and many loud cheers of congratulations on the achievement of our Golden Anniversary.

We invited the whole church to join us later on that afternoon for a tea party celebration in the large room set aside for us upstairs. We realized everyone at New Life wouldn't come, but we had also arranged with friends outside our church, from far and wide, to join with us there. Many from our former church of St. Georges came as well as other people in the area that we'd known for many years. Four of our very distant cousins who lived in the vicinity even turned up to surprise us. It was a very festive and grand weekend for Jim and I, basking in the love of family and friends as we commemorated our fifty wonderful years of marriage.

Cutting the cake.

103. An Afterword: A Glimpse of My Life After My Memoirs

Not long after our wonderful 50th Anniversary, Jim and I began thinking it was time to downsize once again and make a move into Kelowna. Jim's pastoral care work at New Life Church still took him into Kelowna and home again, five days a week. It was clear we needed to put an end to his long highway commutes.

Our wonderful niece Marie, and her husband Les, were a great help to us in our move to town and incidentally, Jim also had the privilege of performing their wedding ceremony back in 2005. Les is an experienced Real Estate agent and found the perfect condo apartment for us in the Glenmore area of Kelowna. And Les made our move easy also, by driving the Moving Van along with the help of Dan and Chris and a group of able-bodied friends from New Life Church. Marie stayed behind and cleaned our empty house from top to bottom. We thanked her for doing such a great job and for truly being one of God's angels in this world!

Our new condo at Brandt's Crossing has made our lives a blessing and continues to meet our every need. And we feel good about having more leisure time to relax, not to say relaxing means retirement, for we don't believe in retiring ever. Pastoral work and involvement at New Life keeps on giving our lives purpose and fulfillment. We were church elders for fifteen years, but now we reap the privilege of being perceived as senior members with over twenty-five years of experience and sort of 'Grandparents' of the Church.

Our lives are full and busy and we still consider ourselves available to do the work of the Lord, even though we're now in our eighties. We enjoy relatively good health and have a desire to live out our remaining years spending our time blessing others around us. There have been ups and downs along the way, especially the loss of our four siblings over the past decade. Hazel, Floyd, Irene and Harold; such great losses for Jim and I. Our one remaining sibling now is our Auntie How, who lives in the lovely Sunrise Living Community in Vancouver.

So, as we journey on our way, we're content and we try to make learning new things our lifetime goal. I think you'll agree, that can be very challenging in this ever-changing world. However, our aim is to keep actively involved in life, both mentally and physically as much as possible.

Blessings and joy are ours with a church family around us and the love of our two amazing daughters, five adult grandchildren, and seven great-grandchildren, who range in ages from sixteen years down to eight months of age. We deeply love each one and hold them close in our heart and prayers, daily. And now I want to bring you an update on the lives of our family members by telling you who they are today, in 2016.

Our oldest daughter, Leslie, is married to Don, her husband of thirteen years. I am reminded of how thrilled my sister Hazel was to find that Don knew the old swing dances. I can still see the time when he grabbed her and twirled her about in a quick dance in the church parking lot. She just thought the world of him. Don made many visits to see us during the years he covered a sales territory in BC, and I remember how I tried to think up interesting dinners to serve the night he would be stopping by. Often, with the shrimp appetizers! Jim and I really got to know him and have to agree with Hazel that he is very special.

Leslie and Don live in Calgary in a century-old character house in the inner city district of Ramsay. They have busy lives. Don now works part-time for Volkswagen and is a dedicated singer with a show choir as well as a member of the church choir. Leslie is a sales representative, selling Christian products and her travels bring her to see us regularly. Such a blessing! Leslie is also pursuing a certificate in Spiritual Direction, having finished her Masters in Religious Studies three years ago. She tries to find time for creative writing, but most importantly, she and Don love to spend time together and with their six children and six grandchildren.

Leslie's oldest daughter, Trish, has built a successful career in new home sales in Calgary. She owns a lovely home in northwest Calgary, and has my creative touch in interior design. Her home is just lovely. Her three children are growing up quickly. Ethan, our eldest great-grandson, is sixteen years old now and in high school. He is a very clever young man with an inquiring mind that is opening up to many new interests. His sister, Jordan, is one grade behind him and at fourteen years of age has a talent for drawing and a passion for music. Isaac, the youngest at twelve, is curious about the world and enjoys games with his many friends.

Tania, Leslie's youngest daughter, is on maternity leave from her position as Associate Director at the Southern Alberta Institute of Technology Polytechnic in the fund development department. She has a Master of Philanthropy degree and has published and lectured in her field. Sixteen years ago, Tania married Dale and Grandpa Jim presided over their ceremony in Calgary. Dale is working hard as an electrician now, following careers in medical-imaging and professional driving. Their oldest child, Charlotte Leslie Ann, our great-granddaughter is such a dear. She is very social, talking all the time and organizing imaginary play. She started kindergarten this fall after a successful year in Montessori preschool and loves her books. Their twin boys, George and Oscar were born in February of this year, completing their charming family and giving us a total of seven great-grandchildren. Those two sweet boys, George with his knowing gaze and Oscar with his contagious smile and laughter, are a joy to the whole family. The love of family is so important to both Tania and Dale.

Leslie's son, Colin, is founder and director of his own computer company, Imperium Incorporated, a thriving career he has spent his adult life creating. He enjoys hunting and woodworking, and has set up an immaculate workshop in his garage. Colin constantly amazes us all with his talent for understanding the inner workings of anything he sets his mind to, having repaired and restored many vintage woodworking tools and their motors, as well as fixing up an old truck he took over from his brother-in-law, Dale. And, of course, he excels at anything to do with the insides of a computer. He, and his partner Amanda, live in the Bowness area of Calgary.

Our daughter Chris, and her husband Dan, are retired now and continue to live in their beautiful home in Trail; they love the small town life and the people. This year, they celebrated their fortieth wedding anniversary and, as in the past, they continue to enjoy travelling vacations. They spend most of the summer at the lake-house in Procter on Kootenay Lake and we still visit them there each summer. They are both active on curling teams during the winter and Dan loves skiing at Red Mountain. Dan is an artist, too, and spends much of his time painting in his studio in the backyard. Chris enjoys contract bridge and playing her baby grand piano, which was her retirement gift to herself! She also regularly visits the local senior care home with her beloved dog Hershee, a trained service dog. Both Chris and her dog are certified with the St. John's Ambulance Association. Dan and Chris enjoy their new role as grandparents to their first little granddaughter, Emi.

Tim, their eldest son, was married to Neko in April of 2015. They had met while Tim was travelling in Japan two years earlier and following their engagement, Neko moved to Canada. Grandpa Jim had the pleasure of uniting them in marriage in a lovely wedding service that took place in The Teahouse in Vancouver's Stanley Park. Now they enjoy living in a townhouse in the heart of the city. Tim is employed as a meteorologist at B.C. Hydro and likes his daily work of mapping and forecasting atmospheric conditions. He has a great love of the outdoors and nature and has inherited his Grampa's green thumb for gardening. His travelling ventures have taken him to many countries around the world and he has a love for learning new languages. In January of this year, Neko and Tim became parents of their first child, a beautiful baby girl named Emi Severn. They are very proud first time parents and Emi is definitely the happiest baby I have ever seen.

Brad, Dan and Chris's youngest son, and the youngest of our grandchildren, married the love of his life, Jillian, in July of this year. Their wedding was held at the West Coast Wilderness Lodge on the beautiful Sunshine Coast, with Grandpa Jim officiating at the service. Afterwards, they headed to Cincinnati, Ohio for a year, where they are currently living. Brad is doing a fellowship of specialized training, as a sports medicine orthopedic surgeon. On their return from Ohio, Brad will be looking for a place to set up practice and we all hope it will be somewhere in B.C. Jillian works for the government in the field of Public Health Policy and we are so very thankful that Brad brought her into our family. Although Brad's medical schooling has taken up most of his free time, Jillian and he love the outdoors and, when time permits, love to ski and snowboard in the winter and hike and play ball in the summer.

And, as an added note concerning Brad. Jim and I have fond memories of the three summers of 2003, 2004 and 2005 when Brad lived with us in Kelowna and played baseball. During that time, he was a member of the pitching staff of the Kelowna Falcons and was focused on a career geared towards the Big Leagues. Incidentally, he still holds a baseball record he set with the Falcons, as one of their all-time top pitchers. However, when his dream of being drafted into the Major Leagues as a pitcher, didn't materialize, Brad wisely switched direction without even breaking stride and entered the field of medicine. We're glad he did, as we believe the world desperately needs more doctors than baseball players.

A famous baseball player of the past, Ty Cobb, once said, 'The crowd makes the ballgame' and we are so happy to have been a part of that crowd cheering for Brad on the mound, and we continue to applaud him now, as he settles into his career as a surgeon. A big 'thank you' Brad, for suggesting I chronicle my life. This book is the result.

Marie and Jim at their home on Skyline Road
beside the rock wall that Jim built.

Acknowledgements

I owe a huge thank you to my husband and best friend Jim, who has always given me his assistance and encouragement in anything I've embarked on, especially the writing of this book. My heartfelt appreciation goes to my two daughters, Leslie and Chris, who have been a tremendous support and inspiration to me, as well as keen editors and genuine helping hands in so many ways. My thanks to Dan, for his help as well. And, to the other members of my family and to my friends, I extend thanks. You know who you are! Having you in the 'wings' cheering me on, has meant so much to me and enabled my story to reach this printed stage. And to all of you reading my book, I want to express my deep gratitude for taking the journey in order to know me better.

Last, but not least, all praise and honour to my Lord Jesus Christ for guiding me by His Holy Spirit to recall the details of my life and to record them in my memoirs. In doing this, I have realized afresh the phenomenal change and transformation that has taken place in my life since I chose to become a Christian. And also, my need to be loved, which dates back to my young childhood, is now more than fulfilled by knowing that I am unconditionally loved by my Father in heaven. I believe that His love has made me a much more forgiving and caring person and has blessed my life with inner peace, regardless of my circumstances. Praise His Holy name.